9.74

£2·25

D1806608

BROOKLANDS AND BEYOND

Brooklands 'Regulars', 1930s
Left to right: Francis Beart, J. Sinclair (mechanic), Jock Forbes, the
author, Frank Baker (manager and mechanic to Noel Pope), Noel Pope

BROOKLANDS
and beyond

~~~~~~~~~~

CHARLES MORTIMER

GOOSE & SON
Publishers

First published in 1974
by Goose & Son Publishers Ltd

ISBN 0 900404 23 x

© Charles Mortimer 1974

Printed in Great Britain by
Latimer Trend & Company Ltd
Plymouth

Acknowledgments

There are those who I must thank for help I have had in setting out this story, and the first is my friend Bill Boddy, for while I didn't involve him once I had started it, it was his advice I sought as to whether the story was worth telling.

The memory tends to fade with time and although I have been fortunate in keeping notes and log books, I want to thank my friends Francis Beart, Geoff Goddard, Denis Jenkinson and Cyril Posthumus for refreshing mine and correcting errors. One of them was good enough to teach me how to spell 'Donington' and I am grateful to them all and for the help I have had from others.

Since the story mainly concerns pre-War cars and motor-cycles, I should like to pay a sincere tribute to both the Vintage Sports Car Club and the Vintage Motor Cycle Club whose hard-working Staffs and Committees make it possible for this early machinery to be seen in action; and also to dedicated Members like Neil Corner and 'Titch' Allen, whose appearances at Meetings give so much pleasure to everyone. Also, of course, to Members like them, whose time and resources inevitably limit their activities, and, no less, to the many non-competing Members whose beautifully restored machines adorn the spectators' enclosures so that, at times, one almost feels one is still watching it happen from the Members' Hill at Brooklands.

I couldn't have written the book without the help of my Secretary, Jenny Hill, who, although not involved in it, took on so much additional work for me that, without this assistance, it could never have been fitted in.

And, finally, I particularly want to thank my Publishers for their enthusiastic support and for 'bearing with' my dreadful typing and odd scraps of paper.

Illustrations

7

I

There was one stage in my life when I thought I should like to be a farmer. I wanted to learn about farming and, as a first step, I persuaded a farmer friend of mine to let me spend some time working on his farm. On about the third day, he came into the cowshed where I was learning the intricacies of milking. How was I getting on? Was I fed up with it yet? And then, 'This is only part of the picture, Charles. This doesn't make the money. The money's made in dealing.' Up to that moment I was happy in what I was learning, but that remark, 'the money's made in dealing', brought me face to face with facts. For fundamentally I'd always been a dealer and I knew at once that not only was he right, but that I could never learn and understand livestock dealing in the way that I understood dealing in cars and everything connected with cars. So my farming career began and ended there and I continued to be a dealer in the sphere that I knew.

Nearly everyone interested in cars at one time or another touches on the fringe of dealing in them. Some, like myself, go through the motor-cycle phase and some, also like myself, discover that they enjoy the cut and thrust of dealing almost as much as using the blessed things. But, although I've always enjoyed this aspect of dealing, my outlook isn't entirely commercial because I've always had a definite idea of the sort of car or motor-bike I like and I've always tried to concentrate in dealing in things that I like myself, rather than in things with purely the profit margin in mind. But, if I haven't been able to acquire enough of the former, I've certainly had to fall back on the latter and very unattractive some of it has been, in my opinion.

So, through this book on Brooklands, on cars and on motor-cycles, runs the theme of dealing, with its thrills and disappointments, its successes and failures and most important of all, its humour—because it can be, and often is, hilariously funny.

There are people who don't think much of dealers and that is understandable, because it must be admitted that there are some really wicked ones. I like to feel that I have never fallen into that category although, to be a successful dealer, one must have a trait of keenness, if not sharpness, in one's character. In common with other dealers, I doubt if I've ever sold a car that was faultless and when offering a car to the customer one has to think about its faults and decide carefully how to describe it. Age and type of car come into it, of course. An aged sports car has usually done its mileage the hard way, but an old touring saloon may have had the kindest of lives.

Towards the end of my motor-trading career, I was a partner with my brother-in-law, Robin Richards and an old school friend, Dick Carr, in a West End business selling mainly new Continental cars. They were all good cars and sold well but, to me, not all were really interesting as cars. So I made an arrangement with my partners that, if I wanted to, I could deal in the older type of Rolls Royce and Bentley, doing it from my home at Weybridge. I concentrated mainly on Rolls Royce 20/25 h.p., Phantom II and Phantom III, Speed Six and 8-litre Bentleys. Tyres for these were always a bit of a headache and I used to get them from a firm of dealers in North London.

One day, having bought a set for a Phantom II Continental, the salesman said to me, 'Like to have a look at our bangers?' and there, on an open site, were seventy or more of the worst cars I'd ever seen.

'What d'you think of 'em?' I was at a loss for an answer, but said what I thought, that I couldn't understand how he could sell such stuff and still sleep soundly.

He was scornful. 'Listen, boy. See that pavement? Everyone who steps over that pavement and on to our site thinks we're half sharp—and we KNOW *they* are. Never sell a man a good car. Sell him a good car and he's always round your neck. The screen wiper doesn't wipe clean. He thinks there might be a slight misfire. The dashboard lights are too bright. Never make a living that way, boy. No, sell him a bad 'un and when he comes back be charming. Take it back? Of course. Take it back—and sell him a worse one.' And they'd made a fortune dealing that way.

Dealing before the War, in the thirties, was fun. Customers were personal friends and if you studied them and looked after them they never left you. But post-War trading, and part-exchange, killed all that. You could sell a new car to a customer who'd keep it for, say, two years. He'd then decide to swop it for another new one and want a part-exchange price quoted on his own. Having got the quote, he'd hawk the blessed thing right round town, finally doing the deal elsewhere for perhaps as little as fifty shillings difference. Then he'd come back and ask you to maintain it. No, there are still bad dealers but I think, myself, that nowadays some of the customers are as bad— or worse. As a dealer friend of mine said once, 'They know more than's good for 'em.'

So, for me, it's the Vintage car or bike, Vintage miscellanea, books, curios and the rest, because the people who buy them are more like the pre-War customers—they become personal friends you never lose.

Why does one become bitten by this dealing business? In my case it was, at first, sheer necessity. I bought my first motor-bike when I was fourteen, in 1927. It was a 1914 Douglas and it cost me £4, which was a stretch for me at the time but one which I could just manage. Within a month I found that I'd paid too much and that bikes of that age, in running order, could be bought for as little as £1. So, swallowing a bitter pill, I sold the Douglas at a loss, for £3, and reinvested in two Zenith Graduas and a P. & M. One Zenith and the P. & M. went for the princely sum of £2 each and I was back to square one with a Zenith standing me in at minus £1.

All this must have been a bit of a shock to my family, who were not very motor-minded. My father did occasionally drive but, to be truthful, we never looked forward to it. We loved him dearly but, as a driver, he tested us sorely as he had no mechanical knowledge and no 'feel' for the car, which was one of the very first post-1914/18 War Austin 20 tourers. Our chauffeur, whose name was Woodham, could always start it first go on the starter, but my father was an expert at getting it over-rich, which meant that poor Woodham was requested to swing it on the handle. At this stage, my father would start to get testy and, with poor old Woodham swinging madly, he would shout, 'Swing the bloody thing, Woodham. Don't turn it as though it was a butter churn.' No, mine was not a motoring family and it remained that way until my father died in 1932. I think, really, that my mother disliked cars in the same way but, for my sake, she disguised her feelings and later came to quite enjoy all the activity.

In 1927 I went to Radley. My father had been at Rugby but it seemed to be agreed that I wasn't academically bright enough to achieve Rugby and, as it turned out, I wasn't sorry because, if it had to be school at all, I liked Radley. One was completely cut off from all things motoring, however, and the nearest I got to it was in achieving

11

special permission to work on a 350 cc. overhead-valve Blackburn engine under the heading of 'Carpentry'. I wasn't at all interested in learning to be a carpenter but fortunately 'Carps', who used to teach this 'Extra', was a motor-cyclist and it was by his grace that the concession was made.

It was during the holidays of that year that I first went to Brooklands, was instantly gripped and never recovered or lost my love for the place. To me it had everything and I resolved, there and then, that a racing motorist I must be—nothing else would do. I said nothing about it at the time, well knowing what the family reaction would be, but I never stopped thinking about it or about the means to that end. Unfortunately, the prospect of it didn't make me work any harder at school, which was a pity because the opportunities were there and I could have learned a lot more, which would have been of use to me, than I did. Looking back on it all now, I don't think I really thought much further than the prospect of driving a racing car.

That initial trip to Brooklands had been a family one but, from then on, I journeyed there whenever and however I could—usually by push-bike from Dorking where we lived at the time—a twenty-eight-mile round trip. I really made the paddock at Brooklands my headquarters, scraping acquaintance with celebrities and ingratiating myself with the officials on the entrance gate with a view to not paying the few shillings charged for spectators on non-race days. The great thing about Brooklands, of course, was that there was always something going on from April to October, when the track was open. Testing, record breaking, practising—always something. Racing cars, racing motor-cycles, sports cars, all out on the track at the same time—it was great.

I first went to see a motor-cycle meeting in 1929—the 200-Mile Sidecars Races for 350 cc., 500 cc. and 1,000 cc. outfits. Up to that time I had been thinking only in terms of racing on four wheels and it had sunk in very deeply that this was going to cost money. The prospect of racing motor-cycles hadn't occurred to me till then, but from then on I became a regular supporter of all the motor-cycle race meetings at the track.

I had had one discussion with my father on the question of a profession when I left school and had trotted out the racing motorist idea while sitting well back for the anticipated explosion. But he was very good about it and said he'd make some inquiries, although it

12

wasn't what he would have chosen, as I must know. I was grateful to him for this because the whole thing must have been a ghastly disappointment for him. My mother, of course, had known for some time which way the wind blew, so I imagine he had probably had some inkling of it before embarking on our chat. It was some time before he mentioned it again and it was then he told me he had discussed it with one of my uncles—up to that time a great hero of mine because he had some involvement with very early motor racing. My uncle's view was that if one wanted the short road to ruin, then choose motor racing as a career, from which I concluded that he couldn't have been such a very successful competitor himself. None of this put me off in the least. I really had decided the issue and it was just a question of how to embark on it. I was saving, and prepared to start right at the bottom of the ladder and, by now, had contacts at the track, some of whom I felt sure would help me.

As it happened, it didn't turn out that way. I left Radley in 1931, earlier than I should have done, my Housemaster's final report ending with the words, 'I am sorry to lose him but feel sure that the time has arrived when he should follow his natural bent.' It was shortly after that, when scanning my programme prior to one of the B.A.R.C. Bank Holiday meetings, I saw an advertisement for The College of Automobile Engineering, in Chelsea. This wouldn't normally have been of great interest, but there was a photograph of the principals standing beside two Brescia Bugattis which the College had bought and which, after overhaul by the students, were to be raced at Brooklands, driven by no less a celebrity than Dudley Froy. I sent for the syllabus, gave it to Father, who immediately approved it (it didn't mention the Bugattis!), and within a month I became a student there. Needless to say, by the time I had attained any degree of proficiency, the Bugattis had long since departed and I don't actually recall them ever competing, although they may have done. But I found that Dudley Froy had himself been a student at the College and there was strong interest in racing, on both two and four wheels, among the students, many of whom were Brooklands fans like myself.

It was during my first year at the College that my father died, in October 1932. He had never known it but I had in fact rented premises in the paddock at Brooklands for the past two years—a tiny shed under the stands in the Finishing Straight—at the vast rent of £10 per annum. Here it was that, in the holidays, I was trying hard to build up the elements of a business—mainly buying and selling and a little elementary maintenance of the less good two-wheel race machinery. Oh yes, and garaging. I used to garage racing bikes—the shed would take two!

I had acquired my first racing bike in the strangest way. I knew quite a few of the riders but there was one, the late Eric Fernihough, whom I didn't know. Eric worked behind locked doors and was quite unapproachable. He was contracted to J.A.P. engines at the time and raced them in Excelsior machines, all of which were turned out superbly. He had been at Cambridge, had degrees, and was a highly professional and successful racing motor-cyclist of the technical and brainy type. I think that if I had known then that within three years I should be partnering him in successful long-distance world record attempts, I should have dropped through the floor—or, rather, the concrete.

He was also a first-class businessman and very thrifty. For a long time, after having met him, I thought he had no sense of humour. I later found out that he had, although it was a sense of humour all his own and things that amused him didn't always register with others, including myself.

Although quite young—in his early thirties—he was, in a way, one of the elders, so to speak. He was rather serious, had no time at all for the lighter side, and was more at home with the senior riders than with others of his own age. In other words, he knew where he was going and, I think, preferred the company of those whose interests he most closely shared. The money had largely dropped out of motorcycle racing at Brooklands by this time. There had been a lot of it around in the twenties, but there was a bit still to be found and Eric was a master at squeezing the last drop out of the orange.

Even in the twenties there was the lighter side. J. S. (Willie) Worters once told me a story that happened to him in his early days, at a time when he was still racing privately and using Blackburn engines. He, too, was brainy and was always experimenting and trying new ideas and, at this particular time, was trying hard to make friends with Hatch, who was competition manager at Blackburns and very much a boffin. Willie had already had several successes, had been noticed by Hatch and badly wanted to negotiate a contract with the firm for the loan and development of engines. He'd also been noticed by some of the older riders in whose classes he was competing and, with so much money around, they weren't so keen to see him get better at it. He had worked on Hatch for a long time, trying to get him to come down to Brooklands and see the lines he was working on, but Hatch, who was rather anti-Brooklands, or rather the lighter side of it, had refused, saying that he remained unconvinced that any serious work took place there.

At last Willie achieved success and, having wined and lunched Hatch liberally at the White Lion at Cobham, took him to the track. As they emerged from the tunnel under the track, into the paddock, a car standing on waste ground nearby was seen to be on fire, surrounded by a small crowd which included several well-known riders. One of the best known of them, Dougal Marchant, rushed up to Willie's car. Handing a fire extinguisher to Hatch he said, 'Quick. Use that. I'll go and get a big one from the Clubhouse.' Hatch duly did so. The fire extinguisher had been drained and refilled with a mixture of petrol and paraffin for his especial use, and Willie told me that within forty minutes Hatch was back and working at his drawing-board in the factory at Bookham, never to be seen at Brooklands again.

My first encounter with Eric took place at the final B.M.C.R.C. Meeting at Brooklands at the end of 1931. The meeting was over and I was strolling round the paddock having a last look when I spotted a notice-board outside his shed. On it were advertised for sale all his racing machinery, including the bikes he had raced that day. Most were in the £80 to £100 bracket—right out of my reach—but there was one, believe it or not, at £10. I hadn't even got £10 at the time because I was fully invested with a stock of £2 and £3 lots. They weren't selling awfully well because the trade recession was already under way and I was feeling the pinch along with everyone else.

The bike advertised was described as a 175 cc. track-racing E.F. J.A.P. I just had to know about it so I knocked on the door and Eric opened it, peering at me curiously through the thick lenses of his glasses.

'Yes?' He didn't look too friendly, I thought.

'I see on your board here you've got a bike for sale at £10.'

His attitude changed at once. Eric was always the businessman, even when it came to the £10 touch.

'Oh yes. Well come in. I haven't got it here I'm afraid. It's down at my garage in Southampton.'

'Could you tell me about it? Is it dreadful?'

15

He looked quite offended, as well he might because, in fact, it was a product of his fertile brain. Finding that he had got a lot of spare bits round the garage in the winter of 1929–30, Eric had ingeniously gathered the lot together and had assembled a racing bike from them, naming it the E.F. (Eric Fernihough). The frame was Montgomery, the forks Triumph, the engine was all J.A.P., but the crankcase was 250 cc. side valve on to which he had fitted one cylinder from a 350 cc. vertical overhead valve experimental twin. But the *pièce de résistance* was the gearbox, which was a two-speed Albion with belt drive to the rear wheel. This was quite shattering because belt drive had been out, as far as Brooklands was concerned, for years. But, according to Eric, it was built up of brand new bits throughout and was a thoroughly usable and raceable bike, even if not very fast. I later found out that this was ninety per cent true. The only untrue part, Eric later told me, was that although he had in fact built and raced such a bike a year or two previously, he had subsequently broken it up to use some parts on other machines and, at the time he and I were negotiating, no such machine existed. So, in fact, I was the ideal customer because he hadn't got the machine but, given time, could build it; and I hadn't got the money but, given time, could raise it—and on this basis we did the deal, with me taking his word that the machine was really nice and usable.

And it was, too. The arrangement I made with him was that I should pay £5 down with the balance at £1 per month, delivery not to be taken until the full sum of £10 was paid. This suited us both and, in fact, I think I completed the deal by the end of the year! To youngsters of today these figures will seem laughable, but there wasn't inflation in those days. No one had much money but what money you had would really buy something.

I took delivery of the bike early in 1932 at home at Dorking and immediately I saw it I was thrilled with it. Nearly everything was new on it, but although new, was out of date. It had the correct Brooklands look with dropped handlebars, the saddle mounted over the rear wheel and a big Brooklands-type silencer, from which the most stupendous crackle emerged, having filled the slim fuel tank with the correct brand of alcohol fuel, Discol R.D.I. Quickly its presence was detected by the family, giving me the task of selling them the idea that it was just another 'buy' to be sold off immediately a buyer came along to offer a profit. Would I have sold it? Not likely!

1. 175 cc. E.F.-J.A.P. First Brooklands mount in 1932. The last belt-driven machine ever to compete there.

2. (*above*) The Brooklands Campbell Circuit, 1939. 1100 cc. M.G. Magnette K.N. 'Who carries your money, Charles?'

3. 350 cc. Chater Lea. Fifth in the 1933 Hutchinson 100. Victim of the 'Colorado Beetle' in the B.R.D.C. Trophy.

4. (*above*) Dieppe Grand Prix, 1935. 500 cc. Norton, No. 58, second place. 'Hard work in vain.'

5. Brooklands Senior Grand Prix, 1935. Norton, No. 61. Result: 'A tremendous crumpet.'

6. Goodwood, 1935. Austin Healey. 'If Jean wins, there'll be Hell to pay.'

From January until April it had pride of place in the garage, stored under a dust sheet, to be got out when all the family were away for the day and run round the local lanes, sans mudguards, tax, audible warning of approach (from the legal aspect) and of course, sans insurance, because there wasn't any compulsory insurance in those days anyway. I had a driving licence, though, and half convinced myself that the lanes were on 'private property'.

2

As the 1932 Brooklands season approached, I still had problems, all of them financial. I'd joined the British Motor Cycle Racing Club which organised all the two-wheel stuff at the track and had entered the bike for its first race, a three-lap outer-circuit handicap.

Most of the short races at Brooklands were run on individual handicap basis, of course, and this was dealt with exclusively by the famous A. V. Ebblewhite ('Ebby' for short) who had undertaken the task since the very early days. By profession, Ebby was a musical instrument maker and I imagine that there must have been some connection between complicated musical instruments and the elaborate chronometers he used for him to have got the job in the first place. Ebby was an institution and his handicap system worked well, on the whole, despite the intrigue and manoeuvre of riders and car drivers to outwit it.

Broadly speaking, it worked so that, in theory, when you entered a race at Brooklands for the first time he had very little to go on and, because of this, you found that in your very first race you had a dreadful handicap and were expected to go much faster than, in fact, you could. Usually, in a maiden race, riders finished well down the field and at the next meeting Ebby would be just a fraction more generous, continuing the policy until the new rider won his first race. In theory, with this system and a field of riders whose abilities were known to the handicapper, the race should result in a dead heat for the entire entry and, again in theory, everyone sooner or later won a race. In fact, the latter did happen, but for many reasons the Brooklands finishes varied in their degree of excitement.

One of the reasons, particularly in the car section, was the presence of bookmakers. Drivers did bet and many surprises upset the system. It was completely accepted in both car and bike racing that unless there was a little jiggery pokery, you could never make your racing pay as it should.

What sort of things happened? Here are some of them. The entry form for a Brooklands race requested details of any tuning or alterations done to the car or bike since it last raced. If, say, a rider had his eye on a particular race later on in the season with a view either to the prize and bonus money, he could plan quite successfully to win it. On a 500 cc. machine, for instance, there was always roughly 5 m.p.h. difference between its lap speed on the outer circuit using a petrol/benzole mixture as against one of the alcohol fuels. Identical machines would also vary in speed even when using the same fuel.

So, assuming that for two or three consecutive meetings the rider admitted to using alcohol fuel when in fact he is using petrol, his outer-circuit lap speed would become established in the handicapper's records at, say, 95 m.p.h. Then comes the day when he has decided to win; the engine compression ratio is raised, alcohol is used, the lap speed goes up to 100 m.p.h. or more, if he is lucky, and the day is good, and the race is won. No one has bothered to check his fuel when he wasn't winning and there is no point in checking it now because he has already admitted to using the more volatile fuel. He wasn't honest, but he won.

Engine and chassis numbers had to be quoted on the entry form and it was common knowledge at one time that there were four identical cars competing at Brooklands all with the same engine number. But there was only one really good engine among the four and, outside the circle of those four drivers, very few people knew which of them had it at any given meeting.

Even discounting things like this, people who, like myself, were based at Brooklands day in, day out, all the year round, could and did make a substantial part of our income by betting because we knew exactly the lap speed capacity of every regular competitor, we could work out the pattern of every race in advance from that knowledge and the handicaps that were printed on the programme and, more often than not, and barring accidents, we had the winner beforehand.

Sometimes races looked too close when worked out on paper beforehand and then it was better to keep your money in your pocket. Sometimes you could pick out two competitors in the same race; one or the other must surely win because both were lapping well in excess of their handicap speeds in practice. Be sure that both knew it. Did they like or dislike each other? If they hated the sight of each other, then it was a race on which not to bet. If they were good mates and both of them betting men, then it was just a case of penetrating the grapevine to discover what had been arranged.

Sometimes it was more complicated. The late George Brough was a great betting man and, in 1935, I was riding a Brough Superior in a three-lap handicap at the track. I had had the bike since the beginning of the year and had ridden it in several short handicaps and one fifty-mile handicap, the fastest lap speed being just under 96 m.p.h. because the handling was bad and I didn't know why. It was also rather tricky to get off the line because, starting with a push and with hand gear-change, it did occasionally oil up the plug of the front cylinder just as one made the final gearchange into top gear, at about 85–90 m.p.h., on the home banking.

The handling baffled me and I talked to Ted Baragwanath about it, for the famous 'Barry' had ridden Broughs for years and was then sidecar lap record holder with his big supercharged outfit at over 100 m.p.h. Ted reckoned he knew the trouble and, after taking the bike into his works for a couple of days, brought it down to Brook-lands for me to try.

I took it out and did three laps, at 100, 101 and 103 m.p.h., the last one with only one quick shut-off because it was going faster than I'd then been before and had run on to the home banking rather high.

We were both very pleased and Ted said, 'There you are. You've got a race in your pocket. But we must get George down. He likes to see his bikes win and likes a bet.'

On the day, George was there.

'Are we all right, then?' were his first words.

'We're all right on handling. But until we're in top I wouldn't be sure. I've twice lost a lung when changing into top.'

'Umm. Tricky. But never once it gets marching?'

'No. Just on the change.'

'Hum. Well, we must know. Tell you what,' he went on, 'we'll be at the fork where the bookies are. If you're on both lungs at the end of the first lap, stick your tongue out as you come off the Byfleet banking. I've got binoculars. Then I'll tell Barry and he'll put the money on before you cross the line at the end of lap one. They'll still take it.'

Even now, I recall the moment of relief at finding that the bike was on 'two' as it began really to take hold in top gear. I didn't spot

21

George but he spotted me, and we all went home richer after a couple of flying laps at over 105 m.p.h.

I knew George Brough quite well, even then, and came to know him even better later on because when Eric Fernihough was preparing his Broughs for his attack on the World's Speed Record, then held by Henne on his B.M.W. at nearly 170 m.p.h., Eric did a lot of his preliminary testing at Brooklands with a sidecar fitted—and I was the passenger. Dear George. A truly wonderful man. Kind, enthusiastic, helpful and getting as much pleasure from seeing motor cyclists enjoying his products as they were themselves from riding them. He was a colourful man, too, and really enjoyed life and everything he did.

Another comic occasion involving handicapping cropped up in 1939, when I was driving the 1100 cc. single-seater Magnette in a five-lap handicap on the Campbell Circuit at the track. The car wasn't tremendously fast because it was unblown and fitted with six Amal carburettors. I had run it on the outer circuit and its top lap speed had been just under 110 m.p.h. But it was a very nice ride and wizard on corners—you could do almost anything with it. Although I knew the Campbell Circuit well, I'd put my money on Reg Parnell. Reg was driving a leviathan called the B.H.W., which stood for Bugatti-Hassan-Wilkins. The idea of the car had been Dick Wilkins' and had been carried out by Wal Hassan of Bentley fame. It consisted of putting the 4·9 litre engine out of the big track-racing Bugatti that had been raced by Kaye Don and Dudley Froy into a newly designed single-seater chassis, independently sprung.

The car was enormously fast, but I think it must have been too heavy because its road circuit lap times were by no means as spectacular as they should have been. However, in this race I'd put my money on Reg because although I liked the look of my own handicap I felt I would have liked a few more seconds start from him.

On the starting-line, Reg, who was scratch man, said to me, 'Who carries your money, Charles?'

'You do,' I replied and he laughed. But it was true.

'I'll tell you something. You're carrying mine.'

'What odds, Reg? I got fives on you.'

'Don't know. Bill put it on. He'll be here in a minute. We'd better think about this.' But Bill didn't arrive and Reg wasn't serious anyway.

Half way through the race I could see Reg coming up astern in his monster, but I also noticed that it was all on top speed because the big B.H.W. didn't seem happy under braking and wasn't at all quick out of the slower turns. But on the last lap between the final turn out from the Campbell circuit on to the home banking and the turn back on to the road circuit, half way down the railway straight, Reg fairly streaked up on me and wasn't more than fifty or sixty yards behind. I was sure it was his race, but although the 4·9 was so much faster once it got moving—it must have been doing in the region of 140 m.p.h. in the straight—he was still only coming alongside as we entered Howe corner over the River Wey.

Suddenly there was a dreadful noise. Reg was out of control. I couldn't look, but I knew well enough what was happening because earth and turf were flying all over the place and stones were rattling into the cockpit of my single seater. So I won the contest, and when I saw Reg back in the paddock he was laughing. 'What d'you think, Charles? Much better than winning! I got "tens" on you, and I put on a tenner!'

Reg was a great friend of mine and a great mixer. There was a strange gulf between the riders of racing motor-cycles and the drivers of racing cars at Brooklands. In those days the social stratas were more clearly defined and there were, of course, a lot of very well-connected people in the car side, including members of the aristocracy. The two elements definitely didn't mix, although one had the feeling that the upper crust would like to be matey and let their hair down—but didn't know how!

There were two quite separate catering sections in the paddock, a very swish restaurant and bar for the car people and a rather tatty cafeteria for the bike boys. But certain drivers, among them Reg, Billy Cotton, Charles Brackenbury and Clive Windsor Richards, would nearly always use the café. Others like Chris Staniland, Cyril Paul and Ken Taylor—one of the 'T's of Thompson & Taylor—always used it, and these were the chaps who really got the tempo of the place, because while the restaurant was just like any other restaurant, the café was 'Brooklands'. Even when I switched from bikes to cars, I never used the restaurant. But more than once I heard it said that you could dine there and never know a thing that was going on at Brooklands but you couldn't have even a cup of tea in the café without hearing something of interest.

23

The menu was shocking and consisted almost solely of tea, bread and butter, toast and poached eggs. The tables and chairs were dilapidated, there were no tablecloths and the cups were cracked and the saucers and plates chipped. But that wasn't the fault of the Brooklands Automobile Racing Club or its catering manager, Emery. It was the fault of the clientele, for a wilder lot never patronised an eating establishment anywhere.

On the motor-cycling side, during the time I was there in the thirties, you would see the same people there on most days. Noel Pope, solo outer circuit lap record holder; Francis Beart, famous tuner; Noel Christmas, Jock Forbes, all with their mechanics and helpers; Freddie Clarke, a super little rider, and Charlie Brackenbury, too. It was Charles' delight, on mild weather days, to flick pats of butter up on to the ceiling, where they would remain until the next warm and sunny day, then to descend and fall with a 'plop' on to the heads of any unfortunate customers who had patronised the place not knowing the risk. One of the first things one did, on entering, was to scan the ceiling and re-arrange the tables to points of safety, always making sure to clear and clean one table and leave it beautifully laid for the unwary, directly under the largest infestment of butter pats. It would be the only table in the place that was clean and not swimming in tea and one constantly wondered why the uninitiated never seemed to ask themselves why!

From time to time, members of the upper crust would penetrate. Here again, Charles was often the reason because, being such a first-class driver, he often partnered the upper crust in their big and expensive racing cars in the long races. One whom he introduced to the café was John Cobb who, immaculately dressed and straight from his London office, had come down in the afternoon to practice in the big twelve-cylinder Sunbeam which he and Charles were driving in the 500-Mile Race. John followed Charles in and made a bee-line for the 'clean' table.

Charles said, 'No, not there.'

'Why not? It's the only one that isn't filthy,' John replied.

Charles answered, 'Sit down here and wait and see,' joining us at our table. Hardly had he done so when there was an avalanche of rancid butter on to the other table. John murmured thoughtfully, 'See what you mean. Glad you told me.' After that, he was a frequent visitor and always welcome.

24

This strange segregation also penetrated the administration. The organisation was undertaken by the B.A.R.C. on behalf of the owner of Brooklands, Dame Ethel Locke King, and the motor-cycle side was run by the British Motor Cycle Racing Club, who relieved the B.A.R.C. of all responsibility on the two-wheel side. If you were a Member of the B.A.R.C. at 5 guineas per year, you could do more or less what you liked. Your membership badge admitted you on all race days and other days and allowed you to take your touring car out on to the track on days when there were no meetings. It wasn't at all a big annual sum to pay for the facilities offered. But membership of the B.M.C.R.C. admitted you only to B.M.C.R.C. meetings and practice days and was, quite rightly, rather restricted because the annual subscription was a mere 2 guineas.

On the other hand, we were all tenants of the B.A.R.C. because we rented sheds in the paddock, but we weren't members, despite often being requested to take out membership. Why should we join? We were wrapped up in the motor-cycle side and had very little in common with most of the car people, although the racing itself was of interest to us. We paid annual rents for our sheds varying from £10 to £20 according to size and there we were, the only section of the community able and wanting to watch the best car racing in the country without enjoying membership of the Club. It suited us down to the ground, but, not unnaturally, it didn't suit the Club. The pressure to become members increased and was resisted and finally, exasperated, the Club introduced the most absurd rule ever.

It was aimed directly at us—racing motor-cyclists who were tenants of the Club and who worked full time at the track. It said: 'As from today, tenants of premises in the paddock who are not members of the organising Club shall not be entitled to spectate at car race meetings'; we were called together to be told this by Mr Kenneth Skinner, Secretary of the Company.

We all listened carefully, our thoughts centred on how to get round it, for get round it we certainly would. Talking it over afterwards, we decided to disregard it and see what would happen. We found out at the very next meeting.

Watching one of the early races at the next car meeting, I was tapped on the shoulder by a large gentleman I'd never previously seen.

'Excuse me, sir. My name is Matthews. I've been appointed by the

25

Club to check on members from time to time. Have you got your B.A.R.C. badge with you?'

'Sorry. Afraid not.'

'But you are a member, sir?' well knowing I wasn't.

'I'm a tenant. I work here.'

'Ah, I see. You are now required to be a full member in order to watch the car racing. Were you not aware of that?'

'Yes I was, but it seems rather silly.'

'I quite agree, sir, it does. But it's a new rule, and I have to enforce it. Perhaps you'd like to join the B.A.R.C.?'

'No. Not at all.'

Matthews—we learned later that he was a retired member of the local police force—stiffened but was still polite. 'In that case, sir, I must ask you to come with me to the office,' and, feeling rather as though I was being arrested, I followed him. I was duly ushered in to the presence of the great man himself, Percy Bradley, Clerk of the Course.

Percy was charming, saw the humour of the thing and its slightly ridiculous side, but was firm and said that the rule had been made and had to be enforced. We conferred again amongst ourselves so as to outwit it. And outwit it we did.

Noel Pope was put to the test at the next car meeting. Watching a mountain handicap, he received the Matthews tap on the shoulder and the whole rigmarole was embarked on again.

In his hand Noel held an empty two-gallon Shell fuel tin. 'I'm not watching the racing. I'm on my way from my shed to get some fuel from the Shell depot.' Matthews was shaken, particularly when he noticed at least another half dozen racing motor-cyclists spectating, all carrying two-gallon fuel tins. But the Club didn't give up immediately. It couldn't literally impose a curfew on its small tenants but it could, and for a time did, insist that although it was accepted that tenants should be able to use the facilities on car race days, they had to be in motion and on the direct route to and from their premises in relation to the premises they were visiting. All it did was to make spectating more difficult and to make life for poor Matthews intolerable. He gave up and returned to his previous task of watching for pickpockets and three-card tricksters and we returned to normal spectating.

In fact, the Club was very tolerant with us. But we weren't being

26

bloody minded about it. True, we did enjoy the car racing, but we were tenants—although minor ones—and in those days 5 guineas wasn't a small sum to most people and quite big to us.

I seem to have digressed a bit, but I do want to give the reader as good an idea as possible of the atmosphere of Brooklands. It was different from any other circuit I've known. Every day brought its own highlight. It was a happy, carefree place, exciting and completely unorthodox—always fun. The ten years I spent there as a tenant in the paddock live with me now and, like many others, I really loved the place. And the people too. There were more characters there who were 'larger than life' than any other community I've known.

One particularly vivid character was Walter Handley, a great rider and almost equally good when he turned to cars. Very dry, Walter had one of the keenest senses of humour imaginable. I was riding a 500 cc. Norton once in an outer-circuit race in which Walter was riding a 'works' B.S.A.

The B.S.A. entry was of great interest because, at that time, the factory had steered clear of racing and on that account were rather 'looked down on' by some in view of their lack of race breeding. It wasn't expected that Walter's bike would be so very quick, but on the other hand we were all rather mystified as to why so well-known a rider should accept such a machine if he were not convinced of its potential.

When the flag fell, Walter leapt into the lead and was becoming a vanishing speck in the distance, lapping at well over a hundred, when suddenly the engine seized and there was debris all over the track, through which we had to pick our way as best we could. Walter was rushed to hospital with quite severe head injuries and unable to receive visitors for several days. On about the fourth day, I made another visit and was immediately confronted with the Matron, whom I knew slightly and judged to be in no good humour.

'Mr Handley?' she piped. 'Are you a friend of Mr Handley's?'

'Yes. An old friend.'

'I see. Well you can't see him.' Obviously something had happened. She was very cross.

The cause of it all was that, having emerged from a period of unconsciousness, Walter had quite quickly requested a newspaper so as to catch up on the news he'd missed. He'd been promised it, again and again, until, having decided that the promises weren't intended to be fulfilled, he took the matter into his own hands. Getting out of bed, he put on his dressing-gown and proceeded down the hospital drive in his slippers, out into Weybridge High Street and across to W. H. Smith's, where he bought quite a collection of reading matter, only being spotted by the Matron as he hove into sight returning along the drive. Her last words to me were that Mr Handley 'was a great nuisance—quite irresponsible' and she would be 'most thankful when the time came for him to be discharged'.

On another occasion, when well-placed in, I think, the British Racing Driver's Club 500-Mile Race, Walter had a monumental accident in George Eyston's supercharged Magnette. The car must have been doing between 125 and 130 m.p.h. at the start of the prang and it ended in the undergrowth towards the end of the Railway straight. It was a difficult place to get to—there was only a track which led to it and very few people knew it. So I was first there and found Walter unhurt but dazed.

'You O.K., Wal?'

'Yes.' Then very slowly the well-known drawl: 'Didn't think much of that at all.' He wanted Eyston to be told and I agreed to do it. On the way back I met Eyston bumping along the cart track in a borrowed car. I told him—but never did tell Walter what he said!

In the spring of 1932 I made my first entry for a race at the track, putting the E.F. J.A.P. in two outer-circuit races at the opening B.M.C.R.C. meeting. Nemesis overtook me because our local paper heard about it and came out with a paragraph about 'Local resident' entering for Brooklands race. Knowing that my father read the local rag from cover to cover, I tore out the page of our copy and, to make doubly sure, rang Duncan Ferguson, who was the Club Secretary, to tell him that I couldn't ride and asked him to suggest someone who would like to take over the ride.

A few days later I had a letter from him saying that Jack King, who was sidecar passenger to Pat Driscoll in his Norton outfits, would be glad to ride the E.F. I had got over the problem of transporting the bike. I couldn't afford transport so decided to keep it in my tiny shed at Brooklands, but it did have to be got there in the first place. I pushed it the fifteen miles from Dorking, coasting down the hills and, even, snicking it into top gear at the bottom so that it would run part way up the next bit. I had thought that the trip would take me most of the day, but in fact I did the door-to-door trip in under three hours.

Next day, Jack nobly rode it to finish about halfway down the field with a flying lap of 54·14 m.p.h.!

While I was thrilled to see it perform, I had to admit that it wasn't exactly a flyer and I still hadn't ridden it myself. Nor did I at the next meeting for, at home, I still sensed that I was under suspicion.

I'm not sure, now, whether Jack had arranged to ride something else or whether he just felt that, having experienced the ride once, he didn't want it again. At all events, he wasn't available so, again, I got on to Duncan Ferguson.

This time, much to my surprise, there was no delay. He had been approached by Chater Lea rider Ben Bickell who was, at the time, in the lead for the Brooklands Aggregate award. Ben wanted as many rides as possible and would be happy to pilot the E.F. Would I contact him? I did, in a half-apologetic sort of way because Ben was a big star. He was awfully nice about it but would like to have the bike at his garage in Highgate for a few days, so as to have a look around it. Would that be alright?

Another push, from Brooklands to Weybridge station, on to the train at Weybridge, and the bike was at Waterloo! I don't recall how I got it from Waterloo to Highgate, but I'm sure I didn't push it this time!

Ben rang me next day. He'd had a look round the bike and was quite happy with it. He'd bring it down to the track in his van with his own bikes on the day and asked whether I'd mind if he made one or two minor engine alterations so as to use his own fuel.

I remember that meeting very well. The van arrived. Ben practised on his own bikes, and then came the E.F. which, according to the programme, was handicapped to lap at around 56 m.p.h. to win. Ben, and his tuner brother Joe, told me that they'd made one or two minor alterations to the engine which they felt might make a big difference. They didn't want to do a complete practice lap because they felt that the bike stood a good chance of winning and, if it did, they aimed to back it. Their plan was to warm it up in the paddock, go straight out on to the track, and gun it hard down the half mile. No one, they felt, would bother to clock it over the half mile, on the assumption that they would be doing at least a lap's practice on it, never having ridden it before. If it would go over the half mile at 60 m.p.h. or more, they aimed to put their money on it. I could hardly take all this in—my relic of a bike being ridden by so famous a rider—who actually thought he might win with it!

It went over the half at just over 63 m.p.h. and, as all the stopwatch-clickers were getting ready to time it at the end of the lap, Ben coasted into the paddock. 'That's it, then. It should win.'

By this time, there was a lot of interest in it because the regulars had realised that there was something afoot.

'Aren't you going to do a lap on it, Ben?'

'No, it's an old bike. And I've got too much to do on the others. I haven't practised with the sidecar bike yet.' He was very crafty.

The E.F. didn't win. It did a standing lap of 59, one flying lap of 63 and then, walking away with the race, the engine stopped. After the meeting Joe said to me, 'Would you like to see what's gone in your engine? Come on, we'll take it down.'

When turned, the inlet valve of the engine opened but the exhaust valve didn't and, as the cambox cover was removed, out fell the exhaust cam follower in two halves. Joe picked it up and looked at it thoughtfully. 'You poor little bleeder. Not your fault. You were never designed to follow cams at those revs!'

From this first meeting, I got to know the Bickell brothers well. Joe's wife, Maureen, had a beautiful sister, Celia, who was on the stage and, at that time, was in one of the Leslie Henson shows. I had a great time escorting Celia round the West End. This, coupled with the racing, made it necessary for me to work hard at my dealing, but it was well worth it because although Celia was gorgeous, I couldn't possibly drop racing, even for her!

My very first ride on the E.F. was in July 1932 and I still have the cutting from *Motor Cycling* describing it.

'H. C. Lones had a 500 cc. J.A.P. twin dwarfed by the body of his Morgan and C. K. Mortimer the limit (utter) man on 4 mins, 42 secs, wheeled out a wierd contraption once familiar to admirers of the Fernihough—an E.F. J.A.P. or, in other words, an old Montgomery fitted with one pot off a 1920 J.A.P. twin and a belt drive. Driscoll's average speed of 83·90 was sufficient to carry him to victory a long way ahead of Mortimer who, nevertheless, motored his bicycle so effectively that he gained second place from R. H. Page (Norton). The E.F. J.A.P. however, had gained enough glory for one afternoon and refused to start for the last handicap, an example that was followed by one of Lones' cylinders and, nearly, by W. C. Marshall's Rudge.'

Not perhaps the most flattering of press notices. Even so, they didn't tell it all because the reason for the E.F. not starting in the second handicap was that it caught fire on the line. And to cap it all, as I fought the flames in order to preserve my treasure, I could hear the voice of a blasé spectator wafting over the railings, 'Leave it alone. Let the bleeder burn!'

None of this worried me at all. I'd been placed in a race at my beloved Brooklands at the first attempt and that really meant something. I rushed back to Dorking to silence the local rag.

The E.F. continued to give me good racing throughout 1932 and notched up several more places, but its days were numbered and I had to have something faster. I did buy another bike towards the end of the season—a 250 cc. New Henley J.A.P. which had, at one time, been raced by Mike Couper, who later achieved fame with the big Talbot, BGH 23 on which he lapped the outer circuit at just under 130 m.p.h. I bought the New Henley from Mike Rawlence, elder son of L. C. Rawlence, who was then concessionaire for O.M. cars in Britain, thereby embarking on a friendship with Mike and his younger brother Tony which lasted throughout my racing span.

The New Henley, while more modern looking than the E.F., was still not fast enough, its best outer-circuit lap being under 80, which won me nothing because, even then, 250's on alcohol were all lapping at 85 and some were doing nearly 90. So, in the winter of 1932–33 I sold both, worked hard and saved.

That was a busy winter because my father died in October and, as I was the only son, there was a great deal I could do to help my mother. We continued to live in the same house at Dorking, for we had many friends there, and in the early part of 1933 I began to think again of racing.

I had reliable racing that year, having bought from the Bickell brothers one of their 350 cc. overhead camshaft Chater Leas which I ran in a number of races, sometimes as a solo and sometimes with side-car. The best solo lap was turned at just under 90 and, with chair, about 76 or 77. I ran the outfit in as many long races as possible because I wanted to have a strong 'go' in the Hutchinson 100 at the end of the season—a flat-out 100-mile blind of 37 laps.

I only had trouble once with the Chater Lea but it was maddening, as this account from The Motor Cycle of October 1933 shows:

'A fifty mile (18 laps) Handicap for the British Racing Driver's Club Trophy was one of the most inexplicable flops Brooklands has ever seen and it is to be hoped that not too many British racing drivers were there to see just how badly track two-wheelers can behave on occasions. Here is the sad story in a nutshell; thirteen(!) started. Mortimer's Chater Lea went out with a bent exhaust valve on lap one and Lambert's Morgan became a single cylinder model. That started the rot. The Colorado beetle, or whatever the infectious bug was, flitted from engine to engine until, by one third distance, just three people were left running.'

The exasperating thing was that it wasn't a bent exhaust valve for, on the Chater Lea engine, there was a little copper pipe which ran from the cambox externally, direct to the exhaust valve guide which it lubricated. The pipe hadn't even fractured. The end had just come out of the tiny hole in the head which led to the guide. The engine faded instantly, just as I was leaving the Railway straight, so the pipe must have had a touch or a knock, possibly as my pusher went to flood the carburettor on the start-line. The exhaust valve was seized in the guide and, not realising that there were going to be so many retirements, I began to push in. Within three minutes bikes were packing up everywhere and I stopped pushing and went to work to try and get the engine running. I got a twig of Brooklands gorse, dipped into the oil tank and laid the bike on its side, swamping the valve stem with castor base. Then I got a stout bit of stick and started to try and free the valve. I got it partly free and began to think that, after all, I might emerge the winner of the slowest fifty-mile race ever run at the track.

Working on the bike was quite hazardous because it had coasted from the Railway straight to the start of the Byfleet banking and, of course, all the solo runners were not using the banking but taking the inside line and cutting the grass verge at the flat part of the track, at the bottom of the banking. As I worked away with my horticultural tools on the Chater Lea engine, bikes were zooming past, eighteen inches away, at between 90 and 110 m.p.h.

In the end I did get it going and rode in, passing others who were in trouble and working equally hard. But it was too late—the race was over. I never got caught again without tools, though, in a long race. From then on I always had tools laid in the grass at four places—the beginning and end of the home banking, half way down the Rail-

7. 1935. The 'Thresher'. £25 winner of the Viscount Wakefield Cup.

8. (*below*) Gatwick Speed Trials, 1936. 500 cc. Norton. Five runs: 13·59, 13·54, 13·29, 13·10 and 13·02 seconds, to win the 'Six Fastest'.

9. Brooklands, Hutchinson 100, 1935, 350 cc. Norton. 'What have you done that for?'

10. Brooklands, 1939.
350 cc. Beart Norton and sidecar. World's Standing Mile and Kilo.

11. (*above*) Shelsley Walsh, 1947. Alta 1½-litre single seater.

12. 1948: 'The nicest racing car I ever owned'—the 1934 1½-litre Maserati.

way straight and half way round the Byfleet. I used to put them there before the start and collect them afterwards, together with plugs, copper wire and tape. Two-and-three-quarter miles is a long way to push on a hot day.

A friend of mine, a T.T. rider, used to do the same thing in the Isle of Man, but he went one better. Having slid off his bike in the Senior T.T. at the Gooseneck he found himself unhurt and the bike undamaged, but he couldn't restart because it was too steep to push uphill—the correct way of the course—and dangerous and against the rules to turn round and push-start downhill. He searched around, found a vast boulder, lifted the machine on to it so that the cradle of the frame rested on it, and putting the bike into first gear, pulled the engine back on to compression via the rear wheel. Then, giving the rear wheel an almighty heave, he succeeded in restarting the engine, finishing the race in replica time. After that, he always had huge blocks of wood parked in the ditches all the way up the mountain climb from Ramsey to Snaefell at mile-apart intervals. He was a nice chap and shared the information with his mates, and several people used the facility over the years. Whether or not the A.C.U. would have liked this broadening of their T.T. Regulations no one knew—or seemed to care.

The last race in which I ran the Chater Lea, this time with sidecar, was the Hutchinson 100, right at the end of October. When the programme came out I was a bit shocked to note that I had to start off the same mark as E. G. Bishop's 350 cc. Excelsior J.A.P. and sidecar, because Bishop was then holder of the outer circuit 350 cc. lap record. I felt that 'Ebby' must have gone out of his mind but, at the start, our engine chimed in at once, while poor old Bishop was left pushing.

As all this happened so long ago, it might be as well to describe the 'Hutch' as it was in those days; 100 miles flat out, individual handicap for all-comers, solo machines of any capacity, sidecars the same and three-wheelers.

So, at one end on the start-line you had the scratch man, in this case Ben Bickell, who would have to lap pretty consistently at between 108–10 m.p.h. in order to win and, at the other, someone on a 172 cc. Villiers-powered two-stroke who could win if he kept lapping throughout at around 70 m.p.h. So there would be an interval of, perhaps, twenty minutes or more between the departure from the line of the limit and scratch men. Obviously you couldn't have a start-line stretching right across the track so we used to form a sort of double queue alongside the timekeeper's hut, moving up to where the starter stood when our turn came.

Sometimes, the gentleman on the two-stroke would be buzzing round on his own for a couple of laps or more before anyone else got off the line, looking and feeling very conspicuous and self conscious but, gradually, the race got under way and then it really was fun. Everything was out on the track and everyone had to take different lines, all of which converged into the same one, hard alongside the Vickers sheds, at the fork.

The Morgans would be right up at the very top of the banking, partly because in order to control their bucking steeds they needed it all, and partly to make life as easy as possible for the rear tyre, which was always rather a worry for them.

With them would be the 1000 cc. solos, because by virtue of their weight that was the easiest path for them, and also because the high line was easier on the rear tyre. Tyre wear was a real worry on heavy machinery in those days.

Lower down on the banking, around the 50-foot line—the track was 100 feet wide at its narrowest point—you would find the 1000 cc. and 500 cc. sidecar outfits, their lower speed making it possible for them to use less banking, which really ended about 25 or 30 feet out from the grass verge at the bottom.

A bit below this group would come the faster 500's, the 110 m.p.h. brigade whose controllability made it possible for them to pass below the slower-moving sidecar people.

There was a painted line right round the track, 10 feet from the top of the banking, and another 10 feet from the inside grass verge at the bottom and here would be all the rest; solo chaps lapping at less than 108 m.p.h., the smaller stuff which might be doing no more than 70–75 m.p.h. and the 350 sidecar outfits lapping around 80 m.p.h. All the speeds quoted are for long races. For shorter events, they would be 5 m.p.h., or more, faster.

The effect of this was that the bottom line—the inside—was a busy and tricky thoroughfare, but in using it, one saved considerable distance. The 50-foot line was the easiest and the top 10 feet, though not so crowded, was also tricky because nearly everyone there was moving, and a mistake made there was usually serious.

What happened if you went over the top? It rather depended where-

34

abouts. The home banking was the most dangerous because, once over, there was a big drop into a thickly treed area. It was here that Clive Dunfee was fatally injured when his big six-cylinder Bentley went over in the 500-Miles race. On the other hand, H. T. H. Clayton went over in an M.G., a much smaller car, staying in the car, whereas I believe Dunfee remained on the track.

It was strictly forbidden to climb up through the undergrowth at the back of the banking, so as to watch from the top, but it was often done and I happened to be there when Clayton went over and was less than a hundred yards away when it happened. I was there with several other riders and it was a regular vantage point for us, well-screened with undergrowth and yet giving a perfect view of almost the whole of the lap.

As Clayton's M.G. appeared approaching from behind the Members' Hill, high up on the banking, the 2·6-litre Monza Type Alfa Romeo of A. P. (Ginger) Hamilton was close behind, even higher and obviously intending to pass. But there clearly wasn't room for him to pass above the M.G. and when both cars were nose to tail he decided this himself. Both cars were doing well over 120 m.p.h. and, as Hamilton changed his plan and decided to try to pass beneath, the front of the Alfa touched the tail of the M.G. Instantly the latter swung round broadside, pointing directly up the banking, travelling sideways and upwards. By this time we were departing at speed and that was all we saw. There was a loud crackling as we ploughed through the undergrowth, which was drowned as the M.G. hurtled through, cutting a swage through the saplings as it landed upside down forty or fifty yards away. For a moment we could hardly believe it. Then we climbed back to the top of the banking and ran along it and down the path cut by the car. As we ran, we met a press photographer—a good friend of ours called Wood. Poor Woody was breathless and dishevelled.

'Don't go down there, for God's sake,' he gasped. 'He's lost his head!'

'What d'you mean, Woody?'

'What I say. His head came off. I saw it.'

Well, he hadn't. In fact he's alive today and in business not five miles from where I live. But he had lost his crash-hat and that was what poor old Woody must have seen.

There was a rumpus about this and poor 'Ginger' appeared before the Stewards. But it was the sort of situation which could, and did, arise at any time at Brooklands and all the fuss died down in the end.

The only other 'over the top' that I saw was in a race in which I was riding. It was a three-lap outer-circuit handicap and I had to go off the same mark as a young fellow—a student—called Hogarth. Our machines were both the same capacity, 350 cc. Norton and A.J.S. respectively. In the past, my Norton comfortably had the legs of the A.J.S., but Hogarth was a customer of Francis Beart's and Francis had told me that, since its last race, a lot had been done to Hogarth's bike and it was bound to be faster than it had been.

Even so, I still felt that I could cope, but when the flag fell I had doubts—the A.J.S. really was fast. In fact, it was all I could do to tuck in behind him and stay there and I was relieved to find that I could stay right with him—but no more—as we came off the home banking into the Railway straight. In the Railway straight I found that this was it. I could do nothing more than stay with him. At the end of the straight we were still nose to tail and doing well over 100 m.p.h. and then we arrived at the beginning of the Byfleet banking. In order to go in really close—within a foot or eighteen inches of the grass verge —you had to be very firm indeed with those old bikes at that point because there was no rear springing—they were rigid frames. You went in and laid the bike over to the left (Brooklands outer-circuit races were run anti-clockwise) and immediately the rear wheel would step out to the right and you were in a full 100 m.p.h.-plus slide which would continue for nearly three-quarters of a mile until the Byfleet ended and you brought the bike back over to the right for the fork. Hogarth laid the A.J.S. over stylishly but, never having been in so fast, the rear wheel stepped out so far that it shook him and, without shutting off, he immediately brought the bike upright. That was bound to be the end. Up it went and before he knew what had happened he was silhouetted against the skyline, still half on the bike. They disappeared from view and I slowed and stopped, trying to make sure that I wasn't collected from behind in doing so. I left the Norton and ran back but there were no marks on the track and I couldn't pinpoint the place. Someone else was already trying to climb the last few feet of the banking which, although not vertical, were very steep.

After a bit of a struggle and with machines howling round way below us, we got to the top but, at first, couldn't see where poor old

Hogarth had gone. The gorse there was so thick that it had closed in behind him and, in any case, both he and the bike had leaped over the first twenty feet or so on their airborne trip. When we did find him he was quite unhurt, apart from a few scratches, and lying on his back in the thickest part. His first words were, 'Where's my bike? I need it to go to work on Monday!' The gorse had broken the bike's fall, too, and the damage amounted only to bent footrests, gearchange and an odd broken control cable. So, obviously, it was possible to take a trip over the top and get away with it. All you needed was luck!

The 1933 Hutchinson 100 was the first of several in which I took part. At that time I was rather badly lacking in experience and organisation because, in fact, had everything gone smoothly and been properly organised, we could almost certainly have won that race. My sidecar passenger was an old school friend, Johnny Waite, and it was agreed that Johnny's father would look after our pit. We had to make a stop at half distance for fuel and oil and, although we had watched pit stops in long races, we were all three of us inexperienced in the technique and I don't think it occurred to us to practice the fill beforehand.

Bishop, also, could have won, if he hadn't oiled a plug at the start. As it turned out, he was just getting under way as we came off the Byfleet banking at the end of our second lap and we came up behind him just under the Members' Bridge on the home banking, finding that we could tuck in behind him and slipstream him all the way down the Railway straight. Neither Johnny, in my sidecar, nor Bishop's passenger were aware of this. Passengers in Brooklands' sidecar outfits didn't ride sitting up. They lay face downwards, facing rearwards. My sidecar had a 'slipper'-type body—that is to say the passenger's head and shoulders protruded from the 'heel' of the slipper so to speak, and although he couldn't see where we were going, he had a good view of everything astern. The body of Bishop's sidecar, on the other hand, had a streamlined tail into which the passenger's head fitted and the poor chap lay on his side with his crash-hat wedged into the tail of the 'chair', seeing nothing and enduring it all.

On the Chater Lea we had, till then, used about a third of the Byfleet banking and, at the end of the Railway straight, I was astonished to find Bishop take a different line, diving right in at the bottom within a foot of the grass verge on the inside. One had to take an instant decision. Our own line or his much more difficult one? He was experienced and we followed him. Within a hundred yards, his side-

37

car wheel had left the ground. Higher and higher it went till it was a foot off the ground—and there it stayed for the whole three-quarter-mile length of the Byfleet banking. One couldn't believe it, because by the end of the Byfleet the wheel was hardly turning—just revolving idly so that you could see the tyre tread clearly. At the end of the Byfleet as he went on to opposite lock for the fork, it came down to earth with a bump, and hardly had his outfit slewed as the wheel made contact, when I noticed our 'plot' do the same—quite a big 'twitch' it was, too! There was less than a minute to think about all this before we would be doing it again but, obviously, if his outfit was performing these antics round the Byfleet, ours must be too. We mustn't lose him, but I had to know!

After three or four laps like this, I elected to have a look, just before we left the Byfleet to straighten up for the fork and was surprised to find Johnny laying not below me and to the left, but level! And you could count the spokes of the wheel as it turned lazily! The result of all this was that we got a wonderful 'tow' from Bishop for more than fifty miles before we got the sign from the pit to come in and refuel.

Arriving there, we found chaos. Our 'tow' from Bishop had put us leading the race on handicap by a huge margin and, spotting this, numerous well-wishers had crowded into the pit to help, well knowing our inexperience. A gallon of castor-based gushed from the re-fuelling gun, some of it into the tank but a great deal more over the rear part of the outfit and neat methanol streamed down from the overflowing tank. About the only thing that was right about that 'fill' was that nobody was smoking! The engine wouldn't restart, which wasn't surprising in view of the liquids poured over it, and we had to change a plug, which lost us a lap instantly. Till then, we had been lapping, with Bishop's help, at over 80 m.p.h. but, having lost him and jettisoned our chances, we could only limp in to finish fifth. We'd thrown away a good chance of winning the 'Hutch' at the first attempt.

In the early- and mid-thirties the type and pattern of bike racing at Brooklands was changing. The big money had gone out of it and manufacturers no longer built special machines for use purely for outer-circuit racing, to be ridden by professionals. The big professionals like Bert Denly, Bill Lacey, Victor Horsman, Wright, Staniland, Worters and others were packing it in or turning to car racing. There was no lack of usable machinery, though, because many manufacturers such as Norton, Rudge, Sunbeam, New Imperial, Velocette and A.J.S. all made Isle of Man T.T. replica bikes for sale to the public and they sold well and adapted well to outer-circuit racing. And, of course, some of the ex-works outer-circuit bikes found their way into the hands of private owners, to swell the entry lists.

But the trend was a strong one and it was from outer-circuit racing to Grand Prix- and T.T.-type events for road-racing bikes fitted with front brakes and in road-racing trim. There were still outer-circuit races at B.M.C.R.C. meetings but more events were held on the 'Mountain' circuit which was just over a mile round, on the finishing straight and the home banking. Outer-circuit races over the full two-and-three-quarter-mile perimeter took up about a third of the programme.

To do both, you really needed two bikes because too much work was involved in swopping saddle mountings, wheels and other fittings to make it possible to use one machine. So I rang the changes for 1934, using a big 996 cc. Brough Superior J.A.P. for the outer circuit and investing in a 250 cc. T.T. Replica New Imperial for the road-racing events.

The New Imperial looked every inch a racer—just like the works T.T. bikes—but, when it arrived, turned out to be desperately slow, with a maximum of under 80 m.p.h. on pump fuel. I had it down for the 100-Mile Brooklands Grand Prix in July, a race run round the Byfleet banking and into the finishing straight where there was an artificial chicane made up of oil drums, and back to rejoin the outer circuit at the end of the home banking.

With Eric Fernihough's help, we got it lapping at about 85, prior to the event, but about a fortnight before the day, the Club announced that they were going to cancel the Lightweight race owing to lack of entries. This upset Eric greatly for he was a certain winner with his Excelsior J.A.P. and he marshalled together all the possible starters, campaigning for the race to be held. In the end, I think, about eight or nine firm entries were whipped up and the Club agreed to hold the race concurrently with the 350 cc. event.

The report of the race in *The Motor Cycle* of August 2nd said: 'Fernihough (246 Excelsior) took the lead from Mortimer (New Imperial) after the second lap and from then onwards proceeded to sit on his lead, frequently looking behind to see that no one in his class came too near. By three quarter distance he was still leading, but T. Cogan Verney (New Imperial) was now second, Mortimer on a similar machine having dropped back to third.' And the reason for that was that I had boobed again and been too mean to invest in the £5 optional extra of a bigger front brake!

So it ended. A very dull race, but we did have a bit of fun with Eric before the start. On the morning of the race a big van arrived in the paddock and on its side was a familiar trade emblem and the words 'Rudge Whitworth. Coventry'. Now Rudges, who were not entered for the race, were the only firm capable of beating Eric in the 250 cc. class, or the only British ones anyway. And when we found the occupants of the van to be none other than Ernie Nott and Tyrell Smith, their star riders, we thought at once that they had put in a late entry. In fact, they hadn't. They were on their way to Dover, en route for the Dutch T.T.

But the opportunity was far too good to miss. Tyrell and Ernie agreed to co-operate and I rang Eric at his garage, outside the track, on the Brooklands Road. It was about nine o'clock and the race was due to start at twelve.

'Eric. Rudges are here. Tyrell and Ernie.'

There was a dreadful silence. 'What are they doing?'

'I don't know. They seem to have come for the race.'

Another silence. 'They can't. Entries closed a week ago. I saw the list.'

'Well, that's what they say. Thought I'd better tell you.'

'I'll come down. We can stop it if we all stick together.'

He arrived within five minutes. By that time, every Lightweight competitor was in the know and all were in favour of Rudges running. Poor Eric was frantic. He rushed back to Byfleet and virtually re-built the machine in two hours, fitting his best engine and biggest brakes, among other things. But, to give him credit, he did laugh about it on the start-line and he beat us all with even greater ease than he would have with his 'cooking' equipment.

Apart from that one third place, I had no success at all with the New Imperial. I ran it in a number of races including the Hutchinson 100, in which it suffered a slow puncture and finally broke one of its roller-type cam followers. Eric won the Hutch that year, on his 175 cc. Excelsior J.A.P. at over 82 m.p.h., a good win and a good speed on a tiny bike, superbly prepared.

The New Imperial began to respond to tuning as the season wore on, but the faster it went the more voracious became its appetite for cam followers. I was fed up with it and arriving back at the paddock one day after a two-mile push-in, I was greeted by a grinning Francis Beart.

' 'Nother cam follower, Charles?'

'I s'pose so. Bloody thing.'

'Give you twenty-five quid for it—and take the chance.'

I thought for a moment. The loss would be a big one—so was the gamble though. The rattle that preceded the silence had been slightly bigger than hitherto.

'Done.' And Francis wrote out the cheque.

I walked back to my shed and changed, passing Francis' rather more imposing premises on my way over to the canteen.

'Charles. Come in and have a look.' The barrel and head of the engine were on the bench. What remained of the piston hung limply by the bosses from the gudgeon pin. The rod had had it, so had the barrel. You couldn't tell about the head till the valves were removed. I just didn't know what to think, but Francis looked at a deal in the same way as I did, and he stood laughing and reassuring me all the time.

The rest of that season was all outer circuit stuff for me, mostly on the Brough. But my rides that year had contrast, if nothing else, for my other mount was right at the farthest end of the scale—a 150 cc. overhead valve New Imperial with engine and gearbox unit construction. It came about this way.

Our local New Imperial agent at Dorking was Henry Nash, and it was he who had supplied the 250 that I sold to Francis. At that time, New Imperials had really excelled themselves in the price-cutting war by designing and producing the little 150 cc. 'Unit Minor' O.H.V. model, to sell at a record low price of 27 guineas, complete. It was quite a sporting little bike and I bought one and did a little work on it to make it look more racy, intending to use it on the Mountain Circuit. It really wasn't fast, though, and I had had enough of New Imperials, so Henry kindly bought it back from me. Having done so, and seeing the start I'd made on the bike, he went further and worked on the engine. We then tried it and, on the form it showed, he entered it in a race. I rode it and won. Henry did more work, entered it again with me as rider and rang the bell for the second time. Altogether,

41

it won three or four races, each faster than the previous one and, finally, Ben Bickell rode it and scored again.

With its Brooklands' handicap so completely wrung out that it was now almost impossible to win again, Henry withdrew the Unit Minor into retirement—but only temporarily. Soon afterwards he produced it again, the engine now linered down to 125 cc., the machine fully streamlined, and departed for Belgium where he successfully broke the World's Standing and Flying Kilometre and Mile for the class, at speeds of over 80 m.p.h. All this with a bike costing 27 guineas, new, and designed to take Mr Everyman to his work!

Hopping off the New Imperial and on to the Brough was an experience to be taken seriously with machinery three times as heavy and nearly seven times the engine capacity. Everything was different. With the New Imp, one was always limit man. You started at the fall of the flag and, if you won, you never saw another machine throughout the race, just tucking yourself in and keeping your head down under the fairing—and hoping! It could be very disappointing because it could, and sometimes did, turn out that in a nine-mile race you would lead the whole way bar the last twenty yards, only to be swamped by half a dozen big 'uns to finish seventh.

When I first got the Brough—it had been one of the late Frank Longman's 200-Mile race machines—I could make nothing of it at all. I had expected it to be hard work, but it was far, far worse than I hoped. Lapping in the early 90's, mostly on about half throttle, and using far more of the bankings than should have been necessary at that speed, it was frightful, going into long weaving wobbles and any other tricks it could think of. In my ignorance, I thought that this was what a big bike was like and that it was my own lack of experience and strength causing the trouble.

Johnny Waite, who helped me with the machinery in between spells of passengering, suggested a long ride in order to get used to it, and we entered it for the fifty-mile Essolube Trophy. Its fuel consumption was immense, as was its tyre wear, both back and front, and on measuring the consumption properly we found that we couldn't do fifty miles on a tankful of fuel, which brought the consumption out at something like twelve to the gallon. So, in addition to finding ourselves on the scratch mark, we also had to make a fuel stop after twenty-five miles, or fit a bigger tank, which we hadn't got and couldn't afford to have made.

In the light of today's specialised refuelling arrangements, ours were comic to look back on. Instead of a refuelling hose running from a churn mounted on the roof of the pit, refuelling in those days was done from two-gallon tins. A powerful man would do the job, up-ending the tin into the tank and then grabbing a large screwdriver off the pit counter. Using all his force, he would bring the screwdriver down on to the bottom of the tin, punching a hole in the bottom to let the air in, but although I saw this done on many occasions I never saw a fire! I don't think there ever was one—maybe fuels were even less volatile at that time than one realised. What the fuel companies did with their ruptured tins, we never knew.

We finished fifth in the Essolube Trophy race at an average of 89 and a best lap of 95 m.p.h., the only runners to have to stop for fuel. I rather think we must have taken part in another short race on the bike before the fifty-miler that day, because thinking back on all this recalls two comic start-line conversations, both involving the Brough and both involving passengers of other outfits.

The first one, I think, was when we were running the bike in a race, earlier on in the season. It was a three-lap outer-circuit thing and we had to give start to everyone except the scratch man, Tommy Rhodes in his Morgan. I didn't know Rhodes personally. He was a quiet Northcountryman who regularly drove at Brooklands and always lapped at a bit over a hundred. On that occasion, his passenger was a rather depressed little chap and, on arriving at the start-line, Rhodes nodded to me and his passenger got out and came over.

We had three seconds start off Rhodes and his passenger opened the conversation with, 'What speed can'st lap at, maitey?'

'Oh, ninety-five to ninety-eight.'

'Aaahh.' He gave it careful thought and then came the punch line. 'Yon Rhodes. Morgan's tricky old lot. Taikes holding.' And he pro-ceeded to unburden the problem. We would both be using the same line—agreed. They might catch us or might not—also agreed. If they did, and if it was at certain points on the track, it could be difficult. Why? Because, if we were too high to allow him to pass above, he wouldn't be able to pull down to pass beneath. Nor could he slow because, like most of the Morgans, he had no accelerator pedal to control the speed, but a Bowden cable from a lever on a rung of the steering-wheel. This wasn't all for, so his passenger glumly informed us, it was Mr Rhodes's habit, once in top gear, to twist a rubber band round the lever and take a half-hitch round the rung of the wheel, making it impossible to shut off at any point where the Morgan required both hands on the wheel—which really was most of the way!

The poor passenger looked quite pathetic about all this and our first reaction was that we were being craftily and professionally demoralised. But, on examining the set-up, Johnny reported that it appeared to be true—all the gear was as described. And, later, on consulting Henry Laird, another star Morgan driver, it was officially confirmed. So we did leave Mr Rhodes all the room he might—and did, need.

The second conversation was with E. C. E. (Ted) Baragwanath, again on the line of a race. Ted, a great rider of big twins and Brough Superior in particular, strolled up and said, 'You're going to hurt yourself with that if you aren't careful.'

We said we knew, but we didn't know what was wrong.

'Well, something is. You'd better let me have a look round it before the next meeting. Meanwhile, be careful. If you think the bloody thing's going over the top, don't you go with it. Let go of the bars and slide off the back. Golden rule.'

From the depths of Ted's sidecar came the voice of his passenger. 'Really, guv'nor? Never 'eard that one afore. I won't 'arf ride 'appy now.'

It had dawned on us, by now, that we were regarded by the stars as a bit of a menace, in the sense that we might get into real trouble with the Brough and involve one of them in a bad accident and, at the end of this particular meeting, Ben Bickell agreed to take it out for a few laps and try to make a diagnosis. I was glad that it seemed generally accepted that it was the bike and not the rider that was at fault and, having tried the thing and lapped at over 101 m.p.h., Ben confirmed that it was 'a pig' and felt that the trouble lay with the damping of the front forks.

At this stage, 'Barry' took over and after two days in his shop the bike emerged, handling perfectly and winning the very next race for us, at an average of nearly 101 m.p.h. from a standing start.

Even now, I can still recall the tremendous contrast of those two machines, the little New Imperial, all noise and fuss, its engine rather rough and harsh, but the machine infinitely controllable as regards handling. The Brough, lapping at around 106 m.p.h., its engine as smooth as a Rolls, so quiet that all you heard was the rush of the wind,

44

but requiring physical strength on many occasions, even in a short race, and far from forgiving if you did make a mistake in line, particularly when running on to the bankings.

At this stage, the autumn of 1934, it was obvious that a lot of careful thinking would have to be done in planning the 1935 racing season. I had ridden solo machines at Brooklands of 150, 250, 350 and 1000 cc. and the 350 with a sidecar on occasions. I knew that the latter didn't appeal. It was fun in its way and it had the added appeal in involving two people rather than one. But the object of outer-circuit racing was ot go as fast as possible and it seemed pointless to attach to the bike a deadweight that automatically dropped its lap speed by at least 15 m.p.h. So sidecars were out. So was the 150 because I was too big a chap to get the best out of it. There weren't a lot of races for 250's and the trend was becoming more and more towards the road-racing type of event, so the 350 cc. and 500 cc. classes seemed the ones to go for.

The question of keeping on running a 'thousand' took some heart searching. There were very few of them running at the track at that time but, to my mind, they had a certain glamour and individuality that no other class had. Inefficient when compared with the 350 and 500's, they certainly were. But they were great to ride when they were on form and exhilarating in quite a different way from any other bike. The sensation of riding a 'thousand' fast in an outer-circuit race, perched high on the banking, from whence you could see the whole way round the two-and-three-quarter-mile track—when you had time—was something quite apart. 'Grass cutting' with a fast 500 or 350, using the bottom line, was utterly different. The most you could possibly see of the track was, perhaps, three or four hundred yards ahead and although it was more exciting, there was no feeling of exhilaration.

Since, as I am writing this, we are at a stage when nobody else possessing first-hand experience may write about it, I'll try to give an idea of what I mean, because I still have all my old logs and records of the machines I rode. The previous owner of my Brough Superior had been Geoffrey Davies and I had bought the bike from him in the spring of 1934. I had taken it home and looked long and hard at it before riding it and had then written to Geoffrey to iron out one or two points. I'll quote his reply in full because not only does it give the 'atmosphere' but it also gives an insight to my own inexperience.

'In answer to your queries, I used to drain the sump as usual just before a race, then immediately on starting give her a couple of shots from the hand-controlled oiler, just to feed her while the mechanical pumps get going. The setting for these pumps should be correct as they are now—I should make a note of them if I were you as the greatest trouble with a big twin is to lubricate the front cylinder. The two differently numbered plugs are correct. You see, the two cylinders have different characteristics, the rear gets most of the oil and needs a well-recessed electrode so as not to oil up. The front cylinder tends to get hot even though it is apparently in the airstream. I imagine there is an eddy from the front wheel which deflects the air flow more to the rear cylinder. Anyhow, the front plug should have a heat-resisting electrode fairly fat and solid. Pay particular attention to the ignition lever position—somewhere about one-third advance for starting, then not quite full, used to give me the best results, but a couple of practice laps will soon show you the best position. Air full open, of course, juice about one-third to start. I have no doubt the rest is common knowledge to you as you are experienced—but start the exhaust lifter with the clutch engaged and bottom gear in. Like that, she is beautifully easy and quick to start. I used to make my first change up just before the Vickers Bridge, just before the climb up the banking at somewhere about 45 m.p.h. Then into top as you swing round the banking—there is a big sign, I believe it is still there, on the edge of the banking—well just about there she should be doing about eighty to eighty-five in second. Let me know anything you are in doubt about. I shall be only too pleased to assist in any way at any time'.

That letter was a great help and even though we had problems of control with the bike, we did at least have a reasonable knowledge of starting procedure. So what was it like to ride a fine old warrior like this in a race?

Once having got to the bottom of the handling problems, we found that, surprisingly quickly, we had got the whole thing taped.

In the first race we won with the Brough there were twenty-five starters, ranging in size from our 'thousand' down to a 175 cc. two-stroke. The distance was over three laps—eight and a quarter miles. We were not on the scratch mark—there was one behind us—Ben Bickell on his 350 cc. Bickell J.A.P. and from Ben we were to receive just three seconds start in three laps. At that time Ben held the 350 cc. outer-circuit lap record on this bike at over 102 m.p.h. and we knew that if he was going to equal this we should have to lap at over 101 m.p.h.

to beat him. At this time, the best lap we had done with the Brough, in a race, was well under 100 m.p.h. Among the twenty-three runners to whom we were conceding start, there were almost certainly dark horses. On the handicapping as it stood, the limit man on the 175 would have to lap at around 65 m.p.h. to win.

No snags with the warming-up. Sump drained, racing plugs fitted after warming up on soft ones—push up to the start-line alongside the Vickers sheds. Some rudery from Ben about having to give start to a 'thousand' but, in fact, we knew that we should almost be departing together, so much heavier was the Brough for the two pushers to launch off the mark. Now we are ready and waiting for 'Ebby' to come along and brief us and he starts way down at the other end of the line opposite the timing-box. On up the line he comes and we can hear his voice. 'You two together, you on your own, you four five-hundreds together.' Then he arrives. 'You on your own, Charles, and then you, Ben.'

He returns to the other end of the line and after a moment's delay there is a flurry and the 175 bursts into life and starts its long journey towards the home banking facing us. A temptation to turn on the fuel is resisted, for the 'baby' will be droning along on his own for some time before anyone else leaves. We watch him toiling up the rise to the banking, the buzz of the tiny engine gradually fading. Now he is out of sight and still we wait. Suddenly there is activity again as two 250's and a sidecar outfit depart together. Then two more solos and a roar as about five 350's depart in a tight bunch. Johnny's voice can just be heard above the din: 'Fuel on, Charlie.' In gear, now goggles down and waiting—he's almost here. The flag drops for the four 500's and Ebby jumps back nimbly, standing beside us. Watch his face—it's impassive, nothing to be gained there. Suddenly the flag is aloft and falls as quickly. For a moment nothing seems to happen except for a shuffling of feet. Now is the moment when the weight of a big twin becomes apparent, for we actually saw Ebby jump back to stand beside Ben. Our big engine is turning, but not fast enough to be able to drop the compression lever. Now it is, and as we drop it—there is an almighty bang from the exhaust and she fires. She takes a second to really take hold and in that split second we can actually hear Ben's engine to the right and almost alongside—dreadful!

At last we are really moving—change into second—good, we're still on both cylinders, and now we really are going, climbing up on

47

to the home banking as though we were in a lift. Should like to look astern to see if Ben's there but it's too risky, so concentrate on line from now on. Into top at peak revs and already it's becoming hard work to keep the old lady on course. Bumps, bumps, bumps, bigger and better and causing the old bike to lurch and twist as she makes her way right up to the top line—within ten feet from the top of the banking. We sweep under the Members' Bridge and, having done so, can see nearly the whole way round the track. Not a bike in sight! No time to worry about that, we must get exactly positioned to negotiate the big bump over the bridge that spans the River Wey—to be wrongly placed there means trouble with a capital T. Here the bike becomes airborne for forty or fifty yards and must land dead straight at the beginning of the Railway straight. It does and now, for a moment, we can relax as we thunder down the straight at between 110 and 112 m.p.h. A quick scan round the horizon reveals nothing— the boys must all be miles away—it just can't be done. But, really, we know it can, for the bike is going as it's never gone before and these first two laps are our chance because there's bound to be a lot of traffic to get through on the third. Line it up, now, for the Byfleet banking and we go on far faster than ever before and, again, have that wonderful sensation of climbing in a lift. Round the Byfleet, high, high up, pulling it down slowly about three hundred yards from the end, so that the kink, at the fork, alongside the Vickers sheds will be ironed out and there'll be room for Ben to pass between us and the sheds, if he wants to. But there's no sign of him, which isn't surprising for had we known it, our standing lap had been turned at over 93 m.p.h., despite the hand gear change—outer-circuit bikes hadn't aspired to foot-change in those days!

Across the wide expanse at the fork—a breathtaking lift up on to the tighter home banking, and one or two stragglers are being passed —earlier than we would have expected. Again the big bump, the Railway straight and the Byfleet and now it can be seen. Bikes by the dozen, it seems, way ahead on the banking, the leaders streaming off the banking and across the fork. Some are a long way ahead but we're coming up on them fast. Passed two or three across the fork but the home banking looks like the Brighton road on a Sunday. This is the difficult bit, for everyone is using the banking here and the faster 500's are using the top. They're nearly all lapping at over the ton and our second lap was done at nearly 106 m.p.h. The bike's too

48

big to weave in and out of them but we have to pass beneath two who are using far more of the banking than they need for their lap speeds of around 103 or 104 m.p.h. Even so, they were so high that we barely had to pull the bike down at all and we were lucky in that they could be seen a long way ahead.

Some of the limit people seem to be crawling as we thunder past them down the Railway straight for the last time, and as we enter the Byfleet we see that the little two-stroke is still in the lead, hardly moving, it seems. Nothing else to be seen now that we're on the Byfleet again and, emerging from the Hawker sheds, we can see all the way to the finishing-line—not a bike in sight. Automatically we ease—but only momentarily, opening up again instantly on the thought that Ben could well be right astern. Now across the line—chequered flag and we ease, surprised that with the problems of passing on that last lap, we completely forgot the problems of handling the bike. The race had been won at an average of 100·82 m.p.h. from a standing start and had taken just five minutes from start to finish. Crawling by today's standards, but exciting nearly forty years ago on bumpy old Brooklands, and without the modern aids of things like sprung frames and telescopic forks! Yes, Brooklands was bumpy.

So, at the end of 1934, the decision was taken reluctantly—no more big twins. It was sad, but it had to be, for the orthodox big twin had by then become like the ageing musical comedy star—all glamour but not enough performance. It didn't have to be orthodox, of course. Noel Pope rode his in supercharged form, but the weight of the big blower mounted low down in front of the engine presented handling problems which Noel was content to grapple with but which I didn't relish. Or, if you were clever and scientifically and analytically minded like Eric Fernihough, you could adopt an altogether new approach which gave you an immensely fast and controllable machine; but, again, I hadn't Eric's knowledge or experience or his sort of brain.

So it obviously had to be a 500 for 1935 with, perhaps, a 350 to back it up. There was a wide choice for Rudge, Sunbeam, Excelsior, O.K. Supreme, Vincent, Norton and others all marketed T.T. replicas; but, for me, the choice had to be Norton. They steered, they stopped they went well and they were reliable.

My first Manx Norton arrived from the works early in the new year of 1935 and from then on my rides were almost exclusively Norton. I ran it exactly as received from the works, on petrol benzole, at the opening Brooklands meeting in one race, a ten-lap Round-the-Mountain handicap, finishing second, a hundred yards behind the winner, Ron Harris. With thoughts of the Wakefield Cup at the next meeting, I entered it—again on petrol benzole—because there was prestige value attached to winning one of Viscount Wakefield's Cups and I knew that it would be a help throughout the season.

The meeting was a success for me and, reporting it, *The Motor Cycle* of May 30th said:

'The Mountain handicap for the Wakefield Cup was run in two five-lap Heats with a ten-lap final, for which the first eight men to finish in each Heat were eligible. Heat 2 fell to C. K. Mortimer (490 Norton) 25.s after a terrific scrap with E. G. Bishop (498 Excelsior Sc) 40.s. Bishop took the lead on the third lap when Mortimer was lying fifth and never looked like being caught. Then, on the last lap, Mortimer seemed to spring from nowhere and led Bishop over the line by about twenty yards. The final was a grim affair from the start. First, Paul could not get his Ariel to fire and had to retire. Then Bishop packed up with a dead engine and, finally, A. J. Rawlence (490 Norton) who had apparently been playing "possum" in his heat, came a beautiful purler under the Members' Bridge, when he had the race in his pocket. This let in Mortimer 50.s who retained the lead to the end to win at 65·21 m.p.h. from R. Harris (348 Norton) 19.s and L. R. Courtney (348 Velocette) 45.s.'

In fact, this race set the pattern of my racing throughout the whole of my two-wheel Brooklands span. I was a good, consistent and quite fast rider all the time, never spectacular but always around. Rather a dull performer, really, but if the leaders retired with mechanical trouble, or overdid it and threw the bike 'down the road', I usually seemed to be near enough to take over and it was surprising to me how often that seemed to happen. Being fairly hefty was a help, too, with those old bikes because I seemed not to tire a lot and could keep slogging on at the same speed for lap after lap. But, if called upon to produce a special effort when it was needed, I seemed unable to do it without casting the machine away so, after having done that once or twice, I settled for being unspectacular, safe and as fast as possible. It never got me into the Norton team or near it, but I had a lot of enjoyable racing and a better measure of success than most.

I had learned two other vital lessons at this stage and both apply still in motor-cycle racing today. The first was never to 'change mounts in mid-stream', that is to say not to start a season racing one make of machine and to make a change to another halfway through, even if the prospects of the change appear rosy on paper. This is an almost certain recipe for failure because something that has been superseded is seldom much less good than that which supersedes it and may even be as good or better. And, in any case, a new machine nearly always takes time to be made really competitive. One saw this time and again and in this connection I took a leaf from Prince Bira's racing with his E.R.A.s and Maseratis for, under the efficient management of his cousin Prince Chula, Bira never parted with his outdated racing car until the bugs had been shaken out of the car that was to replace it. So I did the same with my Nortons.

The second lesson was only to run as many machines as one could comfortably maintain and service. One always wanted as much riding as possible and this was necessary and a good thing. Most of the riders of Nortons ran a 350 and a 500 and I did, myself, as soon as I could afford both. This was alright because the overhead camshaft Manx Norton engine was so good and so reliable if looked after sensibly, that almost anyone could do it in their spare time. But when journeying to races abroad and away from Brooklands the temptation was to say, 'If I'm going as far away as that, I might as well take a 250 as well and have three rides.' This was nearly always a bad mistake because the preparation, maintenance and riding of three bikes at a meeting was too great a load for two people and its even worse now that multi-cylinders, disc-valve two-strokes and sophisticated ignition set-ups are the rule.

Some people, at Brooklands, used to perform near miracles with their Nortons for the frames of the 350 cc. and 500 cc. were one and the same and, after a 350 cc. scratch race one would see engines being torn out and 500 cc. units installed for the next race. Later still in the day there might be outer-circuit races and the same chap would then be tearing off the T.T.-type mudguards and handlebars, replacing them with drop bars and rear-mounted saddles. In many cases it was that or nothing if one just had to do as many races as possible, but the whole thing was essentially a compromise and good results weren't often achieved this way.

The next step I took with my 500 was to acquire a high-compression piston for use with alcohol fuel. But this, too, was only a compromise because the engine had to be taken down a number of times during the

51

season since some races were restricted to 50/50 petrol-benzole fuel regulations whereas others permitted the use of alcohol fuels. The result was that every time the engine was stripped, it took a little time to settle down again and was unnecessarily disturbed many times in a season. So, before thinking about getting a 350, I started saving up for a second new engine for use solely on alcohol. I made this quite a high priority and got it as quickly as I could because, for one thing, I felt it looked a bit undignified, when riding a 500, albeit on petrol, to be receiving starts in handicap races from alcohol three-fifties—whoever rode them!

So, by July, the picture was improving and *The Motor Cycle* said:

'In the ten-lap Mountain handicap, everyone got away well except C. M. Brooks (Norton) whose engine refused to fire. C. V. M. Booth (348 Velocette) took the lead early on, but the back markers were working through the field. On the last lap, R. Harris (499 Rudge) and C. K. Mortimer (490 Norton) closed right up on Booth on the far side of the track and all three came round the hairpin together and roared up the straight with Harris slightly in the lead.'

I was pleased to finish second to Ron in that race for I had had only a very short start from him and he was really good at it all. But I was even more pleased to discover that, because I had been concentrating so hard on catching Booth, I had almost failed to notice Ron come up alongside and had then found that I could very nearly keep up with him. At that time I would never have thought that I could stay close to him in a scratch race, but in the five-lap scratch race that followed I found I could, and finished second to him again when he won at 71·63 m.p.h. with Brooks on his 500 Norton third. This was a pleasing discovery but very surprising.

Quite a few of the regular Brooklands riders were departing, at that time of the year, to take part in the T.T. in the Isle of Man and were then going on to run in Continental races. I thought about this and consulted Eric, who would always listen to me and give good advice. But Eric hated the T.T. and never ran in it because the competition from the big works teams was very strong and he said that the money side wasn't good enough. He was awfully clever about picking the races he ran in. If the Norton and Rudge teams were going to the Swiss Grand Prix, Eric would pore through the calendar and find a less important race in Austria or Belgium, preferring to be a big fish in a smaller pool, both prestige and moneywise.

He put me off the T.T. and suggested I went to the Dieppe Grand Prix in July. He was going and we could make up a party, stay at the White House Hotel on the circuit and he would look after us all. But there was just one thing, we had to behave properly. He had stayed there every year and liked the French and they liked him. That mustn't change.

So we went, and it was great. I took my 500, Tony Rawlence took an identical bike, Neil Christmas a 350 Velocette, Francis Beart the 250 New Imperial I had sold him, and Eric his 250 Cotton J.A.P. I'd never been abroad before and, racing apart, it was a great adventure when we caught the night boat at Newhaven, arriving at Dieppe at about three o'clock in the morning. My very first sight of France remains with me still, but even more vivid was my first experience on its roads because it appeared it was then normal and accepted practice for 'Coureurs' in the Grand Prix to ride their racers from the docks, through and out of Dieppe up to the circuit some three miles away. So that we did, without road fund licences, any form of insurance and with open exhausts and no lights at a quarter past three in the morning! No one said anything and, despite the hour, we were greeted with open arms on our arrival at La Maison Blanche where, prior to practising which was due to start at six o'clock, we sat down to huge breakfasts of ham and eggs in the bar. I have seen this sort of hospitality subsequently, abroad, but never on such a scale or at such an hour. It was really unbelievable!

And it was a super meeting because we were the supporting cast to the car Grand Prix and were in the same paddock and able to see all those great names we'd read about. Chiron and Dreyfus of Scuderia Ferrari Alfa Romeos, Etancelin and Marcel Lehoux on big single-seater 3-litre Maseratis, Benoist and Wimille on 3·3-litre Bugattis—it was all very stirring.

By this time, of course, I knew everyone who raced a two-wheeler at Brooklands and it was strange to be out on a circuit with an entirely new set of riders—Continentals whose names and exploits I had only read about. The organisers made a great fuss of Eric, who had obviously relieved them of quite a useful sum by way of appearance money. Never having appeared before outside England, the rest of us were in no position to make such a request—in fact we considered ourselves lucky to have had our entries accepted.

We all liked the circuit, which was roughly triangular, the first leg being a long straight, mainly flat but with one or two super dives downhill and then up again. Then, at the bottom of a hill, which really called for brakes, you turned right on to the next leg, which was a level and twisty section with fields on the left-hand side of the road and high banks on the right and led into the village of St Aubin. The approaches through the outskirts of St Aubin were really tricky because, like most French villages, it was mainly agricultural and the cows used the high street twice a day. This meant that braking adhesion was virtually nil as one entered the village and, even in the middle, where one turned right at the 'T' road, it was very slippery indeed! No one, ourselves included, seemed to think this at all unusual or dangerous but good for a laugh. Looking back on it, though, I wonder how the Grand Prix car people felt about it because their cars had a lot of power, plenty of speed and were, even then, valuable.

After turning right in the centre of St Aubin, the third side of the triangle climbed up through Les Esses, a series of fast right- and left-hand bends continuing to the right-hand hairpin bend on which was situated our pub, a hundred yards or so before the start-line.

None of us had any serious troubles in practice except poor Francis who, despite having fitted the latest and most modified cam followers to his New Imperial engine, was still breaking them at the rate of about one every three laps. Finally, after having worked the whole of one night, stripping the engine in search of broken bits of cam follower, and by candle light in the potting shed, he gave it up, kicked the New Imperial and rallied round to help the rest of us. We saw very little of Eric, who had a super garage somewhere nearby in which he locked himself and his machinery while we all worked happily and noisily in the open yard at the rear of the hotel. Luckily for us it never looked like raining.

All the races were to be held on the Sunday, the 175 cc. and 350 cc. races concurrently at nine o'clock in the morning and the 250 cc. and 500 cc. together at eleven. Then, in the afternoon, there was a Voiturette race for 1500 cc. cars to be followed by the big Grand Prix. Although the records I still have don't show whether Eric rode in the 175 cc. event, I think it is likely and even think he might have won it. But Neil Christmas certainly won the 350 cc. race and this made the day for us, for it was his first race abroad and he was a good rider and a great chap to have around.

Then it was my turn and, feeling a bit out of it all, I arrived on the line and took my place. Beside me were two superbly turned-out bikes both ridden by Frenchmen, one a Monet Goyon and the other, I think, an F.N. They gave me a friendly nod and almost at once we were off. My old Norton started well and, as we neared the approach to the steep downhill where we braked to turn right, I was quite happy to count only seven or eight machines ahead of me. At the end of the first lap I was, in fact, lying seventh and for the next few laps I was able to pick up another two or three places. I could still see two more ahead of me and when I next passed the pits I got a sign confirming that I was now in third spot.

I began to work hard but progress was slow, although progress there was. When I got closer I could see that the two riders ahead of me were scrapping hard together and I thought that, because of this, they weren't going as fast as they might have if they had had the road to themselves. In fact, as does sometimes happen when two riders are locked in combat, they have the effect of slowing each other by unwittingly getting in each other's way. These two, both Continentals, were doing just that and I hoped they would continue and that I might even be able to make it a threesome or, conceivably, get past them. Unfortunately, this didn't happen because the Monet Goyon rider, Georges Monneret, began to drop back a little and soon it was he and I who were scrapping while the leader, Cora on a Belgian Sarolea, was sitting comfortably ahead. My scrap with Monneret was useful to me because he knew the circuit and I didn't and I was learning a bit more each lap. Once I knew that there was nothing between us on speed I let him draw ahead a few yards so as to watch his line, particularly through the Esses which were, to me, the hardest to learn. That helped a lot and I then felt ready to have a go at him. He wouldn't let go, though, and was using a lot of revs in gears out of the hairpin so that, suddenly, there was an immense bang and bits of Monnet Goyon engine flew in all directions. Then I started to try for the Sarolea and Johnny, in the pit, kept me posted. The gap between us now was forty seconds but I still had plenty of time to do it if it was possible. It narrowed to thirty-seven, then thirty-five and then to twenty-nine. Misguidedly I thought I was home and dry but next time it was thirty and the time after that, thirty-two. Was he going faster or was I slowing? I decided to have a really strong go for two laps and Johnny, guessing what was happening, gave me a sign confirming that my last lap had been my fastest. Now the gap was thirty-eight seconds and I knew I was being played with. So Cora won by forty seconds, as he deserved, and I was more than happy with second place in my first Grand Prix.

I had seen Eric once or twice during the race and noted that he was obviously going well. But being rather preoccupied with my own problems I hadn't had time to see whether he was leading or where he lay in the 250 cc. race which was running with us. The 250's started on the grid behind the 500's, so my first glimpse of him was later in the race when we began catching them up together with the slower 500 brigade. But now I found out that he, too, had finished second in his race, which really rounded off our trip well. I can't recall now who beat him—I have a feeling it could have been a works Benelli which was always rather a worry to him.

Prior to the race, it hadn't occurred to me that I might be placed, so immediately it finished I had to rush round searching for someone with a programme so as to find out how much I'd won. I recall being delighted to find that, when converted into sterling, it amounted to more than £60 which was a stack of money to any of us at that time, and I also found that the awards were being presented at nine o'clock that night in the Casino in Dieppe. So there we all were at a quarter to nine that night, marching up the steps of the Casino, clad in our best city suits, hands itching to get hold of our hard-won French francs. None of us except Eric had ever been to a casino before and he wasn't with us, having been invited by the organisers to a special dinner given before the presentation for the Committee and V.I.P. guests.

Everyone inside appeared to be in full evening dress so we decided to make an informal entrance, not through the imposing glass doors at the front but through the back way which led us via the kitchens. One or two others, also lounge-suited, had had the same idea, for ahead of us trotted Freddie Dixon accompanied by Pat Fairfield, who had successfully driven an E.R.A. in the Voiturette race. As we passed through the kitchens, the opening turn of the cabaret was just preparing to go into action. It consisted of a very large, swarthy gentleman clad in long silk pants and a turban and stripped to the waist. His partner was an extremely glamorous girl, rather less clad and at that moment sitting cross-legged on a huge brass salver which rested on one of the kitchen tables. Obviously he was going to lift this delicious dish up high above his head and make an impressive entrance. But this

56

was too much for Fred who was also exceptionally strong and, trumping the Turkish-looking gentleman's ace, he grabbed the salver and proceeded to carry it in, head high, with the poor girl crying plaintively from aloft. Needless to say they were minutes ahead of their cue, for the speeches were still in progress. But their entrance was so dramatic that the speeches were cut short and the presentations made, perhaps in the hope of getting the mad English out of the building before anything worse happened.

The result of this race was really helpful for little bonuses began to trickle in from accessory people who, hitherto, had promised nothing more than free supplies. I used part of it to make a move from the tiny rabbit hutch that served as a shed in the paddock at Brooklands into a more imposing shack, having my name signwritten on the door. One or two customers came along with Manx Nortons that required tuning and we devised a splendid little racket which became really profitable and wasn't even dishonest—just rather deceitful.

As supplied by the factory, the Manx Norton arrived with either an open exhaust pipe or, later, with a slightly shorter pipe with a megaphone end. The first thing one had to do, of course, before going out on to the track was to fit a Brooklands-type silencer. I did this with mine and ran it flat out for a lap after getting the carburation and jet sizes right and, on petrol benzole, it turned the lap at just under 90 m.p.h. This wasn't fast enough to be competitive and I spent a lot of time improving the finish of the head and exhaust port and this brought the lap speed up to just over 93 m.p.h. It still wasn't good enough because a minimum lap speed of 97 m.p.h. on petrol was essential, but short of raising the compression ratio or embarking on a big exercise in balancing I couldn't see how to make it go faster. The only other thing left was to try some simple experiments with ignition and valve timings and both were simple because the overhead camshaft Manx engine had a vernier adjustment in the camshaft drive which was easily reached by removing a small cover at the top end of the vertical drive. I tried the ignition settings first and found that, while advancing, it dropped the lap speed slightly, a later setting brought the lap speed to 94 m.p.h. Then I tried moving the vernier peg to the next hole and the effect was startling for the bike lapped happily at over 96 m.p.h. Three more moves of the setting before no further improvement was noted and we had the bike lapping at over 99 m.p.h.

So simple, really, and all that it added up to was that these machines were sent out to customers on the reasonable assumption that they were going to be used with open pipes and not with a Brooklands' silencer. Francis, of course, who was a true professional, knew all this long before I discovered it but, although we were great friends and lunched together every day in the canteen, he had never told me and I would never have expected him to do so, for once on the line we were the strictest rivals.

But now that the customers were coming along and wanting to race their Manx Nortons at the track, I could see how the knowledge could be made profitable and the following scheme was devised.

The owner of a Manx Norton would come down to the track for the first time and would immediately be as disappointed as I'd been in the speed of his bike. Could we have a look at it and see what could be done to make it faster? Yes, we could, and this was the way we would do it.

He must take the bike out and do a flat-out lap on it. Eighty-eight miles an hour! All right, we would make that the starting-point. Usually, if he was a bit inexperienced, any one of us, Francis, Jock Forbes or Johnny or myself could have done a faster lap on the bike as it stood, even though he might well have been flat out all the way. For one could alter the line from day to day according to the direction of the wind and thereby use, or cheat, the wind in order to get the best lap speed possible on any particular day.

But in this case we didn't want too high a lap speed from which to start because our charge for improvement was to be at the rate of £1 sterling per mile an hour increase in lap speed so that bringing the speed of a bike up from 88 to 98 m.p.h. earned us £10 for about two hours' work—a very good hourly rate indeed in 1935! Needless to say, we had to indulge in quite a lot of camouflage, involving the necessity of having the bike on our premises 'for about a week' before we could complete the work. And when it was done and the great day dawned for the test we, and not he, would ride it while he timed it with his watch. In this way we could sometimes squeeze the very last drop out of the lemon, particularly if the wind was blowing strongly in certain directions!

This little gimmick became a miniature money-spinner because the Manx Norton was such an excellent bike that everyone was ordering them. But the strange thing was that when customers of ours set off with their 'specially tuned' Manx Nortons, to compete in the Isle of

Man with open pipes, they still proved to be faster than the standard Manx as supplied from Bracebridge Street! And just as reliable.

It seemed incredible, such was the state of racing at that time, that the owners themselves never thought of making experiments with their engines or, for that matter, the Norton experimental department hadn't got round to issuing special instructions for revising timings for use with a Brooklands' 'can'. A few years later they certainly did, because I saw an engine running on the brake, fitted with a Brooklands' 'can'. But, by that time, our fortune was made!

Now and again, the scheme would tend to boomerang when, for instance, owners of Rudges, Velocettes and other makes would ask for their engines to be breathed on. But nothing else had this splendid vernier adjustment that the Norton had and, often, we had to be 'too busy to take on any further work' and particularly when a bike was already going excessively well!

Income was derived by numerous other funny little ways. Garaging bikes, transporting them, betting on them with the bookmakers and on car races even more so, and riding other peoples' bikes. Lots of riders would bring their road bikes down to Brooklands, take them out on the track and scare themselves stiff solely because their machines, which were quite handleable on the roads at terminal speeds, did the oddest things when their owners tried to take them flat out round Brooklands. This service cost ten shillings a lap and was value for money for some of the bikes were not at all nice at their top speeds and a few were lethal. In this instance the owner was required to sign a little chit absolving us from all blame in the event of anything dreadful happening to the bike or its mechanical parts and, in return, he received from us a little chit which let him out if we got hurt!

Car and motor-cycle dealing also accounted for some derivation of income, but here I had a rival. Some of the fuel companies had small petrol stations in the paddock, complete with pumps and forecourt and the manager of one of these, after having put a price ticket on his own car and sold it off the forecourt, decided that he'd try again. He bought another car and sold that, too, and then decided that this was the thing and packed the forecourt with cars for sale. The fuel company would have had a fit if they'd known and, of course, he was always dreading the periodical visits made by the company's inspector. But, in the end, even this eventuality was covered for, on the inspector's arrival at the entrance-gate to Brooklands, a phone call was promptly put through to the vendor of cars in the paddock whereupon he would immediately appear on the forecourt, ringing a large handbell. This was the signal for 'All hands on Deck'. Each of us was responsible for one particular car and, literally within three minutes, every car would be off the forecourt and parked well away in different parts of the paddock. The game was never discovered and no one really suffered except that, if one wanted to get petrol there, one sometimes had to wait if he was out demonstrating a car! It wasn't very good but the poor chap was probably grossly underpaid, anyway.

It was around this time that there were one or two minor 'break-ins' to sheds and premises in the paddock. There was a night-watchman —'Wally'—but although he was always there he seemed to be powerless in the matter and, obviously, the intruders had his measure. Mostly, it seemed to happen at weekends and finally we narrowed it down to Saturday nights. So, one Saturday night, Francis Beart and I mounted guard and what we found was quite amusing. What was happening was that the paddock was being invaded by local lads of the village who got in not by climbing the fences surrounding Brooklands but by boat on the River Wey, entering the paddock via the river tunnel under the track right beneath the famous big bump. All they then had to do was to row the few hundred yards to where the river ran through at the back of the paddock, moor their boats and disembark, so it wasn't at all surprising that 'Wally' hadn't seen them.

The scheme to put an end to this was Francis's and his alone, although I and others helped to put it into action. We waited a week or two and then mounted guard again on a Saturday night. Sure enough, before long, we could hear the splash of oars and from the depths of the tunnel emerged the armada, bigger than before and amounting to six or seven boats. We gave them good time to row well clear of the tunnel exit and, when they had nearly reached the paddock, Francis gave the word of command whereupon my team on one side of the river, and his on the other, emptied two large drums of petrol-paraffin mixture into the Wey while two large paraffin-soaked handfuls of cotton waste and two matches did the rest.

The rout was complete and with the river well ablaze behind them the invaders' exit was sealed. But the fire was rather bigger than we expected and, for a time, we were so hard put to it extinguishing the burning gorse lining the banks that we could do nothing about the enemy. But we did get their boats and these were collected next morning, by the local boatyard who had hired them without, of course, knowing for what purpose they were to be used. After that, there was no more trouble.

One day, when we were lunching in the paddock, Eric came in and the talk turned to record breaking. I had been thinking about records and said that the one I had my eye on was the 500 cc. outer-circuit lap record with sidecar, which stood at the time at around 93 m.p.h. As usual Eric disagreed and, as usual, he turned out to be right.

'Why d'you pick that one?' he asked.

'Only because it seems easier to get than any of the others.'

He looked at me over the rims of his glasses. 'Think so?'

'Yes, I do.'

'Then go break it, lad.'

'You think it's difficult?'

'Very. And when you've done it, what have you got? There's no money for it.'

This was true enough and no more was said. But, as he was leaving, Eric said to me quietly, 'Come and let's have a talk if you want to have a go at some records.' So I did.

It turned out that Eric himself had got a plan to break records in the 250 cc. solo class. All the short records in this class stood at astronomical speeds, so it meant a long ride.

'How long, Eric?'

'Well, the five hundred kilometres stands at seventy-seven. You couldn't go for anything shorter with our bikes. You'd need a lap speed of ninety to make sure, even, of that.'

'Just the five hundred kilos?'

'Good Lord, no. Keep going as long as the ruddy thing hangs together. If we could break that one, the four-hour would come at about the same time and then you could take them hourly, right up to twelve hours. And the five hundred miles, possibly.'

'Whew! What a marathon! So what d'you suggest?'

'Well, I'll provide and prepare the bike. We'll both ride hour-and-a-half spells. I'll negotiate the contracts, we'll share anything to come equally. Timekeepers' fees and track fees to be shared between us equally—but you pay them if we fail.'

It was a very fair proposition and we agreed to go in October when the racing had finished. The bike was to be a Cotton, the engine J.A.P.,

Burman gearbox, Dunlop tyres, Esso fuel and oil and any other accessories Eric could conjure up.

By this time the next big race was coming up, the 100-Mile Brooklands' Grand Prix for 250, 350 and 500 cc. classes. I had just bought a 350 Norton from Steve Darbishire, who was a friend of Johnny Waite's. Steve only raced once a year, in the Manx Grand Prix in the Isle of Man, buying two new bikes for the race and selling them immediately afterwards. Nortons themselves used to prepare the bikes for him and Steve always did well with them. But, although this bike had only done the one race, it was very slow indeed with the Brooklands' silencer and, in the time available before the race, it proved too stubborn to be really competitive. This was a bit depressing but it just had to be accepted for the time being.

Then, at the last moment, I had a super offer from Velocette rider Les Archer, whom we all knew to be the almost certain winner of the 350 race. He felt sure he could win the Junior race on his own 350 Velocette but the factory were anxious to make quite sure of it and had agreed to send down two special works' bikes for him and for Neil Christmas. If I liked, I could have his 350, but if the works' bike gave trouble or was no faster he would still want his own bike. Needless to say I jumped at it because all Les's bikes were fast and were beautifully prepared by his father. It would be a responsibility because, on the assumption that the two works' Velocettes would finish first and second, I should be expected to finish third; if Les felt he could have won with it, I ought to be able to finish ahead of all the rest.

The Archer transporter duly arrived at Brooklands on the day before the Grand Prix and 'Pa' Archer immediately took charge. It was a delightful equipe in which to be because it was super efficient, very successful but also very amusing because both 'Pa' and Les had their own opinions as to how things should be done and frequently disagreed, but always in the most friendly way. 'Pa' always won and Les would concede victory with the words, 'All right, all right. So be it. You're the gaffer', insinuating that from that point on things were really going to go wrong. 'Pa' would reply, 'That's right. So long as you realise that. I'm glad you realise that, Leslie, it was nice of you to mention that.' And, of course, things never did go wrong or, if they did, it turned out to be something on which they had been in complete agreement in the first place.

Dear 'Pa' always gave his instructions in a benign voice which boomed across the paddock and this time he began with me. 'Now, Charlie, we've brought down these three motor-bicycles' (they were always motor-bicycles, never bikes). He went on to explain to me in detail the exact position about the arrangement, with Les standing by muttering 'I've told him all this, I've told him all this, you don't need to tell him this 'cos he knows it.'

So, all in 'Pa's' good time, we got our instructions. What had to be established was how much faster, if at all, were the two works' bikes. To establish this we were to go out and cruise round for two laps and then, as we passed the Vickers' sheds where we were to be level with each other, we had to open up and remain flat out for another two laps. This, 'Pa' thought, would show whether the works' bikes were faster and whether they accelerated better.

And it certainly did show, for as we all three got down to it, the works' machines simply streamed away from me and at the end of two laps Les and Neil were almost out of sight.

Back in the paddock, 'Pa' was all smiles. 'Very good, boys. Well now, Charlie, you lapped at ninety-three on Les's little bike which is about what it always does on petrol. And you, Neil, and you, Leslie, lapped at over ninety-seven miles an hour which, in my opinion, is marching for a petrol three-fifty.'

Next day, as the flag dropped, both the works' Velocettes again did their vanishing act and I was left scrapping away with the rest of the field. The two works' A.J.S.s ridden by George Rowley and Reg Barber were the biggest headache for I just couldn't get clear of them, and once or twice George got ahead. Half way through the race we were lapped by Les and Neil, who were still together, and Les rode up alongside us shaking his fist in mock anger at George and Reg and making comic signals to them to leave me alone! Then he came in ahead of me and tried to give me a tow to get me clear but they hung on like leeches and all that happened was that the lot of us went a bit faster together. Neil had taken a back seat to watch the fun and was tailing Reg. Together we went on for lap after lap, nose-to-tail, until 'Pa', in the pit, began to feel worried about what he would say to Velocettes if someone dropped it and we all came down. So out came a sign, 'Les, push on', and that was the end of it. In the end, Les won with Neil two seconds behind him. I was third—but rather a dreadful third because I was five minutes behind them with one of the A.J.S.s still only a second behind me and the other within sight.

On the Norton in the Senior Grand Prix in the afternoon I was laying fourth with the others still in sight when it seemed to me that they were getting a bit too far ahead, so I decided to push on and be ready to step in and take a place as soon as someone made a mistake or had a blow-up. 'Ginger' Wood was leading on the works 'V' twin New Imperial and I felt that he was only a fairly likely finisher. So I pressed on and immediately came a tremendous crumpet negotiating the artificial chicane right in front of the Grandstand, doing the bike no good at all.

The other big bike races at Brooklands that season were the twenty-five-lap Senior and Junior Mountain Championships run on the 1·1-mile Mountain Circuit to decide who the champion rider was in each class. I entered the 500 for this but with no great hopes because, being not really a long race, it tended to be a sort of medium-distance tear-up. All the regular bright lads were in it as well as Harold Daniell and it was generally thought that, whatever else happened, Harold would win both. It proved to be just that, with a lot of pushing and shoving, frames and exhaust pipes grounding and bits of bicycle flying everywhere. But half way through, I was amazed to find that only Tony Rawlence lay ahead of me—all the others had gone. So, press on I had to, and managed to get by and win, at an average of 70·43 m.p.h. with Harold winning the Junior at 69·97 m.p.h.

This race gave me a nickname—'Champ'. It was bestowed on me by Charlie Brackenbury, George Harvey Noble and 'Mort' Morris Goodall—and it stuck. We all saw the humour of it because although they were all three star car drivers, they followed the bike racing and each of them knew that I was no more the rightful 'Champ' than they were. Looking back on that race now, I just can't imagine what happened to all the star names—the retirement rate must have been a record!

The next item on the agenda—and the last of the season—was the record attempt and, because it was something new and different, I had been looking forward to it enormously; and also because I felt honoured to be partnering Eric at the end of only my third year in racing. The fastest of the twelve possible records was the four-hour, which stood at 77·54 m.p.h., and the slowest, the twelve-hour, stood at 67·56 m.p.h. Even then, the speeds didn't look very frightening but they became significant when one bore in mind that we would be making eight stops for rider changes and refuelling, quite apart from any troubles we should have—and we knew we must have troubles. In addition to all that, we were advised by Dunlops that they were far from sure that we could run for twelve hours on a back tyre but that the chances would be improved if the speed could be kept to a steady lap speed of 80 m.p.h. We didn't want to have to make a rear wheel change—there were no knock-out rear wheel spindles then.

This wasn't as easy as it sounded. To keep a machine capable of lapping at 90 m.p.h. at a steady 80 m.p.h., lap after lap, hour after hour, was quite a problem and would get worse as we got more tired. But Dunlops knew what they were talking about and it had to be done.

The date of the attempt was fixed for mid-October and for a fortnight before that I had a meeting with Eric almost every day. The bike was superbly prepared and fitted-out. Every tiny nut was wired or split-pinned but nothing so that it couldn't be easily removed. The ignition was waterproofed and the control cables duplicated. There were two quite separate and different riding positions. The first, and the orthodox one, had the footrests placed well forward so that the rider took most of his weight on the footrests themselves. The second was devised by placing a thick sorbo squab on top and slightly to the rear of the big fuel tank, so that you rode with your weight taken on your chest, with feet on footrests placed well to the rear of the bike. Only Eric could have thought this one out and it turned out to be a godsend. He was very confident about the weatherproofing of the engine to the extent of saying that where there were puddles of water on the track, as there usually were, we should keep the bike running through them to cool the rear tyre as much as possible. He'd had a lot of heart searching before deciding on hairpin-type valve springs instead of coil springs because he was sure that we would break either type and possibly more of the hairpin type. But in the end he had opted in favour of them because they could be more quickly changed without stripping the top half of the engine. There was even a long metal strip running down from the steering head lug of the frame, on either side of the front down-tubes, to the front engine plates so that, if the frame did break, we might still be able to get along with this taking the strain! Asked whether the bike would steer very well in that condition, he said that that would be the time to find out!

We then began testing, at first with a hack engine to try out the

E   65

cycle parts and riding positions, and then had a short ride each with the engine that was to be used. These tests revealed a snag which couldn't be eradicated before the attempt because, although Eric had competed successfully with the bike in a number of long-distance road races that season, it was now found that at a constant 80 m.p.h. or more the Burman gearbox consumed oil at such a rate that it, too, would have to be topped up at every stop. The reason was elusive but it was obviously allied to running conditions at a constant speed.

The problems now became a bit clearer because one could easily see how tricky it was going to be to break records standing at 77 m.p.h. and yet never exceed a lap speed of 80 m.p.h. while standing so long during the day refilling and servicing. And when you took into consideration the fact that, under the A.C.U. of F.I.C.M. ruling, every record had to be broken by a clear mile an hour, it virtually seemed to mean that every lap had to be turned at 79·5 m.p.h.! I was surprised that Eric wasn't worried—because I was by this time.

The day before the attempt we had a meeting with Francis Beart, who was going to run the pit and the signalling station, checked the arrangements for booking the track, as we should be the only vehicle using it during the day, and telephoned George Reynolds, the official timekeeper. We were all due to meet at the track at seven next morning and to start running at eight.

Everything continued to go smoothly. Eric sat astride the machine and George stood alongside. 'O.K., Eric, off you go.' All very informal and just like George.

The bike came round for the first time and then again and again, and at the end of an hour and a quarter I began getting ready to take over. Another fifteen minutes and in he came.

'All right, Eric?'

'Yes. Jump on.' Away again. A few laps getting signals from Francis and we settled down. It really was a gorgeous little bike and one felt that one couldn't possibly get tired on it. At eleven o'clock I was called in and Eric was waiting.

'Anything to report?'

'No. Seems fine.' He was away and I strolled over to see George.

'How do we stand, George?'

'We're all right. Quite all right. If Eric can keep this up until about five minutes to twelve, about another fifty-five minutes, you'll have the five hundred kilos in the bag.'

That was the longest fifty-five minutes of the day, but it passed, and once we had netted the 500-Kilometre record we all felt better. Less than four minutes later we had the four-hour as well and half an hour later Eric was in again. Still the engine felt lively as it lugged its vast load up on to the home banking but, two laps later, it suddenly lost its edge. Back to the pits—broken exhaust valve spring, and Eric was waiting with the very tool in his hand!

George stuck his head out of the timing-box window and said to Francis, 'He'll have to press on a bit now if you want the five-hour. I'll tell you, lap by lap, what signals to give him.'

Off again and a faster signal at the end of the lap and for the next three or four. 'Lap Speed 85 now' and then a signal to ease.

And so, amazingly, it went on through the day, five, six, seven, eight and nine hours, each record fell one by one. The 500-Mile and 1,000-Kilometre as well, so that by six o'clock we had built up such a margin that all that had to be done was to get off and park the bike against the pits. We had built up such a margin that we had broken the previous eleven- and twelve-hour records inside ten hours.

There was quite a big crowd of spectators milling round by now, although it was nearly dark. Eric, who had had a fairly recent operation for appendicitis, looked really tired and said that nothing would induce him to get on the ruddy thing again. I wanted to go on and he said, 'Do what you like. I'm going to sit in the car till eight o'clock.' I talked to Francis, who was quite happy to go on, and then saw Dunlop Mac about the tyre. Mac said it was all right for another hundred miles—but how were we going to do even fifty miles in the dark with no lights? I wasn't worried about that—I felt I knew Brooklands well enough!

So off I set again. It was cold now, and I did feel tired. And it certainly was getting dark and was much more difficult than I thought it would be. At 6.45 I was back in again.

'No, George, it's too tricky.'

Eric appeared out of the gloom. 'George, can we light the way with my car?'

That was a good idea. Eric had a Light Sports Railton which could do over 90 m.p.h. But George wasn't too keen.

'You've got to be so careful about this question of pacing. But provided the car is behind and not ahead of the bike, I think we can.'

At this, Charlie Brackenbury spoke up.

'Now you're in for trouble, Champ.'

'Why? George seems happy.'

'Oh, not that. But car headlights will bring out every rabbit in the district. Chris Staniland and I used to get them that way. Just motoring round slowly with a greyhound sitting on the running-board of my big Buick. In the end the concrete played havoc with the greyhound's feet, but we fitted it with chamois-leather boots and kept the local butchers in rabbits for years. You'll see.'

We did, and it was really tricky because the rabbits came out in swarms. You couldn't avoid them and every time you hit one the bike went into a 'tank slapper' and sometimes veered right out of the headlamp beam into total darkness. When this happened it was really quite nasty, so back we came again to the pits, just after seven o'clock.

Now that there was a problem to be solved, Eric, who had lost interest in things, suddenly regained it. 'Look, if we run side by side you won't be in bright light or total blackness. You'll be in a sort of half light. You should be able to spot the rabbits and swing in between them.'

'Can we do that, George?'

George sighed. He must have been very tired and cold. 'You boys. Well, all right. But listen, Eric. The front wheel of the bike must be ahead of the front wing tips of the car—all the time.'

Eric agreed.

'Keep it at seventy then, Eric.'

He shook his head. 'No. Sixty.'

'Meet you half way. Sixty-five.'

'All right. But don't get into trouble.'

And in this way we continued till eight o'clock, with every record we had gone for in the bag with a good margin. In fact, the final figures were:

	Hrs	Mins	Secs	Speed (m.p.h.)	Previous record
500 Kilometres	3	56	43·9	78·74	77·53
500 Miles	6	23	11·8	78·29	75·75
1,000 Kilometres	7	59	16·4	77·79	74·63

	Distance		Speed	Previous
	miles	yards	(m.p.h.)	record
4 Hours	314	1526	78·72	77·54
5 Hours	389	1160	77·95	76·95
6 Hours	470	1069	78·43	76·00
7 Hours	546	354	78·02	75·34
8 Hours	622	665	77·80	74·81
9 Hours	698	1702	77·66	73·99
10 Hours	771	335	77·12	73·60
11 Hours	831	112	75·55	73·19
12 Hours	877	177	73·09	67·56

The previous records had all been held by Hewitt McCudden (Excelsior J.A.P.) except the five-hour, which was held by Nott and Lamacraft (Rudge).

This really was a fabulous effort of Eric's because, apart from broken valve springs, nothing broke or went wrong at all. And we were both as comfortable as we could possibly have been after a ride of that length on a rigid frame. We certainly had some bruises and chafes, but it was a small price to pay for the results we got.

The bike was running just as well at the end of the twelve-hour run as it had at the beginning and the engine stripped perfectly. So we were all very happy indeed and it was a fitting end to an exciting season.

3

At this stage of the proceedings I sat back and had a long, hard think. For me 1935 had been a very good season with a number of racing successes and twelve World Records in the bag. But there were two things which made me realise that I was never going to be one of the world's great racing motor-cyclists and the first was that I now knew that I hadn't the ability to be an inspired rider—one who could pull a near miracle out of the bag at the moment it's desperately needed.

And I wasn't going to ride in the Isle of Man, either. I still lived at our family home in Dorking and my mother, who had been so good to me, dreaded the idea. Eric, in whose footsteps I had always tried to follow, had put me off it for reasons of finance. He never went there himself after, I think, just one ride in the T.T. and in any case, I had no burning desire to ride there as nearly everyone else seemed to have.

I still wanted to race a car, and even then one couldn't help noting that the probability of war breaking out seemed to get greater and not less. I was twenty-three years old now and enjoying life tremendously while making no great mark for myself. There were two other possibilities. Francis Beart had served an apprenticeship with Eric and this would have been a splendid thing for me. Moreover, I think Eric would have taken me because, although we were so diverse in nature and character, we both had the same interests and the same principles and seemed able to get along when together. But this would mean very hard work and very little, if any, racing. And, in the nicest way, Eric drove not only himself but everyone who worked with him. And both he and I had tempers and that was no good at all if you worked with him. You needed a certain outlook and mentality in order to work with him and we had an instance of it when we were testing the Cotton, just prior to the World Record Attempt.

He had a little hunchback chap called Charlie who worked with him and Charlie's principal function was to keep Eric's fleet of racing bikes spotlessly clean. He did this superbly and to an exact rhythm. The machines would be brought back from wherever they had raced and would be handed to Charlie, straight off the transporter. Newspaper had to be laid down on the floor of the garage before a machine could be taken in there and, if they were very dirty, they would have to have a preliminary clean outside, whatever the weather. Charlie accepted all this and even seemed to like it and he took the greatest pride in his work. Eric had a phobia about cleanliness and his first action after having ridden a bike, either in practice or in a race, was to insert in the air intake of the carburettor a cork, specially cut to shape, to prevent any speck of dirt entering. Charlie was never allowed to sit on a machine, much less start one, and the starting procedure was for the machine to be handed by him to Eric who would first inspect it before loading it on the transporter and then, when he got to the paddock, remove the cork and start and warm up the engine.

Charlie often came to Brooklands with Eric whose garage and filling station was just outside, on the Brooklands Road in Weybridge. The object of his being brought along was to help unload and reload the bikes and to push-start them. On the occasion of the Cotton test, Francis and I were both in attendance and as Eric, aided by Charlie, set off to push-start the bike, Francis murmured to me, 'This is going to be good, Charles, they've forgotten to remove the cork!'

Eric's bikes always started immediately, but they pushed the Cotton right across the paddock and stopped—and Eric swore. He looked down to make sure the fuel was turned on and then galloped it back to where we stood watching. You could then see how it had happened, because this particular cork was a thin one and didn't protrude from the bell-mouth of the carburettor intake but went right down into its depths. Still, Eric didn't spot it and Charlie was impassive. They changed the plug with much bad language and several other people in the paddock, some of them riders, came over to watch, never before having seen a Fernihough bike fail to start with more than a five-yard push. Another push across the paddock and back and by now Eric was in a raging temper. Suddenly he spotted the trouble. 'Holy Mother, the bloody cork's still in.'

Still absolutely impassive, Charlie said, 'Yes, Mr Fernihough.'

'What d'you mean, yes? Did you know it was there?'

'Yes, Mr Fernihough. I thought you'd left it there for a purpose.'

Charlie was completely unmechanically minded and would have

been just as happy and efficient at cleaning desks as motor-cycles. By now, Eric was puce in the face and beside himself with rage.

'You bloody fool, you're sacked.'

Charlie looked at him and really stood up to him for the very first time in his life because, although he liked and respected Eric, he was quite scared of him.

'No need to speak to me like that, Mr Fernihough, it's your fault.'

At this stage we thought Eric might burst a blood vessel, but he calmed down and said, 'What d'you mean, my fault?'

'Well, Mr Fernihough, it's never been my job to take the cork out. Or put it in. You said I was never to touch it. Always been your job.'

Eric looked away. 'Load the bike back on the transport.'

For a moment one felt that Charlie might refuse, having just been sacked. But he didn't and as Charlie was re-tying it Eric said, 'Sorry, Charlie, you're right.'

'I know, Mr Fernihough. That's all right.'

'What d'you want to do? D'you want to go?'

'Go, Mr Fernihough, go where?'

'Well, I've just sacked you, you idiot. Are you going or aren't you?'

'No, sir. Of course not. You've sacked me several times afore when you lost your temper. I never thought I was going.'

So Charlie was obviously a man who could work with Eric and accept his shortcomings. But, had it been me, I would have left him to reload and take the blessed thing home on his own. Francis had accepted this because he recognised that it was necessary for him financially and because he knew how much he could learn and needed to learn. But Eric nearly crucified him at times, as he did everyone. So that was out for me. But I still could live a similar life to Eric's and set off to the Continent each year, with a couple of good bikes, and travel from one semi-important Continental race to another and could probably make more money that way than I was making at the time.

But I loved Brooklands and it was the thought of leaving Brooklands that made it impossible to do any of these things. And I felt that, if there was going to be a war, I should probably see quite enough of the Continent, anyway.

It was at this time that something else happened to influence these things for the fuel companies began to bring pressure on people like myself to add the Isle of Man T.T. to their programme. Reg Tanner, who was the Competition Manager of Esso, to whom I was contracted, came to see me and put it really strongly. They had been very good to me and Reg was a great friend but, in this, his hands were tied. If money was to continue, it had to be the T.T.

This really decided the thing for me. I wasn't going to do the T.T., so it seemed to mean a switch to cars. But there was one other thing I could do and that was to continue as I was at Brooklands and to team up with someone else just for the T.T. so that I could look after the machinery and have them ridden for me. So I decided to do this.

Who could do it? It wouldn't be easy because he had to be a good rider, free to ride in the T.T. alone and this would be difficult because, if he was good, he would probably want other rides besides the T.T. And he had to be 'liveable with'—that is to say someone whom one was happy to have around apart from the riding aspect. This was important because riders and their supporting staff spend a lot of time together and you must be able to enjoy life together in a small equipe. There was no hurry, but that was what I would do.

Having left Eric's employ early in 1935, Francis Beart had moved into the paddock to manage a newly opened motor-cycle-tuning establishment for Myles Rothwell. Robin Jackson ran a similar establishment for car people in the paddock, looking after cars like the big single-seater Bentley Jackson for R. R. K. Marker, Thomas Fotheringham's Type 35 Bugatti and a host of M.G.'s. Thompson and Taylor had their premises over at the Aerodrome where cars like John Cobb's big Napier Railton, the twelve-cylinder Sunbeam, Rose Richards' similar car and many others, mainly Bugattis and Alfa Romeos, were garaged and maintained. And although nearly everyone who raced motor-bikes and had a shed in the paddock would do a certain amount of tuning and maintenance on racing bikes, no one had ever put themselves out to run a really well-equipped tuning and maintenance firm for two wheelers.

And Francis was the man to do it, for not only was he qualified, having served his time with Eric, but he was very nearly as commercially minded. And since he was to be the full-time manager, and wasn't going to become involved in racing and journeying to race meetings himself, there was every reason why the establishment should go like a house on fire—because the demand was most certainly there.

Something of interest was hatching in Eric's place, too. For whenever

74

one went to see him one was no longer welcome in the workshop but was ushered either into the office or into the house. Secrets like that just had to be laid bare and before long the answer emerged. Eric was building a big twin!

This news was electrifying to all of us because, for years, Eric had been established as predominantly a 'small bike' rider. His road races were always done on 250's or 175's, he did a few outer-circuit races on a very fast 350 cc. track set-up and he regularly ran in sprints with a super-efficient 500. But all these bikes were Excelsiors and Excelsiors didn't make a big twin. And what was he going to use it for? Sprints, obviously, but what else? Was he going to use it on the outer circuit? It seemed unlikely because, great tuner that he was, Eric wasn't the greatest of riders. If it was to run on the outer circuit he could only be thinking in terms of the outer-circuit lap record which then stood to the credit of Joe Wright at over 118 m.p.h. This had always been accepted as a dangerous record. Wright had had some nasty moments on his big Zenith and no other big-twin rider had approached his speeds. The A.J.S. company had built a big twin with a view to attacking the World's motorcycle speed record and they had brought this machine down to Brooklands from time to time. It was a superb-looking bike, looking something like a Brough, the engine of which really consisted of two 500 cc. overhead camshaft cylinders on a common crankcase, but it had either hurt or frightened everyone who had ridden it and, in the end, it had been taken back to the factory and put under a dustsheet after one or two abortive outings at Southport in Wright's hands. On this basis, then, one couldn't really picture Eric coping with a 'thousand' and trumping the tough Wright's ace. But we just had to wait and see.

One day, when I called in to Eric's filling station for petrol on my way to Brooklands, a railway delivery van pulled up and the driver unloaded a very beautiful racing sidecar. I knew that Eric had no sidecar customers and this 'chair' was hefty as regards the chassis and was obviously going to be used with his new brainchild. There were sidecar classes at all sprints and that added up. Moreover, knowing him, I felt sure that he had in mind doing some of the initial tests of the bike with a sidecar as a means of cutting down its performance and top speed so as to get used to it. So, taking the bull by the horns I knocked on the door of the workshop and when he opened it I pointed to the new delivery and said, 'Sorry to bother you, Eric, but when you've finished building your "thousand" I should very much like to ride with you in that.'

I didn't know what his reaction would be but his old face broke into a grin and he said, 'What the hell makes you think I'm building a "thousand"?'

'I don't *think* you are, Eric. I *know* you are. So do a lot of people. And you've been at it so long now that the ruddy thing ought to be pretty well finished.'

He seemed quite pleased, which was surprising.

'All right, then. Come in and have a look.' And there stood the most beautiful Brough Superior I'd ever seen.

In conception, it was entirely different from the orthodox big twin of that time, particularly as regards the engine, for the engine of this bike really did consist of two 500's mounted on one crankcase. Everything was separate; there was a carburettor to each cylinder, two magnetos, both exhaust pipes going out forwards—ending in Brooklands' silencers on either side of the rear wheel, instead of the orthodox arrangement of both silencers on the offside. The rear cylinder was more heavily finned than the front, which seemed to dispose of Geoffrey Davies' theory that the front cylinder of a big twin ran the hottest!

So this was why Eric had been doing so many standing-start tests with his sprint 500 at the track recently. He always used an extremely lightly finned cylinder barrel on the sprint 500—to save the last ounce of weight—but we had noticed that, on a number of occasions recently, the engine of the sprint 500 had had a heavily finned barrel. We'd even asked him about this and he'd said that he was doing a batch of J.A.P. racing engines for export and that they were to be used for road racing!

'Well,' he said, 'What d'you think?'

'I'll tell you. It's the most beautiful bike I've ever seen.'

'It ought to be. It's taken enough time and thought. Come in and have a cup of tea.'

Over the tea, he said, 'D'you really want to ride in the chair?' I really did, but I wondered whether I might be too heavy.

'No, not to start with,' he said. 'I shall be glad of a bit of weight. I've never tried to control that much horsepower yet. Anything that will slow it down a bit will help.'

I didn't have many rides in the sidecar of that bike but the memory

76

of every one remains, even today. Most of the rides were standing half-mile and mile during testing at Brooklands and, later, I rode with him when he broke the Standing Kilometre Record on the seafront at the Brighton Speed Trials, although this was only the course record and not a World Record.

You lay on your right side, facing the rear wheel and about a foot away from it and the outfit had so much power that, when starting a sprint, it had to be pointed not up the road along which it was going to travel but almost at ninety degrees to the right of the road, facing the right-hand kerb. When the power was applied, the rear wheel would disappear in a cloud of smoke and, with the rider applying full right steering lock, the outfit would leave the line sideways with the bike itself fighting to run round the sidecar in an anti-clockwise direction. At peak revs in first it would be going straight, but a lot of right-hand lock had to be applied again on engaging second, quite a lot in third and some when it was doing well over a hundred, when the change was made from third into top. It was dragster stuff—but thirty-five years ago.

Very soon after that, Eric broke Joe Wright's Brooklands' outer-circuit record and subsequently raised it to over the two-mile-a-minute mark. Later still, with a supercharged version of the bike, Eric regained the World's Motor Cycle Speed Record for Great Britain by covering the Flying Mile and Kilometre at 164 m.p.h. Subsequently Henne regained it for Germany when he raised it to 169·016 m.p.h. in October 1936.

None of us could believe it when we heard the news, not so long afterwards, that Eric had been killed in trying to get it back. As far as I know, no definite reason was ever given about the cause of the accident but the blow to us all was made so much heavier in view of Eric's expert preparation, care and thoroughness whenever he took out a bike. For a long time one was conscious of the fact that, if this could happen to him, it could happen to anyone.

But sad chapters like this do pass and, when you are young, sadness tends to fade more quickly. And Eric was a man who certainly achieved something in his life.

It has always been the case that, when an accident of this nature occurs, there is publicity which sometimes leads to people drawing comparisons between the danger aspect of racing motor-cycles and racing a car and, usually, the conclusion is reached that the two-wheeler is the more dangerous. Personally I think that, when we are talking about racing, the exact reverse is the case. At the time Eric Fernihough met with his fatal accident, he was exploring the unknown and, without any doubt at all, this is always dangerous territory either on land, water, air or, of course, in space. I don't know what the statistics are concerning deaths in ultra-high-speed record attempts but one has the feeling that, against distance run, water is probably by far the most dangerous and, in this connection, three names—Segrave, Cobb and Donald Campbell—come instantly to mind. And bear in mind how many car and motor-cycle record attempts there have been compared to record attempts on water.

I used to read of Eric's motor-cycle racing exploits for years before I met him and, during the years I knew him and raced with and against him, I can only recall him being involved in one other racing accident. On the other hand, I have known good and successful riders who just couldn't get through a season without at least one accident and, very often, more than one. But, in nearly forty years connected closely with motor-cycle racing, I seem to be able to look back on comparatively few fatal racing accidents when compared with the long list of drivers killed when racing cars.

I think this applies more so today than it did when I was racing between the wars. My own son, now twenty-two years old, is a fully professional racing motor-cyclist, has won a T.T. in the Isle of Man and is now contracted to ride for one of the big Japanese factories. In a discussion we had on the subject not so long ago, he told me that he and, he thought, most of his contemporaries, would normally expect to part company with a machine at least twice in a racing season. That is a very much higher rate of departing than in my own day and is accounted for, I think, by the fact that road adhesion of the modern racing machine, car or motor-cycle, is so much better than it was in my day that the rider (or driver) can 'lean out of the window' further, and more often, before actually 'falling out'. But, with modern machinery, the break, when it comes, is instant and there's no warning whereas with our rigid-framed bikes, one felt that adhesion was barely ever there! In this connection, I've often thought how interesting it would be to put one of our good pre-war alcohol engines into one of Colin Seeley's 1972 frames, just to see what the improvement in road adhesion amounts to.

During the time I was racing at Brooklands I saw a great many

78

accidents to both car drivers and motor-cyclists but, as I write now, I don't recall one motor-cycle racing fatality at Brooklands between 1932 and when the track closed in 1939, whereas there were several car accidents that proved fatal in the same period. Of course the risk becomes greater where true road racing is concerned but, even there, I believe the bike to be, on distance run, safer. You can argue it both ways, I know. You can maintain that the motor-cycle is more dangerous because the rider has no protection. But I have seen more people survive racing car accidents by being thrown out of the car than by staying within its 'protection'.

Right now I can think of several bike racing accidents which I saw happen at Brooklands, all of them potentially very dangerous, all caused by human error, in which no one was badly hurt and which, in two cases, provided all concerned with quite a laugh when the danger was past.

The first, and the most frightening, involved the well-known Velocette rider Les Archer who is still around and in bursting health, I'm glad to say. The race was the Junior Mountain Championship which I was watching from the home banking end of the finishing-straight, looking down the straight with the riders coming towards me. It was at the end of the race and Les was well in the lead but as he approached at over 100 m.p.h., his rear tyre punctured. Continuing and succeeding in crossing the finishing-line in first place, Les slowed and veered inwards to turn sharp left into the paddock whereas, had the puncture not occurred, he would have gone on and completed a slowing-down lap. Coming up fast behind him was a rider who, although he must have seen how slowly Les was going, obviously didn't realise just what had happened. For, as Les turned left into the paddock, he was hit broadside and the result looked like a bomb explosion. The machine that had hit him slid for a long distance, with its throttle jammed wide open, then rolled, reared up on its back wheel and with its front wheel two feet off the ground, motored off riderless across the track and right through a bunch of riders completing their last lap, without touching one of them. No one was seriously hurt.

On another occasion there was a knock on the door of my shed and it was Arthur Dobson who later drove E.R.A.s so successfully. At that time, Arthur was a successful rider of racing Douglas machines and he wanted to know if I would time him on a practice lap he was about to set out on. It was a machine capable of lapping at over 100 m.p.h.

and Arthur was dressed not in racing leathers but in grey flannel trousers and a sweater. I did ask him if he thought that a good idea? But he was in a hurry and only going to do one lap so out he went. He wanted the lap to be timed from the Vickers' sheds and, as the bike approached the sheds at the start of the lap, it needed no expert to see that it was going to be a very quick lap indeed. I started the watch and saw the bike run past the sheds and well up on to the home banking and then it disappeared behind the Members' Hill. One did this so often that, instinctively, one knew when to anticipate seeing the bike shoot out again from under the Members' Bridge and, immediately, I knew that Arthur was overdue. Then, just as I was about to climb down from the timing tower a wheel appeared bowling round the banking—all on its own—at between 70 and 80 m.p.h. I didn't wait to see where it went—I jumped into the car and went out to find Arthur walking back—heavily gravel-rashed but otherwise quite unhurt.

The next one was hilarious but could just as easily have been very serious. H. Trevor Battye, who was a good rider usually on Scotts and on Velocettes, also had a big twin Zenith on which he had aimed, for some time, to win a Gold Star which used to be awarded for a lap at over 100 m.p.h., whatever the capacity of the machine. While he was consistently successful with his Scotts and Velocettes, he had no luck at all with the Zenith and he and I used to talk for hours about the virtues and drawbacks of big twins generally. He was a most genial and pleasant character who always enjoyed his visits to Brooklands and meeting and talking with racing friends and he sometimes got so involved in this that he almost appeared to have forgotten the main object of his visit which was, of course, to put in some practice laps.

On this occasion he had only the Zenith with him and vowed that this was the day on which it would go round at over the 'ton' for the first time with him on board. We all lunched in the café and then dispersed and when we collected together up there for tea, Trevor was there but had not yet been out with the Zenith which, once again, had proved temperamental. But this was usual and he was quite unperturbed by it so we had an enjoyable cup of tea and then went back to our respective sheds to resume work. The track used to close at five o'clock, whereupon Jack Cann, the head gateman, used to first shut the gates from the paddock leading out on to the track and then drive down to the fork where the Vickers' sheds were. His next task was to erect a barrier of hurdles right across the track at the fork and, once this had been done, Vickers were able to bring out the aircraft they had completed that day, cross the track and park them on the aerodrome ready for testing next day. I was closing up my shed at a few minutes past five when, suddenly, I heard the Zenith burst into life and from around the Clubhouse it and its conductor arrived with the obvious intention of doing a fast lap. I still didn't worry because I thought Trevor would see the paddock gate shut and would turn back but, instead, he pressed on to the gate and peering to see if it was openable, found that it was, opened it and went out.

Sprinting to the control tower, I shinned up the steps to try to draw Jack's attention but could see at once that I was far too late because the barrier was right across the track and the front part of a Wellington bomber was already well out on to the track. There was nothing I could do except hope that Jack just might hear the bike coming round the Byfleet, and this he did. I could see him and someone else frantically tearing a gap in the barrier but it was much too far to one side for a big twin to get through it and not end up in the pits and I knew it was useless for Trevor to try it. So I nipped down again and made for the fork, in the car.

There it all was. Bits of Zenith and wooden barrier all in one scattered area of desolation. And in the middle of the disaster stood Trevor, convulsed with laughter at the sight of poor Jack's ashen face.

One sidecar incident, which happened in the 1934 Hutchinson 100 in which I was riding the little 250 cc. 'Grand Prix' New Imperial. Half way through the race, in which I was lapping around the 85 m.p.h. mark, I was passed by Les Archer's Velocette sidecar outfit. They came past quite slowly and quite close to me and immediately they were ahead of me I found myself gazing into the face of his passenger, Offord, who was, of course, lying down and facing rearwards. Slowly and deliberately Offord raised a hand to his nose and extended five fingers whereupon, at that very moment, the sidecar wheel detached itself from its spindle and bowled merrily away into the undergrowth! Offord's face was a study as he covered his eyes with one gloved hand and gently tapped Les on the behind with the other! But there was no real danger here because Brooklands' sidecar chassis were always fitted with a skid to guard against this very eventuality and in any case it happened when we were all 'grass cutting' round the Byfleet bank and the sidecar wheel was airborne anyway.

And, lastly, two 'funnies', both of which happened within the precincts of Brooklands but neither on the track itself. The first involved a customer of Francis'—an Indian—who used to race a Morgan. Francis used to garage and maintain the Morgan but, on race and practice days the customer looked after himself. His technique for starting was to gallop it across the paddock in neutral and, having previously set the hand throttle, snick it into gear and jump in. It was always hazardous and we always enjoyed watching it but none of us saw the beginning of the final disaster. Sometimes when he snicked it into gear it would depart quickly, nearly leaving him behind; on other occasions, having done the gear bit, he would take a flying leap into the cockpit, whereupon the engine would kick back just as he landed and he would take a header over the bonnet and radiator into the road. On this last occasion he tripped and I only saw the end bit —when the driverless Morgan came belting across the paddock at astronomical revs to be brought up sharply by a head-on collision with Reid Railton's brand new Railton coupé, which was parked outside the Clubhouse!

The last one is so disgraceful and stupid that I hesitate to mention it but, as all the others have been stories against other people and this one was against us, I think I had better. But it just shows how assinine you can be when you're young. Noel Pope, who finally held the Brooklands' motor-cyle lap record on his Brough Superior—at over 124 m.p.h.—called at my shed one day, driving a wreck of a 1924 Austin Seven chummy tourer. 'Charles, how about it? A pound a wheel. One wheel still vacant. Francis, Freddy Clarke and myself have got the others.' So I put my pound down and owned a quarter share in the Austin.

The Vintage Sports Car Club would be cross with us, today, if they could have seen what happened to the Austin. We drove it all day and every day, seated in the front seat, seated in the back and we even drove it sitting on the bonnet and it took it all. But after one motor-cycle meeting when we had had a very good day, having won six out of the eight races between us, we took it to a party over at the Aero Club. Leaving the party there was a rush to be driver—each thought he could do slightly better than the others. Francis won, by virtue of his long legs, and away we went, our first obstacle being a fairly high heap of brick rubble and our second the remains of a derelict privet hedge. Then we were on the perimeter road—the aerodrome road—which led back to the paddock and suddenly Noel spotted a haystack. 'Go on. Straight into that,' he urged. But Francis wasn't having any and there was a short wrestle for control of the Austin before the wheel snapped right off the column and they were left still grappling with it in mid air. Meanwhile the front wheels went on to full right lock, the nearside rear collapsed and we were over and going down the road upside down, cocooned in the hood which was filled with plate glass from the broken windscreen. No one was badly hurt. Noel, who deserved to have been hurt most, was unscratched; I had some unpleasant cuts, Francis a broken finger and poor Freddy Clarke who was really the innocent of the party and just enjoyed any fun that was going, came out worst with a broken collar bone, so the Triumph motor-cycle company had to find a new works' rider for a time.

Even then we weren't proud of it and it cooled us down for a long time. And I had an awful job convincing my family that my injuries had nothing to do with motorcycles!

This one only cooled Francis down temporarily, however. At that time, it was usual, if one came up behind a Brooklands mate, while motoring anywhere, to greet him with a gentle bumper to bumper nudge from astern. Charlie Brackenbury started the thing with his big open Buick two-seater and it grew and became a standard form of greeting. Francis, apparently, was motoring through Kingston when he saw, ahead of him, what he thought to be me, in the 1933 Austin Ten I had at the time. Creeping up stealthily astern, but fairly fast, he was about to give the standard greeting when his foot slipped off the brake pedal and he rammed the Austin rather hard, doing some damage to both cars. The driver turned out not to be me, but a rather important civic official and, while waiting for the police, a fairish crowd gathered. Both the driver and the police constable concerned found it hard to accept Francis' explanation that he was only greeting a friend, the latter expressing the opinion that, 'If that's how you greet your friends, Heaven help your enemies.'

This form of greeting is still used, or was, until recently. Only a few years ago, I went up to Silverstone and watched the Grand Prix from the inside of the circuit, at Stowe, motoring down the long run-way, only to run up against a rather riotous re-union in progress, on arrival. Those involved included Tony Rolt, Duncan Hamilton, James Tilling, Bill Ruck Keene and others and when the meeting ended, Bill kindly asked everyone back for drinks at his home. My mount that day was nothing more exciting than a Herald fixed-head coupé and, as we left Stowe, I was a bit unhappy to see the radiator of Duncan's Silver Cloud silhouetted very closely in the mirror. Contact was made and no Herald has ever been down a runway faster. Needless to say, the Rolls was unmarked after the episode, but the rear bumper of the Herald bore the marks of Rolls' over-riders till the day I sold it!

On another occasion, a very well-known post-war racing motorist was involved in a tricky situation which arose following a Club dinner in town. Motoring home through the back streets of the West End, in the early hours of the morning, having wined and dined very well, he spied what he thought to be a number of ladies of easy virtue gathered together on a street pavement. 'Look,' he said to his crew, 'girls on the game. Let's make 'em run.' And before he could be dissuaded, he had two wheels on the pavement and make them run he did. Unfortunately for him, two among them were highly respectable women, one of them a Duchess who was alert enough to take his number. We never did hear the end of that one, I think. It was well before the arrival of the Breathalyser!

Both Jean and I had two rather unusual accidents, both of them very different in character. Hers involved an Austin Healey which we were due to race at Goodwood one Saturday in the mid-fifties. The night before the race I dreamed that she'd had a prang in the Healey and, although nothing like this had ever happened to me before, I tried to put her off driving the car that day, finally succeeding with a small financial inducement so that she could go shopping instead. I drove the car down to Goodwood myself, intending to run it in the one race in which I'd entered, practised, and then had a look through the programme. It seemed to me that the handicapping of the ladies' race was way adrift and when I saw Lew Ebblewhite I said so, since Jean was now no longer involved in it. Lew said, 'Come up into the timing-box,' and, closing the door behind him, handed me a large blank sheet of paper.

'Could you make a better job of it?' he asked, and when I said I felt I could, he answered, 'Right. Do it your way. But remember this. If Jean wins, there'll be hell to pay.'

This was a bit of a sobering thought. I really did think I could do it better and I wasn't worried about our car since it wouldn't be competing. So I sat down and rehashed the whole thing, basing it on what I knew our car could do, setting one or two competitors farther back and putting others forward. One car I put forward was Angela Lane's Healey which had been down to go off the same mark as ours. This was obviously not on, since we had quite a bit of experience and she hadn't. I gave the sheet to Lew and said I'd stand behind it and thought it should be close but, when I went back to the paddock stall, there was no Healey. I then found that Jean had changed her mind and was out practising with it! She came in, all smiles, hand outstretched to give me back the cash I'd given her and as it seemed a *fait accompli*, I sat back to watch.

It was a very good race and everybody agreed that it was. Our Healey kept coming through from its back mark, all the way, followed by Carol Fisher's Kieft Bristol which, while much faster on the straights, was slower round the swerves. On the last lap, both cars finally overhauled the back markers on Lavant straight and, as they went into Woodcote, the Healey led, followed closely by the Kieft. It did look as though we had it but, then, I was staggered to see Mrs Fisher go right round the Healey, on Woodcote, in a desperate 'do or die' effort to pass. One felt sure it wasn't possible—and one was right. Immediately, the Kieft swung broadside, right in the path of the Healey and, sure enough, there it was—an almighty shunt.

I trotted down to Woodcote, to be met by photographer George Phillips. 'Not Jean's fault, Charles. She hadn't a chance. I'll send you the prints and you'll see for yourself. Don't lead off at her, will you?' And that was it—nothing is predictable in racing, they say!

There was another rather comic incident at Goodwood shortly after this. Some brand new and rather elaborate observers' boxes had been set up at each corner and the Duke of Richmond asked me if, in my capacity of Deputy Chief Observer, I would go round in between races, look at each and see if they seemed to be sited correctly. I took a quick trip round and the only one that seemed doubtful was the one at St Mary's so, after the next race, I went there to see a race from the box itself.

As soon as you were in it you could see that it was vulnerable for as you stood watching from its raised balcony, it was obvious that if a car did go off, it would be the box that it would 'collect'. Needless to say, it happened in that very race! The balcony was packed, the rear door was small and never was there such a jam of retreating observers as there was at the moment of impact. But although the beautiful box was demolished—and so was the car—no one was badly hurt.

I always held Duncan slightly accountable not for my biggest road prang, but for the sequel to it, for when we were racing together, he it was who formed 'The Club'. Membership of 'The Club' wasn't particularly coveted, there was no entrance fee and no annual subscription and it was reserved for all who had enjoyed at least one monumental prang either in racing or on the road. Duncan used to dub me 'Charles the Cautious', reminding me at the start of each meeting that I still hadn't qualified for membership and saying, 'Now, Charles, do remember about membership. Today's the day. Have a really good one. You're long overdue after all these years. You'll go much better once you've done it. Think about it won't you?'

At this time he lived at Bracknell, while having his business at Byfleet, and my daily route was via Byfleet to my office at Bracknell so that, nearly every day, we used to meet on the road and, if we were both in a hurry, it was something to remember. On the day it all happened, I really was in a hurry, but at the moment of impact I hadn't reached the point on the road when it was likely we would meet. I had a big six-cylinder Citroen at the time and really was pressing on when I noticed a Ferguson agricultural tractor towing a big trailer about three hundred yards ahead and going my way. We were on a de-restricted stretch and, while the road between me and the tractor was straight, he was approaching a fast left-hander and I did wonder whether I would have time to pass him before the bend or whether I should have to slow and follow him round it. As I came up to him, I realised I would be able to see right round him and know if anything was approaching from the other direction so I kept way on and, immediately I saw that the road was clear, pulled over to the off-side and began to pass. At that very moment, giving no prior signal, he turned sharply right into a gateway. If he had had no trailer I could have got behind him, but he and his trailer completely blocked the road and all I could do was to try to turn with him in the vain hope of lessening the impact. It was a vain hope and a really immense prang, the nearside wheel of the car being pushed right back to the front door, together with the drive shaft and all the suspension and steering units.

Despite the impact, neither the tractor driver nor myself were serious casualties. While he was being given a cup of tea by his mates, I strolled back to enlist the help of the local gendarmerie and it was while particulars were being taken and statements made that Duncan hove into sight. His face was wreathed in smiles when he saw it was me and, getting out, he came across to where I stood with the constable.

'Well done, well done, well done,' he chuckled. 'Boy, what a prang. Look at those ruddy skid marks! Life membership, Charlie, nothing less. Splendid! Couldn't have done better myself.'

Up to that time I didn't know what was in the P.C.'s mind but now he said, ponderously, 'Yes, sir. I noticed the skid marks myself. They seem to indicate very high speed and I ought to caution you that there is a possibility of a dangerous-driving charge here.'

This staggered me but reduced Duncan to convulsions and ended in him saying that, if such a charge was brought, he would see to it personally that, in addition to life membership, I would be made Honorary Vice-President. None of this helped at all, I felt, and in due course I did get the dangerous-driving charge. A subsequent visit to the scene of the prang, accompanied by my solicitor made him think that representation by a Q.C. would be well advised and this was duly arranged.

The Q.C. turned out to be a wonderful man but, although he was concerned about the length of the skid marks, he was more worried on seeing the photographs of the car, feeling that such immense damage could only be caused by an extremely high-speed impact, even after all that braking.

His opinion was that it would help greatly if we could produce expert evidence to say that damage as great as this could be caused even at a comparatively low speed if a car collided with something as solid as a tractor, at a particularly awkward angle. At the time, I could think of no one who would conceivably say this so I rang Duncan to see if he had any ideas. Dear old Duncan. By now he was really concerned. 'Well, yes, Charlie. Of course it could be so. The Citroen took it right on the quarter—the worst possible angle. I'll say so myself, if you like. But I was there, wasn't I? Maybe I'm not the right one. I'll put you in touch with someone, though. A consulting engineer. Always dealing with this sort of problem. Here's his number.' At this stage, I forgave him.

We all assembled at Court on the day. My Counsel handled our part of the thing impeccably, forgetting nothing and stressing that the road was de-restricted and that forward visibility was clear. The tractor driver went into the box and he handled him courteously and gently.

'Now,' he said, 'This was all most unfortunate for you. Perhaps you could tell us exactly what happened from your point of view?'

'Yes, Sir, I will. One moment I was on my tractor, and the next I was in the bloody ditch.'

'Yes, of course. But let's go back a bit further than that, to where you were approaching the gateway and knew you were going to turn right into it. You'll have had a mirror on your tractor so, knowing you were going to turn, you'll have looked into it. What did you see?'

'Nothing, Guv'nor.'

'Nothing. Really? But the car must have been there?'

The old gentleman scratched his head. 'Well, Guv'nor. I've got two tractors. One's got a mirror and the other hasn't.'

Quick as a flash came the reply: 'Ah, yes. And you were driving the one that hasn't.'

He agreed, readily.

That seemed to be it, we must be in the clear. But we weren't and he knew we weren't, feeling that the Bench and one member in particular were worried about what the speed might have been, de-restriction or no de-restriction.

They retired for a very long time and, on returning, announced that they had decided against convicting for 'dangerous'. But they felt they had to convict for driving 'Without Due Care' and this they did, fining me £10, very politely and almost apologetically. This helped but, at the time, I felt a bit hard done by although, in retrospect after many years, they may well have been right.

The police were very fair in this case and I've always found them to be so. But one of my business partners, Dick Carr, never agreed with me about this. Dick, I thought, tended to be a slightly aggressive driver, although very experienced and capable. But he did like to challenge the boys in blue and one day it boomeranged. We were going down to Croydon to collect a new Peugeot and he was driving us in a Renault Caravelle. As we approached a set of lights at Clapham Common, they were at red. Two cars were stopped and waiting and there was a gap for a third, which was being slowly approached by a rather hesitant driver in a Minor 1000. Not very politely, Dick passed him and, swinging back, nipped into the gap. The lights changed and we were away to a fanfare of hooting. I said I didn't think it was very polite but Dick said 'Not at all. He should have made up his mind.'

We were stopped again at the next set of lights and the Minor driver drew up alongside and wound down his window. Seeing this, Dick did the same, receiving the information that the chap had taken his number, to which he replied, 'Good', adding his suggestion as to what he should do with it. None of it was mannerly and all rather unnecessary and on the way down we forgot it. But on the Purley Way we came across a Police car, stopped rather awkwardly on a blind bend and this was just Dick's cup of tea. 'Just look at that. Disgraceful. If we did that, they'd have us at once.' He slowed and, stopping, got out and started to walk back. Although embarrassed, I had to see this and strolled back myself.

'Good morning,' said Dick. 'May I ask whether you're on duty? Ah, I see one of you is smoking, so you can't be. So why are you stopped here?' This time he obviously felt he had them. And he might have, too, if it hadn't been for the fact that at that moment the Minor hove into sight and stopped.

'Good morning, officer. I'm glad you've stopped this man. I should like to tell you about his driving farther back and tell you what he said when I protested.'

Deadlock, of course. Dick was deflated, the gendarmerie relieved and the driver of the Minor assured that the matter would be looked into. It was, very casually. And then Dick was told, 'Think you'd better scarper, mate.' Yes, accidents and encounters like this can become complicated. Better to avoid them altogether!

4

At the end of each season there was always a great rush to the Norton factory at Bracebridge Street in Birmingham. Dennis Mansell and his staff must have dreaded this because we all used to arrive on the door-step, our cars loaded with tired Manx Norton engines, coaxing, cajoling, even bribing anyone in the Competition Department who would give us even the glimmer of a hope that, in the spring, we should have engines doled out to us that were slightly better than anyone else had achieved.

We used to collect our engines in February or early March together with the Brake Horse Power curve for each unit, over which we used to pore while trying vainly to find out the b.h.p. figures of our rivals. In the meantime, we had dealt with the cycle parts of our bikes our-selves, working in our chilly, paraffin-heated sheds throughout the winter. We never noticed the discomfort of it all and there was, of course, a lot more to the winter than that aspect of it. The British Motor Cycle Show which ran for a week at Olympia; a lot of skull-duggery happened here regarding the fixing up of contracts for the season ahead. And then there were the local motor-cycle club dinners where we were kindly asked along as guests of honour in return for a short speech about motor-cycle racing, ending in proposing the health and prosperity of the club.

At this time I had an absolutely top-grade girl-friend, Strelsa, who couldn't, unfortunately, accompany me to evening functions because she was a showgirl at the London Casino supper restaurant and was on and off stage at various times between nine o'clock and midnight. But at weekends I used to collect her from the theatre and we would motor down to her parents' cottage at North Berstead, leaving the theatre soon after one in the morning and returning to London in time for her to get ready for action again at about eight o'clock on Monday evenings. These floor shows were run by an impresario, Clifford Fisher, who had three separate shows running at the same time in London, Paris and New York and they were generally held to be the most glamorous productions of that era. The costumes were superb and all sorts of unusual props were provided for the girls. In one scene they each had a sea-lion and Strelsa used to dread this because her sea-lion was particularly stubborn and wilful. I got on with her parents like a house on fire, for dear Strelsa was an unpredictable, mercurial character with whom I could easily bear, for she was such great fun, and her parents liked the idea of this. It was a love-hate relationship which lasted quite a few years partly, I suppose, because from time to time she would suddenly and without much prior warning be posted either to Paris or New York in order to fill a gap. Paris I used to manage, but New York was out, so we only really saw each other for about eight months of the year. She was working in New York when the war broke out so we didn't meet again until the nineteen-forties and by that time I was married and she had been, and was now widowed.

But the comic thing is that, only a week ago, when Francis Beart came to see me to help me with his notes in writing this story, he said, 'What happened to Strelsa?' and when I told him he said, 'That's interesting because she was mentioned in the *Daily Telegraph* last week as being the first British model ever to pose in the nude.' That took me back because, very much under protest, I had driven her down to Lulworth Cove where the photographers were waiting to take the photographs. And I was with her when her father, who happened to take the paper in which they appeared, confronted her with them. Even now I recall her lightning reaction: 'Fantastic, Daddy. Not me, but isn't she like me?' And it worked!

There was a great social side to racing in those days and the pace was hot although not, generally, as hot as it was in the field of car racing. I enjoyed it for it was part of the racing scene.

The Cambridge University Automobile Club was very active under its enthusiastic Honorary Secretary, Jock Forbes. In addition to Jock, 'Spug' Muir, J. H. 'Crasher' White, Steve Darbishire and J. H. Fell were all highly skilled Brooklands performers and you could always tell them by their light blue crash-helmets. All rode in the Isle of Man and 'Crasher' became an official member of the works' Norton team. They had mostly started on grass tracks in the Cambridge area and, even in those days, grass-track racing had come under the administration of the Auto Cycle Union to which the C.U.A.C. had to be affiliated. Despite this and despite the fact that to ride on a non-affiliated 'pirate' track meant the immediate suspension of one's A.C.U. Competition Licence, they all did it and were even encouraged by their Honorary Secretary, who did likewise! Names like 'Q. Ack, J. Strapp and A. N. Other' always hid the identity of one of the Cambridge crowd at a non-affiliated race meeting. The money was better and all sorts of events were staged which would never have been permitted under A.C.U. rules including, on one occasion, a race between one of them on a grass-track bike and another in an aeroplane, over a quarter-mile circuit! This drew a record crowd which far surpassed any that ever attended an A.C.U. Affiliated meeting.

So, when the time came for me to look for a rider to conduct my bikes in the T.T. it was Jock I asked. But, sadly, he was already offered a works ride by the Vincent H.R.D. company and, although he hadn't actually signed with them, they were offering him rides throughout the season, which I didn't want. If I could have offered the same, I think he would have veered my way although he did like the Vincent people and their bikes and, also, the idea of riding for a works. Later, he told me, he regretted it because my Nortons turned out to be faster than the works' Vincents and we teamed up together in 1937, but for 1936 I soldiered on alone, riding where I wanted to and not in the Island.

I had three little private ambitions for 1936. I wanted to get a Gold Star in the 500 cc. class and knew that, barring trouble, this was something that I ought to manage. I wanted to do the same with the 350 although I realised that this might not be so easy and would require the right day. Everything would have to be right for this, the machine itself, the wind and me because I was none too small to put in quick 350 cc. laps. And, thirdly, I was keen to average over a hundred for a two-lap race. I had done this in a three-lapper with the Brough, with a standing lap at 93 m.p.h. with hand gear change and a three-speed box and felt that, on the 500 with four cogs and foot gear change I ought to manage a standing and flying lap at 95 and 105 m.p.h. respectively.

We made up a party and all went up to Donnington as a curtain-raiser. We stayed at the Queen's Head in Loughborough, four or five of us and some with girl-friends. Socially it was a howling success but disastrous from the racing point of view. It wasn't the girl's fault. It was the usual story—batting on the local cricket pitch. We didn't know Donnington like the Midlanders and they trounced us even worse than we used to trounce them when they came down to Brooklands. Jock always went well there but for me it was a catastrophic day. I lay nowhere but was having quite a good scrap with a chap on a Velocette who had no more idea of where he was going than I had, when suddenly he dropped it on the sharp right-hander coming out of the woods into the long straight. Then I found that I, too, was 'on the floor' and followed him into a vast clump of rhododendrons. Once in the undergrowth it became a very noisy prang and as I picked myself up I found I was laying not on a Norton or a Velocette but a steaming hot Rudge; while I pondered the mystery we were joined by yet another unfortunate, this time Excelsior mounted! Obviously someone had dropped oil at the approach and if we didn't evacuate quickly, we were likely to be far more hurt staying where we were than we had been in our respective prangs. So there was an ugly rush to get clear!

The opening Brooklands' meeting that year was a big one and, as I had won the Wakefield Cup the previous year, I was keen to have a strong go again. This time it was a five-lap race on the outer circuit, so I entered the 350 because the only time 'Ebby' had seen it was when it was going slowly in practice for the Brooklands' Grand Prix in 1935 and I hoped he'd remember that when working out his handicaps! He was coming to like the 500 less and less from a handicapping point of view so I entered that for the Fitzgerald Cup race, also on the outer circuit.

On the day before the meeting, both were going well and I did six or seven practice laps on the 350, all at 99 m.p.h., including two at 99·99 m.p.h., but not one at a hundred! The big Norton went even better, 107 m.p.h. being its best, but when I had done four or five it felt a bit rough and, on taking it back to the shed, I found that the big end was on the way out. This was a blow because it was a brand-new big end. So I seemed to be out of the Fitzgerald Cup race.

I was depressed and decided to try and forget it by going up to Town to hit a bit of night life with Strelsa. But on the way up to the wicked city I spotted a very aged International Norton among the stock at Comerfords, the big Thames Ditton motor-cycle dealers. It was marked up at £25 so I felt it couldn't possibly be very much good, but I just had to stop and have a look, thinking it might be worth buying for resale.

At this stage of the proceedings I was arrayed in my best city suiting, en route for La Dolce Vita, but we got the Norton out and I took it down the road. It was a super old bike but nothing would make them take less than the £25 they were asking and, as I stood there arguing, I had a bright idea. I would have it and go straight back to Brooklands, work on it all night and try to bring it to the line for the Fitzgerald Cup race next day! I had no lighting in the shed, so I bought half a dozen torches and twice as many batteries; heating was no problem for it had been a blistering hot day and was still very warm and mild.

Within an hour I had the Norton back in my shed at Brooklands. The International Norton, of course, was the road-going version of the Manx T.T. Replica, fully equipped with lights and magdyno and generally a more 'civilised' machine for road use. The tank, although approximately the same shape, was slightly smaller and had a bright chrome finish instead of the dull of the Manx machine.

I had no problem here about removing the lighting equipment—someone else had forestalled me—but the bike was filthy and I spent two hours, first of all, in giving it a thorough clean. That done, I looked it over for cracks and found nothing frightening there. The engine had the standard cast-iron cylinder head which, at first, I aimed to change for a bronze one but, having removed it, I decided to keep it because it didn't appear a bad head at all and I was proposing to use alcohol fuel which would make the unit cooler running, anyway. I removed the barrel and piston, and looked around among my spare alcohol pistons for one which seemed to like the idea of marriage to this particular barrel; the favourite was one which we had experimented with at one time, the experiments ending in seizure—but not to the extent of the piston being reduced to scrap. I wanted one with a big clearance because there would be no time at all for running in—it would have to go straight out and race.

I replaced the magdyno with a B.T.H. racing magneto and replaced the carburettor with a spare racing carburettor we had previously used with an alcohol set-up. I was stuck for valve springs. I would normally have replaced them as a matter of routine, but it was an old engine with coil-type springs and my spares stock only included hairpin type, with which all my bikes were fitted. Luckily the race wasn't a long one and they seemed to have some life left in them but, if we were to meet with failure, they looked the likely source to me.

I also fitted a Manx-type fuel tank, mainly for the sake of appearance, although I felt sure that it was less likely to spring a leak than the bike's own tank which showed traces of repair in more places than one. Time was a factor. Some jobs had to be done however long they took, but one on which I had to put a time limit was the work to be done on the sphere and ports of the cylinder head. In fact, I was so badly up against it for time that I had to set myself a time limit of an hour for the head, to include removal of valves and springs, decoking and polishing, grinding in the valves and reassembly.

Then I stopped for a tea break and, while 'brewing up', gave thought to the work ahead. It was three o'clock and I still had to devise the exhaust system, the gearing and do something about tyres. I was going to have some sleep because I never liked the idea of racing with no sleep at all so I set a time limit of two hours for gearing and exhaust set-up, after which I was going to get as much sleep as I could between 5 a.m. and when the paddock noises would start to wake me around eight o'clock. Then I would have breakfast in the café, after which I would take the wheels to Dunlops across the paddock and get 'Mac' to slip the covers off and replace what had to be replaced.

Had I known that all this was going to happen, many willing hands would have helped me, but I hadn't got back to Brooklands with the bike until after eight the previous evening and it was such a crazy scheme that I hadn't the heart to start phoning round for assistance. In any case, when I started the job I felt, with the optimism of youth, that I had bags of time and it was only as the job progressed that I found out how quickly nine hours can pass!

On the assumption that the machine would be at least 5 m.p.h. slower on lap speed than my own Manx, I decided to gear down a tooth and a half on the top gear ratio I normally used. You could gear to half a tooth variation on the Manx Norton because both engine and rear wheel sprockets were removable. One tooth down obviously wasn't going to be enough, and two might be a fraction low for this rather aged set-up if it did decide that it was going to develop any power at all. I thought, myself, that it might possibly lap at between 96 and 98 m.p.h. against the 105 or 106 m.p.h. of my own, whatever the conditions.

Finally I attacked the exhaust system and this proved less easy than I had anticipated. The swapping of exhaust pipes from one machine to another was bad practice. An exhaust pipe of a machine running on Brooklands appeared to undergo quite substantial stresses with the mountings of those days but fractures seldom occurred provided you always kept the same pipe with the same frame. Using different engines didn't seem to matter but if you started swapping exhaust pipes from frame to frame you could soon find fractures and cracks in the exhaust. So I aimed to use the pipe that was on the bike and fit a Brooklands' silencer to that. I knew exactly the length of pipe I wanted for maximum efficiency but, when I went to measure up, I found that on this bike, at any rate, there were lugs brazed to each of the rear fork blades, to take pillion footrests and the one on the offside blade fouled or would foul the big Brooklands' can. This was a nuisance because the length of the pipe as it stood was almost exactly right. It mustn't be shortened for efficiency so it had to be lengthened which wouldn't make it any less efficient 'extractor action wise' but would mean that the big silencer would be rather farther back than usual and this wouldn't improve the handling of the machine round the Byfleet because the rear end of the machine would be sliding out there and this big weight so far rearwards would increase the tendency to do so. And I had no welding set—so I decided to 'kip down' after first hiding the car because I knew that anyone seeing it would immediately start banging on the door of the shed to see if I had died during the night!

I slept from about four until eight, nipped down to Weybridge and got a shave, breakfasted in the café and then took the exhaust to Robin Jackson's works in the paddock to get eight inches welded on to the end of the pipe, having first taken the wheels to Dunlops. Dunlop Mac's comments on the wheels—'A rough old lot there, Charlie. You've got new tyres and tubes', made me know I'd done the right thing in that direction.

Having fitted the wheels and the silencer, I found I had an hour for practice. I was ahead of schedule. I put in a very big jet, for safety, galloped the old warrior across the paddock and it burst into life, sounding more than healthy except for chronic piston slap and rather a lot of oil smoke. I warmed it up and it got a bit quieter and then I took it out for a lap and found it had lapped in 1 minute 45·2 seconds—96·52 m.p.h. I was delighted and wondered if I could make it go faster in the time available. It handled and steered perfectly, even round the Byfleet, but there was noticeable engine vibration at the top end.

For that first timed lap I had managed to enlist that valuable asset, a knowledgeable spectator, as a timekeeper and, as there were still some forty minutes left for practice, I asked him if he would stick with me in this capacity. There wasn't much that could be done but I wanted to try the effect of the 'valve timing trick', although my helpful assistant mustn't know what I was doing.

So, having explained to him that a lot of things had to be tried in a very short time, mainly ignition and carburation settings, I asked him to go up to the control tower and stay there with the stop-watch and time me for a lap from the same spot on the track, every time I went out. If he wasn't back at the shed when I came in after doing a timed lap, I would assume that it had been an improvement over the previous one and would keep on experimenting from lap to lap until he was waiting for me at the shed or until time ran out.

I had noted in my work book the ignition, valve timing and tappet clearances that I had set the engine up with but there wasn't time now to put a degree disc on the engine between each test—we should just have to keep experimenting and take the readings later on. I did three more laps before practice ended and, having checked what had been taking place, the book then read as follows.

Inlet: 52/55 (12).

Exhaust: 74/38 (20). Lap: 1.45·1. 96·52 m.p.h. (which meant, of course, that with a tappet clearance of twelve-thousandths of an inch, the inlet valve was opening fifty-two degrees before the top of its stroke and closing fifty-five degrees after bottom dead centre. With twenty thou clearance, the exhaust was opening seventy-four degrees before bottom dead centre and closing thirty-eight after top. From then on the book read:

1 later on vernier giving Inlet 46/59.

Exhaust 68/42. Lap 1.42·2. 97·27 m.p.h.

1 later on vernier giving Inlet 40/63.

Exhaust 62/47. Lap 1.40·3. 99·01 m.p.h.

1 later on vernier giving Inlet 34/70.

Exhaust 58/54. Lap 1.40·2. 99·21 m.p.h.

In view of the fact that each change of settings involved removal of the fuel tank and cambox cover, this was all that could be done in the time but it didn't really matter because the improvement on the last run was so small that it showed that going any farther down that particular road would make no further gain and might even result in the lap speed being slower. So that was it. The old warrior still felt quite happy but the engine vibration was bad, manifesting itself through the handlebars rather like one of those electric-shock machines that one used to see in funfairs and on piers. It didn't matter in a race of this length but it would have skinned one's hands in anything longer than fifty miles and it couldn't be doing much good to things like exhaust pipes, carburettor flanges and engine mountings.

By now, some of my racing mates had arrived and I had to put up with a lot of rudery about my new mount. Someone took it for a personal test down the aerodrome road and returned with a report that it was more like a threshing machine than a racing bike so, from then on, it became known as the 'thresher'.

The programme was out and the 350 cc. Norton handicap looked quite promising. It looked as though a lap speed of around 97 m.p.h. might see it well-placed and I knew it could do this. My spectator friend was now firmly installed as a permanent member of the staff, for that day at any rate, and I told him that if he was a betting man he could do worse than risk a few shillings on the smaller bike for the Wakefield race. He went off, gleefully, in search of a bookmaker, returning later to say that he had put a pound on at 'fives'. An old friend of mine, 'Tich' Cogan Verney, who also lived at Dorking, had a spot of bother with his Norton and I told him that if the 'thresher' was still in one piece after the Fitzgerald Cup race, he could ride it in his race, the Wakefield Cup Mountain Circuit race but, secretly, I rather doubted whether it would manage to survive the whole day. But I knew the prospect of it would raise Tich's morale on what would otherwise have been rather a frustrating and dreary day.

There was one preliminary race and then the time came for us to take the bikes down to the starting-area at the Vickers' end of the finishing-straight. The Wakefield outer-circuit race was first, so I took the 350 and Tich the 'thresher' with the knowledgeable spectator seated on the back, for they had agreed to be my pushers at the start of each race.

In its report of the meeting, *The Motor Cycle* of May 28th said, 'The second race was a five-lap all-comers' handicap for the Viscount Wakefield Cup and caused "Ebby" and Mr Secretary Ferguson to commune in regard to the future. C. K. Mortimer and his 350 cc. Norton went much too fast! So did the second man, L. J. Archer (348 Velocette Sc). Mortimer won by a mile or thereabouts at a speed of 95·59 m.p.h. Archer was second.'

But despite the average, which was respectable for a 350 cc. at that

99

time, three of the four flying laps were over 99 m.p.h. average—no Gold Star this time!

The report went on, 'Only seven came to the line for the next event, another five-lap all-comers' handicap for the Fitzgerald Cup. Again there was backchat between "Ebby" and Ferguson—this time it was to the effect that there would be no more of these five-lap events as the comparatively long distance did not appeal. With so small an entry it looked as though the race would be tame in the extreme. On the contrary it provided a real good scrap. Mortimer on a 490 cc. Norton this time, and J. H. Greenwood (499 Rudge) cleaved their way to the front. At the end of lap 4, Mortimer was a mere hundred yards ahead of Greenwood. And Greenwood won by less than eighty yards at 100·01 m.p.h., having put in a lap at 104·63 m.p.h. Mortimer, too, had been moving, one of his laps being at 100·61 m.p.h. Third was R. C. Hogarth (346 A.J.S.). Whether these three-lap events have a greater appeal than those over five laps was amply proved by the next event, a three-lap all-comers' handicap for the Prof. A. M. Low Cup. There were no fewer than twenty-four starters with three of them—Wicksteed, Mortimer and Archer—all rehandicapped on account of their speeds in earlier events.'

This was good, but there was more to come and the *Dorking Advertiser* waxed lyrical. After reporting my two races, it went on to say, 'T. Cogan Verney, also on a Norton, won the other Viscount Wakefield Cup in a Mountain race which he rode at an average speed of 67·18 m.p.h. He also came second in another mountain race. To bring both the Wakefield cups to Dorking was a fine achievement.'

That was a great day's racing and one of the most rewarding I ever had. The thought of that great old bike—twenty-five quids' worth—standing dirt-encrusted and forlorn one day and winning one first and two seconds at Brooklands less than twenty-four hours later endeared us to it no end, so that we just had to keep it—and keep it we did, for a long long time.

It was a long time, too, before the memory of that day was erased from 'Ebby's' memory. 'Ebby', of course, was never influenced by anyone. He was very influential himself and, to those who only knew him slightly, he could be a rather formidable and overbearing figure. He regarded our little band of 'regulars' as naughty schoolboys but at the same time he also had real regard for us. His manner, where we were concerned, was that of a rather distant schoolmaster. On his day, he could be jocular, even friendly, but if at one meeting we were able to outwit him too obviously he would be quite austere and almost unfriendly for several meetings afterwards. And he was an autocrat. I remember, once, when passing the window of his timing-box, he called down to me, 'What are you doing, Mortimer?'

With that feeling of guilt that overwhelms the young when brusquely questioned by someone in authority, I replied, 'Nothing.'

'Well, come up here and help us. We're two timekeepers short.'

In fact it was a compliment, although he didn't mean it to be, because no one unqualified was ever allowed to handle chronometers in the timing-box unless they were known and, after that, I had frequent invitations and always enjoyed it. It could be quite humorous because I was by far the youngest and all the rest of the official time-keepers at motor-bike meetings were well in their sixties and one or two were over seventy. Usually there were six of them and the field was divided among them so that, if there were twenty-four starters in a race, each timekeeper was responsible for four riders. I well recall one race in which there was a 'photo'-type finish, or should have been, for the first eight riders thundered over the finishing-line in one solid mass.

Both Judges were also in the box and, from the silence that followed, I knew at once that no one had the remotest idea of who had won and that they possibly didn't even know the finishing order. Had I, a rider and a young one at that, not been in the box, there would have been no problem. They could have discussed it freely and decided the result on a majority vote but they couldn't bring themselves to having to admit such a course of action in front of me for they firmly believed that we riders considered them infallible. The silence continued and I was about to request permission to be excused so as to go to spend a penny when, in terms so definite that I had never before heard their like, 'Ebby's' voice rang out: 'Lamacraft, Pope, Archer. Winner's speed ninety-six point five six.' I can't remember now whether these were the right names—it isn't really important. It was the air of absolute certainty that was so funny.

But to be fair, the timekeepers at Brooklands did a very, very good job indeed and the handicapping was as good as it possibly could be, bearing in mind all the forces that worked against it. Being older than we were, the timekeepers were always a source of amusement and humour, and stories, some of them scandalously untrue, were recounted concerning what probably went on in the timekeepers' box. One, I can recall now, concerned the timekeepers in the Double Twelve-Hour Race for cars. This was a very long race—it was run over two days of twelve hour's racing each day and every available timekeeper was brought to the line including one or two who were very old men indeed. One of them, so the story went, arrived each morning wearing a bowler hat which he hung on a peg in the timing-box. During the practice days which preceded the race it was noticed that he never left the timing-box without wearing the bowler. During the first morning of the race, the hat was replaced by someone who shall be nameless, with an exactly identical hat, made by the same hatters, but two sizes smaller so that, when its unfortunate wearer tried to don it, the hat stood on top of his head like a pimple. He left for his lunch break carrying the hat, having never been parted from it when in the open air, and returned still carrying it, and hung it on its peg. During the afternoon's racing it was replaced with another bowler, again identical but, this time, four sizes bigger so that it took in not only his head but his ears and nose. At this stage his timekeeping must have become rather erratic but he left Brooklands that evening, still carrying the hat, but was not on parade next morning when the other timekeepers rostered. His wife answered the phone call that was put through to his house at Esher with the words, 'Oh, I'm so glad you've rung. I'm afraid my husband won't be able to come to Brooklands today. We're waiting for the doctor at this moment. My husband's extremely worried about his head!'

The majority of the Brooklands' staff were fairly elderly. There was a delightful old gentleman called Walker whose two main duties were the maintenance of the lavatories—and first-aid. Walker was absolutely fearless and supremely confident in all matters concerning first-aid—he would tackle any injury, however serious, with an air of confidence that calmed everyone. His resources as regards equipment seemed very limited, even to us, but he made up for this by the lavish use of iodine which he seemed to be able to acquire in ten-gallon drums. Walker used iodine in the treatment of the most unusual injuries—but everyone survived and it was generally agreed that in the matter of first-aid Walker knew what he was doing!

The safety arrangements, from the point of view of marshalling, would hardly have met the approval of the A.C.U. or R.A.C. today. At Brands Hatch, today, for instance, in practice or in a race, there are marshalls placed at intervals round the circuit so closely that each one can see his neighbours. At Brooklands, on weekday practices which went on continually, there was only Jack Cann on the exit gate from the paddock—no one posted at any point round the track although there were observers on race days. But the strange thing was that it all worked very well. There *were* accidents, but they were always noticed quickly, either by someone who was using the track for practice or someone on the aerodrome, or working in a shed in the paddock or by Jack himself. I really don't think there was ever an accident in practice that wasn't spotted immediately or a case where helpers weren't on the spot within a very few minutes or seconds, and I feel sure that there was never an accident in which the victim's injuries were in any way made worse by lack of prompt attention.

Some quite extraordinary vehicles, never seen at race meetings, used to put in appearances at Brooklands for testing and experimental purposes. One of these was a tiny cyclecar, the brainchild of Myles Rothwell, I believe, and its purpose was record breaking in the ultra-small-capacity engine class. It was quite an attractive looking little car, well streamlined, with full enclosure for the driver, and the power unit was a motor-cycle engine. Its regular driver was a Mr Stafford who had taken over the management of Myles Rothwell's interests when Francis relinquished them and it was a constant source of amazement to us that Stafford could even get in the car for he was a huge man and one would have thought it impossible. We used to worry a bit about this and, sure enough, one day when we were enjoying our tea up in the café, there was the sound of a most tremendous accident and there lay the lovely little single seater strewn in small pieces all over the track. There was a rush for transport and, when we arrived at the scene, the driver, whom we had assumed to be Stafford, turned out to be someone we had never seen before. He was badly hurt and still in the car and this was its last public appearance.

But the strangest vehicles of all were the products of an inventor whose name escapes me, although anyone who saw them could never forget them. They consisted of one huge wheel roughly the size of the rear wheel of an outsize traction engine. Its bearing surface on the road was not flat, like a traction engine wheel, but very slightly curved in the shape of a car tyre so that, if weight was transferred to the right-hand side, it rolled in a right-handed direction and to the left if weight was transferred to the left. Its diameter was in the region of eight feet and its width, I should say, roughly four feet. The power unit was behind the driver's seat and integral with it and the whole unit started its journey inside the wheel and at the bottom. On power being applied, the engine and seat unit, which was attached to the wheel by inverse-toothed rails, would move slowly forwards and upwards on the inside of the wheel, its weight as it rose causing the wheel to turn forwards. Once under way, the engine, driver and seat could be moved sideways in either direction in order to steer the contraption. The driver, it seemed, had virtually no forward visibility and not very much protection from the mud and water that used to stream down from the top of the wheel. Maximum speed was in the region of 5 or 6 m.p.h. which was, perhaps, enough in view of the fact that shutting off the power or braking tended to take the operator complete with power unit backwards and upwards, sometimes as much as forty-five degrees. We never saw him loop the loop but always expected to. This vehicle interested and amazed us, besides causing us a lot of amusement. It interested us, not only because it was so ingenious but because several versions appeared with fresh modifications which only an intelligent creator could have thought up. On the other hand it amazed us that such a man could conceivably have thought such a vehicle could have a commercial future—because all this was happening in the nineteen-thirties.

Inspired by this, Jock Forbes bought himself a monowheel cycle, the sort of thing that trick cyclists ride in circuses. We none of us had any doubt that Jock would be monowheeling round the paddock before long because his sense of balance had always been quite exceptional. Among other parlour tricks, Jock could ride a Manx Norton either standing on the saddle with arms outstretched or sitting on the fuel tank facing rearwards. But the monowheel defeated him and became a source of worry to all because every time he parted company with it, Jock remained lying where he'd fallen, while the monowheel continued faster, it seemed, than when he'd been aboard it. It would appear riderless, at great speed, from all points of the compass and sometimes round blind corners so that, in the end, we persuaded its gallant conductor to abandon his ambition in the interests of our safety as well as his.

There were, too, many amusing sprint cars, mostly motor-cycle engined, which gave their owner-constructors endless pleasure and despair in equal amounts. Robert Waddy's Fuzzi, a tiny car powered by two 500 cc. J.A.P. dirt-track engines; the Glegg brothers' J.A.P.-engined 'Dorcas', a 1000 cc., with front-wheel drive and twin tyres on the front; and Charlie Martin's 'one and a half litre' special with four 350 cc. racing J.A.P. engines in line, were among them. Fuzzi could be a great performer on her day, but every successful minute seemed to be matched by an equal number of hours of work. Dreadful things, usually connected with transmission, seemed to happen to 'Dorcas' on nearly every occasion and Charlie's 'fifteen hundred' was dangerous even to start because, if one of the four racing J.A.P.'s backfired, the drive chain to the countershaft would break and depart among the spectators, leaving that one engine to scream its heart out while the other three used to run so badly out of balance that the car was almost shaken to pieces. In the end it was conceded that John Bolster stood alone in being able to make this type of car competitive and I recall, once, asking John what were his first impressions when, having built his twin-engined 'Bloody Mary', he drove her on her maiden run. Without a moment's hesitation and looking straight at me, he replied, 'Well, of course, I knew at once that I was to take my place amongst the world's great automobile designers.'

My own E.F. J.A.P. with its belt drive and vertical overhead valves had been almost the last 'comic' bike to appear at the track but there was one other, a duplex-steering O.E.C. which appeared by courtesy of Granville Grenfell, who had removed its J.A.P. engine and sub-stituted an Austin Seven engine. Ridden by Freddy Clarke, it was an enormously long bike, seemed never to go very fast but gave all who saw it a lot of pleasure.

One thing stood out when watching products like this performing and it was the tremendous cost in man hours and money that was put into them in relation to the results achieved. Each of the cars must have cost as much as an E.R.A. but driving an E.R.A. and winning races with it wouldn't have given the special owner the same sort of satis-faction. But, from the bike aspect, it was obviously better to stick to Nortons if you wanted to win races!

My 500 gave me another good day at the B.M.C.R.C. June meeting, finishing third in the five-lap Mountain Handicap and winning the ten-lapper. This one was a really open race and *Motor Cycling* agreed, saying, 'Finally, a ten-lap Mountain Handicap was hotly contested from all marks. Pope, who had been put back to scratch with Ron Harris, got away from the latter at the start and the pair of them got really cracking, tail to tail. Lap after lap they tore round, Pope perhaps fractionally increasing his lead over Harris and the two of them just creeping up on Mortimer who had a short start of them. Out in front, Whitworth was catching the limit men on the seventh lap and Pope was now fifty yards in front of Harris, Mortimer just in front of them. It looked Pope's race when, at the end of Lap 8, much blue smoke and a lack of urge showed that the 515 cc. Norton had had enough at last. Pope had some consolation in having established, subject to official confirmation, a five-lap record for Class 'D' (750 cc.) of 70½ m.p.h. Harris just failed to catch Mortimer and Whitworth, not far away as usual, was an excellent third.'

Our 500 Nortons usually became overbored, partly by accident and partly by intent. Boring out to give a capacity of over 500 cc. was a simple operation and put one up into the 750 cc. class. There wasn't much competition in that class and its records usually stood at about the same or even lower speeds than did the 500 records. So it wasn't something you set out to do unless you were unlucky enough to have a 500 cc. engine seize so badly that the cylinder barrel and piston were damaged and would not bore out again and stay within the 500 cc. class. Then, rather than scrap the barrel, one would bore it out for use in sprints or records in the class above, although the difference in speed wasn't great.

The Brooklands 100-Mile Grand Prix races followed in July. My 350 Norton, which had been going well throughout the season, decided that it didn't like petrol races after a number of alcohol ones and seized fairly early on in the Junior race. On the line for the start of the Senior race, Ben Bickell said to me, 'Mind you don't do what you did last year in this race. I was just behind when you threw it away. Don't want to see that again.'

As soon as we were away, you could see that it was going to be a very competitive race and, for me, it had to be a question of sticking around and waiting for things to happen. Harold Daniell on his big Norton was soon a speck in the distance, although I could see the others nearly all the time and lay eighth in the early stages. Then I managed to pick up a few places and was following Ben when, suddenly, he dropped it at the very same chicane where I had done it the previous year, but whereas I had come off at the exit, he parted company at the approach, through braking too hard and too late. For a moment it was really nasty because Ben was bowling along the concrete at about 70 m.p.h. right in front of, and almost being touched by, my front wheel. But, by the time we got there, the speed had dropped and there was room to go between Ben and his machine. I did say something to him about it afterwards, though!

When the race was about three-quarters run, I was lapped by Harold who was still hammering away as though he hadn't a minute to live. I couldn't understand the urgency of it in view of the big lead he'd got, but apparently his strategy was to ease off as soon as he'd lapped the second man. So, in the end, the race result was:

1st	H. L. Daniell	(Norton).	1 hr 14 mins 43 secs. 80·01 m.p.h.
2nd	J. W. Forbes	(Norton).	1 hr 16 mins 51 secs. 77·71 m.p.h.
3rd	R. H. Newman	(Norton).	1 hr 17 mins 53 secs. 76·59 m.p.h.
4th	C. K. Mortimer	(Norton).	1 hr 18 mins 36 secs. 75·88 m.p.h.
5th	J. W. Beevers	(Norton).	1 hr 18 mins 56 secs. 75·58 m.p.h.
6th	D. C. Minett	(Rudge).	1 hr 20 mins 23 secs. 74·15 m.p.h.

One of the Sunday papers said, 'There was a great fight in the early stages of the Senior (500 cc.) contest. C. B. Bickell crashed into a barrel marking one of the corners. C. K. Mortimer, who was just behind, escaped a collision only by making a hurried swerve which almost carried him off the track.'

It would have been nice to be able to claim that this incident with Ben cost me a place. But it didn't. The plain fact was that there were now too many Nortons around, all of them reliable, and too many good riders on board them. Harold, of course, always stood out and if he was about, no one else really counted. Jock was lighter and a better rider than I but I was disappointed to find Newman so far ahead and Bill Beevers close behind. It amounted to the fact that I should either have to improve as a rider or have faster Nortons. Both difficult alternatives.

I had relied too much on retirements. There'd been retirements in this race—quite a lot. But they'd been behind me instead of in front and, among them, there'd been practically no Nortons.

In September each year, we all used to have a day out, competing at the Sunbeam M.C.C. Speed Trials at Gatwick. There was no money or prestige attached to it. It was just a delightful day spent hammering away at a standing-start quarter mile and although it didn't matter if you won or lost, we all used to take it just as seriously as the big races held at Brooklands. On this occasion, I took 350 cc.

and 500 cc. alcohol-engined Nortons and won the 350 cc. class from Eric Oliver, our respective times being 14·16 and 14·61 seconds. The whole thing was very competitive for most of the runners were sprint specialists, whereas this was the only sprint, apart from Brighton, that the Brooklands people did. There were the usual capacity classes but each was subdivided into Experts and Experts Barred. To become an Expert in the 350 cc. class you had to have bettered 15 seconds and, in the 500 cc. class, 13 seconds. I had been upgraded as a 350 cc. Expert at a previous meeting but was still eligible for the Experts Barred in the 500 cc.

This particular day was great fun. Noel won the 500 cc. Experts' class with 13·19 seconds and Francis was second, both on Nortons. I managed to scrape home first in the 500 cc. Experts Barred with 13·29 seconds, the second man L. E. Good on a Rudge being close behind with 13·35 seconds.

In the unlimited Experts Barred, Francis came first with 13·21 seconds and Eric on his big sprint Brough Superior won the Experts and made fastest time of day, recording 11·80 seconds, to my second place time of 13·10 seconds.

The day always ended with an invitation event for the six fastest riders. Eric, sportingly, didn't compete in this, provided he'd achieved what he set out to achieve, Fastest Time of Day, and provided there seemed little chance of his time being improved on. But Noel switched from his 500 Norton to his big supercharged Brough so it seemed likely that the 'Six Fastest' would be his. Everyone was fiddling around with alternative jet and sprocket sizes and it was hard to think of any way of improving one's previous time. I tried to think of another approach and, at last, hit on one which might be disastrous or might conceivably work.

The course was a straight quarter mile on tarmac with quite considerable road camber at the start. This meant that a competitive 500 or 1000 was a great handful for the first hundred yards and the risk was always that, in spinning and making its long black streak on the road, the rear wheel of a bike might possibly slide down the camber and into the gutter, although this could always be prevented if one eased the power off a bit to bring the rear wheel back to the crown of the road. But this wasted a lot of time and ruled out a good run.

The final gearchange, from third to top, was made about a hundred yards before the finish-line and I couldn't help thinking that if one geared the bike up, rather than down which most people were doing, one might score in two ways. Because, firstly, it would mean that, in pulling a higher gear, the machine would spin its rear wheel much less and thus be more stable although, admittedly, slower away. And, secondly, I felt that one would gain in only making two gear changes instead of three. So I geared the plot up one whole tooth.

I then sat looking at it, trying to imagine getting it up the course and this led me to think of exhaust arrangements in relation to revs. Normally one used an ordinary open exhaust on a sprint bike and a megaphone exhaust for road races because the extractor effect of a megaphone was greatest when the revs were high.

The set-up I had contrived would have low revs at the start, because of the high gear it was to pull. But over the finish-line it would still be in third, not top gear, and then it really would be revving. Open pipe or megaphone, that was the question.

I decided to stick to the open pipe and took the bike up to the start-line. But there was some delay, for someone had dropped oil there and officials were trying to clear it. So, thinking that we should have wheelspin anyway, I fitted the megaphone.

The result was quite comic because Noel's Brough was uncon-controllable on the slippery surface and recorded only 13·27 seconds, while I won with 13·02 seconds, the best I had ever done even on a dry road. It put me within a fiftieth of a second of becoming an expert, too, and who could get closer than that!

Those little day outings to Gatwick were the greatest fun and you really did have to try hard if you hoped to compete with the sprinters. And you had to be consistent, too! On this occasion my five runs were 13·59, 13·54, 13·29, 13·10 and 13·02 on the bigger bike.

Once again, the Hutchinson 100 marked the close of the Brooklands season and, this time, there was a rather comic innovation. Money was very short around that time and a number of would-be com-petitors just hadn't the money to invest in big-capacity long-distance fuel tanks. So the Club ruled that, when filling in entry forms, entrants must state whether or not they were proposing to use standard tanks and stop for fuel, or use big ones and go through non-stop. Com-petitors could use big tanks but, if they chose to do so, they would be penalised one minute so as to even things up for those who would have to stop.

This caused quite a flurry and everyone was rushing around with tanks of all sizes, measures ranging from half pint to half gallon, slide rules and other impedimenta and when all the commotion subsided no one seemed to have reached any firm conclusion at all, which seemed to indicate that the Club had thought it out very fairly to everyone.

I was keen to do well in this race. I had never achieved anything in the 'Hutch', which had always seemed to be an unlucky race for me. So I thought carefully about it. There were two initial decisions to make. Which bike, the big or the small? Stop for fuel and accept the credit of a minute, or go right through and relinquish it? With hindsight I reckon I made one wrong decision and one right one. I chose the 350, which was wrong, and chose to make a stop, which was right. Later still, I made another wrong decision and that, I felt sure, cost me four places.

It was right to make a stop. If you knew how to make a refuelling stop it did appear that you could gain a very few seconds. But, again with hindsight, I think one would have gained more on the 500 with its far better acceleration from the pits up onto the home banking.

There was no excuse for my other mistake. I was so keen to 'ring the bell' in the Hutch that I handed the machine, complete, to J. S. (Willy) Worters, for him to prepare for the race. Willy was an ex-racer of the generation just before mine and knew everything there was to know about Brooklands and how to prepare racing bikes for it. When I got the machine back from him there very few external differences except for the handlebars. Most of the experts used dropped handlebars for the outer circuit so as to bring the rider's shoulders as low as possible and thus reduce frontal area. Others used the same technique but with narrower bars pointing almost downwards and this was good because it brought the rider's arms closer in towards the fuel tank and made even less frontal area. But there had to be a compromise here because if the bars were too narrow, you hadn't enough purchase and the machine was a brute to control. These bars of Willy's seemed to me only slightly wider than the tank itself! So I took them off and fitted a pair of road-racing bars that I'd used previously both for Mountain races and on the outer circuit. When Willy saw this, he nearly had a fit! He was extremely professional, a bit of a martinet and had no great opinion of our generation either as professionals or as riders.

'What have you done that for?' he growled.

'Yours are too narrow. You can't hold the bloody thing.'

'Why not? What's wrong with it?'

'Nothing's wrong with it, Willy. But it's not a sprint. It's a hundred miles.'

He grunted. 'And how much d'you think those bars'll cost you in a hundred miles?'

'Half a second a lap. No more.'

'Thirty-seven laps. Eighteen or nineteen seconds. Races have been lost by fifths. And it'll cost you more than that.'

'Well, I'm sorry. But I want to be comfortable.'

Willy gazed at me disapprovingly. 'And I thought you were dedicated. I'll tell you one thing. If one of my riders had given me the reasoning you have, it would have been his swan song.' And away he walked.

I didn't feel happy at all. But I stuck to my guns and the race result was:

	Start	Time	Speed
1st S. H. Goddard (246 O.K. Supreme J.A.P.)	13 m. 34 s.	1 h. 15 m. 51 s.	85·87 m.p.h.
2nd R. Harris (490 Norton)	2 m. 28 s.	1 h. 16 m. 50 s.	98·04 m.p.h.
3rd D. C. Minett (499 Rudge)	2 m. 28 s.	1 h. 16 m. 58 s.	97·85 m.p.h.
4th J. B. Moss (348 Norton)	5 m. 33 s.	1 h. 17 m. 3 s.	93·09 m.p.h.
5th C. D. Allen (490 Norton)	0 m. 37 s.	1 h. 17 m. 15 s.	100·31 m.p.h.
6th C. K. Mortimer (348 Norton)	4 m. 19 s.	1 h. 17 m. 20 s.	94·50 m.p.h.
7th N. B. Pope (348 Norton)	3 m. 19 s.	1 h. 18 m. 17 s.	94·59 m.p.h.
8th H. Laird (1096 Morgan)	2 m. 42 s.	1 h. 22 m. 47 s.	
9th M. A. Clement Smith (246 New Imperial)	16 m. 39 s.	1 h. 23 m. 58 s.	
10th R. Board (246 Excelsior)	13 m. 48 s.	1 h. 27 m. 4 s.	

Ten minutes after the race had finished I came face to face with Willy. He handed me a slip of paper with these figures on it. 'Thirty seconds between the second and sixth men, Charles. Cost you second place.' I didn't reply. There was nothing to be said.

There was one other race I enjoyed that year, but in retrospect, because it wasn't an enjoyable race to ride. The B.M.C.R.C. staged a two-lap outer-circuit thing for Gold Star Holders—riders who had previously covered a 100 m.p.h. lap. The field was small—seven in all—

but it became more select the nearer one went to the scratch mark. Eric, on his Brough Superior, had that honour, and Noel, on his blown version, received just two seconds from him. Tom Atkins on the supercharged Douglas was on the six-second mark, Ben Bickell on his copper-plated Bickell J.A.P. had eighteen seconds and the three limit men, including myself, twenty seconds.

Two big twins, and five 500's. Although only over two laps, it was going to be a quick race whoever won it and it did seem strange to be on the limit mark with a machine that was going to lap at not less than 105 m.p.h. The flag fell and we were away with Jock West on the works' Triumph in the lead, but only by a few yards. Jock increased his lead as we went higher and higher on to the home banking but, on the run down to the Railway straight, my faithful old 500 slowly overhauled him and passed just as we began 'grass cutting' round the Byfleet. Now there was no one ahead and nothing to worry about till we reached the same spot on the next lap, because not even Eric and Noel could make up that amount of ground before then. And no one did come by, for we won at 99·51 m.p.h. with Eric second and Ben third. The old Norton had done a standing lap at 93 m.p.h. and a flying one of 106 m.p.h. But Eric was the moral winner for, having done a standing lap at 102·69 m.p.h., he then got momentarily held up getting past Noel so that, although his flying lap was 117·46 m.p.h., he just failed to win. But, my word, he was close and as he came by almost as we crossed the line, my poor old 500 seemed to be nearly stationary.

The last full season I did with bikes at Brooklands was 1936. I felt that the bikes I had deserved a better rider and it was then that Jock Forbes and I teamed up together. We did a full season in 1937, which included Brooklands, Donnington, Crystal Palace, the North West 200 and the Ulster in Ireland and the Junior and Senior T.T. in the Isle of Man. Jock rode and I maintained the machinery and we hardly stopped for breath! We found that, although we both had our odd quirks, we got on well together and we won far more races than we could possibly have done had we competed against each other. We had our fair share of troubles and the first one came up on our very first 'away' trip, the North West 200.

I'd never been to Ireland before but Jock had and he knew nearly every member of the Committee organising the race. They gave us a night out on the town and when the time came for practice, next morning, I had such an appalling hangover that I gave him the wrong machine to take out, the 500 instead of the 350. Had that been all, it wouldn't have mattered too much. We should have put up a cracking 350 practice time and everyone would have been greatly impressed. What did matter was that if the main oil feed from the tank to the pump was left connected overnight on that particular engine, oil used to seep through the pump and into the crankcase and, to prevent this, we used to disconnect the feed pipe and plug it, reconnecting it again when we were next going to take the bike out. Jock discovered it halfway through the first practice lap, when the whole unit seized with a bang and I found out when, believing I was about to reconnect the feed pipe on a 500, I found it was connected already and, looking further, discovered that it was a 350 I was about to go to work on.

That was a dreadful start but it was about the worst thing that happened during our two years' partnership. Earlier on, I said that Jock was a better rider than I, and that was true. But I felt he was almost too light to be able to get the best out of the 500 and was rather keen to see what he could do with a 250. He wasn't very keen on this idea—riders never like transferring to a lighter class. They appear to feel that there is some loss of prestige, but it's all right to go up a class! So I didn't press it.

For years I had resisted the annual pilgrimage to the Isle of Man for the T.T. in June, but now I had to go. I think, really, that I hadn't liked the idea of going there without riding but now that I had a job to do in maintaining the bikes I didn't mind the prospect of it at all. In fact, as time went on, I really came to prefer the organisation and management side of bike racing, which was just as well. Once in the Island, I fell in love with it instantly. In those days we were so much more fortunate than are the young riders of today, because our race bikes were, by comparison, so simple and so reliable that we had a lot of time to enjoy ourselves and to really see the Island. Two things have made this less easy for today's competitors—money and the sophistication of the modern racing bike. Money did enter into it when we raced in the Island in 1937 and 1938 but to nothing like the extent that it does now. Now, when one listens to a group of riders talking together, you only have to be with them for two minutes before there is a reference to money. I mean, of course, a reference in relation to racing. Start money, appearance money, prize money, bonus money. It does seem rather a pity because while money is very important indeed, it is good to have as much fun as you can when you are young. On the other hand, while we had very little money in the nineteen-thirties, what we did have went a long way and really bought something. New Manx Nortons were to be had for between £90 and £100 whereas, today, it isn't at all unusual for a young rider to have to fork out a four-figure sum for a good 250, even.

Sophisticated machinery, water cooling and disc-valve two-strokes add up, also, to hours of complex maintenance involving a high degree of mechanical knowledge and this is certainly essential if one is going to do well in racing today. So, inevitably, the racing motor-cyclist of 1973 has less time, by far, to enjoy himself and really see the sights of the places where he goes racing. Nothing can be done about it and, in any case, he probably doesn't mind!

To us, though, the Island became almost a holiday trip because, provided the machinery was really properly prepared and one's own organisation was reasonably efficient, there was plenty of time to be spent in enjoying oneself once one got there, barring accidents, and even then they seemed to happen less frequently than now.

Our day in the Island was a long one. We were up at four o'clock each morning and at the start with the race bikes at five. Practice until seven-thirty and then back to breakfast, after which we would work on the machinery until mid-day. From then on, the day was usually our own. We stayed at the same place each year, Jock, Noel Pope, Noel Christmas, Franz Binder the Austrian rider, and myself, and the house was right at the top of Bray Hill and run by a wonderful woman, Mrs McCall, who had an attractive daughter, Nell, and a son, Archie, both of whom used to work in Douglas. We never once were allowed to leave for practice in the morning without tea and toast and every meal was waiting for us when we came in. They were really great to us and I'm afraid we gave them a dreadful time—although they used to insist that they enjoyed it. We had our own cars in the Island but the McCall family had a wonderful Austin heavy twelve tourer, vintage about 1927, and in the afternoons we all used to pile into this and go out to see some remote part of the Island chosen by Archie, who did the driving. Today, I really think that many people who go there see little more than the T.T. course and the main beauty spots such as Greeba Castle and the Laxey Wheel but, in the Island, there is really more variety of scenery condensed into a small area than any-where else I know. T.T. Race week is probably the worst week of the year in which to visit the Isle of Man but I still do, and spend more than half the time in parts where there are no crowds at all. In fact, every year I've been to the Island I make a point of navigating on the map to some part I've never seen before and still haven't seen a lot of it.

The McCall Austin was a tremendously willing and robust car and the family never worried about it being overloaded and it was on one of these occasions that Noel Pope discovered a small round hole in the floor, at the back, through which you could see the prop-shaft revolving. That was the sort of thing Noel rather liked and, when we stopped for tea at the next village, he disappeared into one of the small shops and returned carrying a huge paper bag in which were a number of large balls of string. One knew what was going to happen—the string was going to be threaded through the hole and tied round the propshaft and when we returned to the car, Noel was already seated in the back ready for take off. At first it wasn't too difficult. The string began to wind nicely on to the shaft but, as the diameter of string round the shaft became greater, it had to be fed through more quickly and everyone in the back was working like mad finding the ends of each fresh ball, and joining them together. Archie was pointing out all the beauty spots, quite oblivious to what was happening, and gradually things began to happen. The propshaft began to vibrate but the driver was used to odd noises and vibrations. Then the huge ball of string round the shaft became so vast that it touched the underside of the floorboards, making them jump up and down. He did notice that and a good thing he did because, by that time, the lot was on fire!

The Island was very hard on transport and 1937 was the first and only year that we took our own cars. In 1938 Jock and I invested £5 each in a quite presentable Morris Oxford square-radiatored saloon, the first that followed the bull-nose and this particular car must have had one of the hardest fortnights of its life. We bought it two days before leaving for the island and it had a blown head-gasket which we replaced before rigging up a towbar for the trailer and bikes. The head gasket blew again almost immediately and, assuming that the head was warped, we then fitted two gaskets together. They failed on the way up to Liverpool and, realising that we had trouble on our hands, we bought a big stock of gaskets and this time fitted three. From then on, the only time that the engine was cold was when we had to replace blown gaskets. It would still be warm when we set off for practice each morning soon after four o'clock, because someone would have borrowed it for a night out before hand, from which it probably hadn't returned until about two in the morning.

Although we had enjoyed the T.T. in 1937 and hadn't come back empty handed, Jock had never really been happy with the 500 and, this time, we had agreed to drop the big class and to do the Lightweight and Junior races. So, instead of the big Norton, we had a little 250 cc. overhead-camshaft Excelsior to keep the 350 Norton company. And a super little bike it proved to be although not quite so well-finished and nice to work on as the Norton—but just as reliable. In fact, the Excelsior gave us our best T.T. placing, finishing on the leader-board in sixth place. We were very happy about this although Jock felt that he would have liked to finish just one place higher, ahead of Maurice Cann, because that would have meant that we should have been the first privately entered machine home, behind the works' bikes.

5

Yes, Jock and I had two very enjoyable seasons together and, in many ways, we would have liked to go on. But the war clouds seemed to be gathering fast and I did want to have a go at car racing before I got too old. I had, in fact, already had one drive and this is how it came about.

I had noticed that, among the cars at Robin Jackson's tuning and maintenance establishment was a virtually new M.G. racing 'Q'-type supercharged 750 cc. and I had seen several different people driving it on the outer circuit from time to time. I imagined that it was for sale but then discovered that it was Robin's own property and that he let it out on hire from time to time to customers who wanted to race but who hadn't got cars of their own. So I had a word with him and the upshot of it was that he agreed to hire it to me for an outer-circuit race at the next Bank Holiday meeting at Brooklands. I forget what the hire fee was. I think it was £15 or it might even have been £10 and, having agreed it, it was then planned that we should meet up on the Saturday prior to the meeting which was on a Bank Holiday Monday.

I duly reported on the Saturday to find Robin's emporium under tremendous pressure because a number of cars belonging to valued clients were all giving trouble at the same time and no mechanics were available to look after me and the 'Q'-type. I knew Robin very well and he knew that I was happy to wait and I did this for most of the morning, while watching all the activity. One of the cars in dire trouble was Fotheringham's Bugatti and another which was taking a long time was the huge Bentley Jackson 6½-litre single seater which George Harvey Noble was driving. I was looking at the vast rear tyres of the car, on which George used to lap at well over 130 m.p.h. They looked thoroughly tired to me and I said so. George shrugged his shoulders. 'Well, you know, Charles, they always look like that. There's probably more meat on them than you'd think. But I'm going to let Mac see them.'

On the Monday morning I noticed, on looking at the programme that George was driving the car in two consecutive races—rather unusual for a big car at Brooklands and when I saw it in its paddock bay it still had the same rear tyres as it had had on the Saturday. I got involved in the 'Q'-type later and I didn't see George until after the meeting when, spotting me, he hove into sight wearing a huge grin.

'Charles, you remember mentioning the tyres on the Bentley Jackson?'

'Yes, I do.'

'Well. Bloody funny. You'd have laughed if you'd seen what happened. I drove the car in the first race and, as I was slowing down to come in I took a look at the rear tyres and saw that the breaker-strip was showing on one. That put me in a spot because I was almost sure I wouldn't have time to get the car back to the paddock, through the crowd to Dunlops, change the tyre and get back on the line for the next race. I was just trying to get it through the gate into the paddock when I heard a shout. There was Mac, shouting to me to stay where I was and when he'd got through the gate I saw he'd got a jack and two wheels with him which looked even bigger than ours. Before you could say "knife" the Bentley was jacked up, our wheels were off and the others on. The car seemed even bigger and higher than usual as I drove it back to the line but it was alright in the race. No sooner had I backed it into its bay after the race, than a jack was under it and before I was even out of it our wheels were fitted and the huge ones had vanished through the crowd. When I asked him where he got them he said "They were lent" and when I asked who'd lent them he said "Barnato". I said I must thank Barnato and Mac said, "Don't do that. He doesn't know he lent them." I didn't know I'd borrowed them either. They must have been off the eight-litre Barnato Hassan.'

It was a lovely story and Mac could have been telling the truth. If so, the idea of the big Barnato Hassan sitting, jacked up in its paddock bay, minus its rear wheels, unnoticed by its crew, conjures up a picture worth remembering.

By lunch time, on the occasion of my first car drive, Robin's chaps were still hard at it and it was suggested that I take the car out for a few laps and look after myself for the afternoon. I did this and took the car round quite slowly for a few laps and then came back to ask just what I was allowed to do. Could I take it as fast as it would go or as fast as I wanted to? I just didn't know what it was going to be like, after a bike. The answer was that they left it to me—I could do what I liked. So I took it out with the idea of having a strong go, after finding a friend who'd got a stop-watch. But as soon as the revs got high, there was a tremendous bang from the supercharger blow-off valve and I came in again, bought four new plugs from Robin's storekeeper and tried again. This time it was better and lapped at 105 m.p.h. But it was so easy after a bike that I could hardly credit it and, in any case it still didn't want to rev and still occasionally kept blowing off.

I felt I'd gone far enough on my own so I took the car back and when I saw that they were still working like demons I left them to it after arranging to have a mechanic meet me at the track early on the Monday morning, with the car, so that we could get it right.

At eight o'clock, on race day, I was back and was relieved to see the car and mechanic down at the fork. I was happy as soon as I saw the chap because although I never did know his name I had seen him at work on other cars and knew that he was among Robin's best. I told him exactly what I'd done and, after he had had a check and made one or two small adjustments I set off again. This time it lapped at 108 m.p.h. but it was still unwilling to rev and far from exciting to drive. But nothing we could do in the time would make it go faster—it was 108 m.p.h. every lap no matter how hard you kept the pedal down.

In the race it lapped at 109 m.p.h. due, I felt sure, to a convenient tow from G. L. Baker's huge Graham Paige. I was glad to have had a go but not very thrilled by it.

I knew, at least, now, what a car was like on Brooklands and realised I should want a faster one than the 'Q'-type. So I started looking around. In the meantime Robin, who was probably relieved to get his car back in one piece, asked me if I'd like to have a drive of his 1½-litre supercharged Alta single seater and this I found much more exciting and pleasant, although not as reliable, it was comparable in performance to the E.R.A. and Maseratis.

My first competitive drive in the Alta was at the Brighton Speed Trials, in 1938, a standing kilometre sprint along the seafront. The Alta was quite a useful car for this sort of thing because its brakes, which weren't as good as the E.R.A., didn't have to be used and, being a sprint, it only had to be reliable for rather less than half a minute's running.

On this occasion, the car behaved quite well, finishing second in the

$1\frac{1}{2}$-litre racing car class to Howe's E.R.A., just ahead of Hugh Hunter's similar Alta. A month later we took it to the Lewes' speed trials where it again won the $1\frac{1}{2}$-litre racing class with 20.36 seconds to Peter Monkhouse's 20.72 seconds on the E.R.A. But, running in the two-litre racing car class, the tables were turned and the E.R.A. beat us with 19.41 seconds to our 20.75 seconds.

I was looking around hard, now, for a car of my own but the trouble was that I wanted a fast, reliable and exciting car for not much money. Both Jock and I felt that we had had enough of bike racing and I had, in fact, sold all the bikes in the Island, immediately after the T.T., together with the trailer so we made our way slowly back from Liverpool in the gallant old Morris, now fitted with six gaskets, all of which we had to replace on the way down!

It was Charlie Brackenbury who found what I wanted. Charles had always been interested in the bike side and usually came to the small meetings as well as the major ones and he and I spent quite a lot of time together socially. We had a common bond in our love of Brooklands and I of course, admired his skilful driving of big cars like the Napier Railton and the twelve-cylinder Sunbeam, when he had part-nered Cobb in long races and on record attempts. Had it not been for him I probably wouldn't have known that Andrew Leitch was selling his Type 35 G.P. Bugatti, a single-cam full Grand Prix Straight-eight. I knew the car very well. It had a very good history and had had only four owners, Charlie Martin, the Hon. Jock Leith and Andrew being the last three.

So I got in touch with Andrew and we had a bit of a bargaining session and I bought the Bugatti for £125! Not a thing had to be done to it and I suppose that, today, it would be worth, possibly, £8,000. I don't worry about that, though. I had it when I wanted it and now that I'm nearly sixty I should look pretty stupid in it anyway. But I do remember my impressions of it and it still remains one of my great favourites. It was no different from any other Grand Prix Bugatti but it felt just as right as they all do. I had the same feeling about the car as I had about the three single-seater Maseratis I owned later and it seemed to me that, at that time, the Continental manufacturers knew more about building racing cars than we did. I also had an E.R.A. at the same time that I had one of the Maseratis but I held on to the latter until I'd tried the E.R.A. and, after having tried both, it was the Maserati I kept and raced and the E.R.A. that was sold.

120

But, as my first racing car, the Bugatti was pretty well ideal. Ever since Charlie Martin had owned it, it had been kept and maintained at the same place, Byfleet Motors, a mile from the track, and they knew everything there was to know about it. Charles had told me quite a bit about it before I bought it. He told me that, although no reason could be found, it didn't handle as well as others of its type on the outer circuit and that was why Martin, Leith and Andrew Leitch had all used it only on road circuits where its handling was just as good as the others. I was a bit sorry about this because I would have liked to use it on the outer as well as on the Campbell and Mountain circuits and I aimed to try it on the outer and form my own opinion although I accepted Charles' word because he really did know about Bugattis.

He also told me that all four of the aluminium wheels had hair cracks but that Hugh McConnell, the B.A.R.C. Scrutineer was aware of this and had sketches and measurements of the position and length of each crack on each wheel, as he had of the aluminium wheels on all the other Bugattis using wheels of this type. Andrew didn't mention this when we were doing the deal and it took me some time to find one of the cracks. When I did, I said, 'Holy Moses, Andrew, one of the rear wheels is cracked!'

'It's nothing. Most Grand Prix Bugs have got cracks in their wheels.'

'Never on your life. Look, here's another. And another.' And that little bit of knowledge saved me fifty pounds.

I did try the car on the outer circuit and found that Charles had been right. It really was very nasty and the best I could do was a lap of 118 m.p.h. which I improved on later, when I knew the car better, to 121 m.p.h. But you couldn't keep it flat out all the way—it was too risky.

The first race in which I ran the car was on the Campbell Circuit at the Dunlop Jubilee Meeting in September 1938. I made a point of being around when McConnell came along to scrutineer the car because I wanted to meet him. He was a bit of a doyen but, I thought, a wonderful man who had responsibilities on his shoulders that I certainly shouldn't have liked to carry. He knew everything to be known about every car that ran regularly at Brooklands and I sometimes felt that he didn't really get the credit that was due to him. So many cars could have been turned down on account of age and the possibility of what might happen and it must have been appallingly difficult for him to know just where to draw the line. On this occasion he was assisted by Maurice Hudlass who I knew well because he was the senior scrutineer at most of the bike meetings. Maurice introduced us and McConnell said, 'So you're the new owner. This car's an old friend of mine, you know.'

While Maurice did his usual check of the silencing system, running long rods up into the expansion box to make sure that nothing 'clever' had been done such as running a straight-through pipe down through the middle of the silencer, McConnell did the usual checks, bonnet straps, king pins, steering-arm, drop-arm, front axle, etc., and then he turned to the road wheels. Pulling out a sheet of paper from the dossier he had on the car, he began to check and then suddenly turned to me.

'D'you know what I'm looking for?'

'I think so. Cracks in the wheels?'

'That's right. Shall I find any?'

'You could. You might find three in the nearside rear, two in the offside rear, one in the nearside front and another two in the offside.'

He roared with laughter. 'And you're happy about that?'

'No, not at all. But with Bugatti wheels at a tenner each I can't really do much about it.'

'Well, see if you can find some cheaper. It'd be in both our interests you know.'

I thought it was great of him. He could have turned the car down flat. From then on, all that he used to do, after having checked everything else was to say to me 'Good year for cracks?', and I used to reply, 'Yes, they're coming on very nicely this year.'

Predictably, the car had rather a nasty handicap in its first race with me, partly because it was known that Charlie Martin had once gone very fast with it, quite a bit faster than either Jock or Andrew, but also because it seemed to be tacitly assumed that racing motor-cyclists were bound to go fast on four wheels as well as on two. It finished fifth with a best lap of two minutes and one second, but could have done better if the standing lap had been better. This was dreadful—two minutes thirteen seconds.

The final meeting that year was the autumn one in October and I put the car again in a handicap on the Campbell Circuit. I watched the Campbell Circuit practice carefully for a lot of the time and it seemed to me that a lap time of about one minute fifty-seven seconds would be required in order to win my race and I knew that I just couldn't get the car down to that. I was handicapped to go off with Charlie Dodson on the big unblown 3½-litre Delahaye and we had to give a start of six seconds to Fay Taylour who was driving an identical car to mine. I was sure we could catch her, but there was some rather strong stuff just behind us including Ansell's E.R.A. and Percy Maclure's Riley. Charlie, of course, had been a big motor-cycle star for years, the spearhead of the Sunbeam team from which he had gone to ride Excelsiors, finally becoming a member of the works' Norton team.

I did a better standing lap than before, two minutes seven seconds, but Charlie did slightly better still and all I could do was to sit right on his tail for a lap or two to try to see where I could get by him for there was obviously nothing between the performance of our cars. I was still a yard behind him as we turned off the outer circuit on to the Campbell, about a mile from the start but, when we reached the first right-hander, he took the big Delahaye in very close so that both offside wheels were actually off the concrete and the rear began to shower me with earth and stones. I was quite cross with him although I should have anticipated it and might even have done the same to him if the positions had been reversed. As it was, it cost me about thirty yards and a lot of discomfort but I found at once that I was making ground up on him and I noticed that it was only on the first lap that he took that particular line! We both got by Fay about half way through the race, all of us passing slower cars at the same time but, on the last lap I found that we had company in the shape of Bob Ansell and Percy Maclure who were having a tremendous scrap of their own so that the finishing order was Ansell, Maclure, Dodson and myself—and it was close. I was quite happy with this race and a lap time of two minutes and two-fifths of a second, and this ended the season.

During the winter I worked and saved a bit of money with the aim in view of getting a second car. It wasn't so much the racing that was keeping me poor—it was my girl-friends and Strelsa in particular. It had been agreed that she would come with me to Brooklands for that last meeting and when we had talked on the phone the night before the race, she told me that two other girls in her show wanted to come. I was going to collect her as usual and the other girls were being driven down by one of the boy dancers in the show who had his own 'sports car'. The 'sports car' was waiting outside her flat in Earls Court when I arrived—it was a 1934 or 35 four-seater S.S.I. tourer!

Both the girls were as pretty as I had expected and both were good fun. And so was the boy although he was—how can I put it?—'artistic'.

We set off in convoy and my first impression was that I'd never seen an S.S.I. driven like that because they were out of sight of our Bentley Speed Six before we even reached Hammersmith. But we caught them up, by dint of furious driving, at Roehampton and that was how we continued all the way to Brooklands. I never thought, really, that they'd get there, but they did. Once there, it was hilarious because, in the Brooklands paddock one never could be sure of retaining the attentions of one's girl-friend unless one actually held on to her and all these girls were whisked off as if by magic so that, when the meeting was over and I said to Strelsa, 'Did you enjoy the racing?', she replied 'Racing? I didn't see any.' Then there was the same mad rush back to town, quite necessary this time because the girls were supposed to be at the theatre and made up by eight o'clock and we didn't leave the track until seven thirty, this time a convoy of four cars, the party including several quite well-known Brooklands' drivers!

Brooklands didn't close down with a bang immediately the last meeting had been run in October. There was usually another month's activity, partly for testing but mainly for the purpose of record breaking. November may not have been the nicest of months from the point of view of weather, but it was convenient because every time records were being broken, only that one car or motor-cycle could be on the track. The theory being that if one was going for records with an Austin Seven, it could find itself in the slipstream of a Bugatti or an Alfa, if other cars were allowed to be on at the same time. And, as the track was, in any case, less used in November, that was the best time for records. So it was an interesting month and by the end of November one was ready for a rest anyway.

Then the repair gangs would appear, hacking up and repairing the concrete all the way round, seeking the worst places and dealing with them first. How the decisions were taken as to which bits needed doing most, we never knew. I never heard of a driver being consulted. The administration seemed to decide this for themselves. We were never very confident about all this because the Railway straight which was flat and easy to repair, received a lot of attention each winter but it had never seemed particularly bumpy to me and was, of all places on the track, the easiest on which to go fast if the surface had been bad. On the other hand, there were some nasty spots high up on the home banking which seemed to be left as they were, year after year and one did rather suspect that their inaccessibility had something to do with it. But we could have been wrong and there may have been some very good reason.

Brooklands became almost a home to those of us who worked there and one hated the idea of it closing for the winter. In a way it was more like the village pub than anything else in that even on the most desolate day in mid-winter, you could always look in and find someone you knew even if it was only one of the gatekeepers, most of whom used to become labourers, carpenters and painters during the closed season.

Although I did work in my shed there in mid-winter, I wasn't there every day. The small sheds had no heating or lighting and it was so bitterly cold that even the strongest paraffin stove seemed to make little impression. I used to continue there until there seemed no more prospect of further record attempts, and then, on the way out for the last time, I used to go up on to the Members' Bridge and take one last look. I always did it—the old track looked so impressive and huge with not a soul in sight and the memory of it and the prospect of it opening again kept you going in the weeks ahead.

I used to aim to take something out on the track again on my birthday in mid-February. Sometimes I did but if the weather had been bad, the track repairs would be running behind schedule and it wouldn't be possible. The winter of 1938–39 must have been mild because, in my old log book of the Bugatti there is the entry—on the very day—10 outer-circuit laps—revs to 5500. Half mile 124 m.p.h.

Nothing more then until early March. I had got my second car by this time. It was the little single-seater 1100 cc. Magnette that had come from the Bellvue Stable. Not a K.3 but designated KN which suggested that it had parts of both. The car had been raced by the Evans family, Kenneth and Dennis and their sister Doreen. They had a huge stable of M.G.s and this had become surplus when I bought it. It was a very odd car both in appearance and in some of its mechanical details. The body was offset to the right, like Dobb's 2-litre Riley, and like the Riley, it had a motor-cycle type Amal carburettor to each cylinder. Again, it was Charles, who influenced me over this car. He kept saying to me, when we were talking about the best cars to own: 'It depends what you want from a car. If you just want excitement and pleasure, get the fastest car you can afford. But you won't

125

win many races with it—fast cars tend to be handicapped right out of it. If you want to win races, use a slow one.'

He was quite right about this. I suppose that the theory on which the handicappers worked was that the fast cars had their chances in the few big scratch races that were held at Brooklands, races in which the slower cars just made up the field. So it seemed quite fair that in the handicap races the balance should be slightly in favour of the slower plots although the scratch men had another problem of their own, that of passing and getting through the crowded fields.

But, as I wanted both fun and to win races I thought that the Magnette would give me the prospect of the latter. So it was this that I took out to practise on March 6th which, according to my notebook, seems to have been one of the coldest days on record!

The Magnette, when I got it, had slightly larger wheels on the front than it had on the back and, on trying it I found that this was done by intent because, with the small wheels on the back, it was ideally geared for the Campbell and Mountain circuits, and reversing them gave you the correct outer-circuit gearing. On this occasion, with the big wheels on the back, it lapped at just over 101 m.p.h., flat out all the way with maximum revs of 5800 round the Byfleet banking, dropping to 5400 at the fork. It was very comfortable and there seemed nothing more to be done until it could be tried on the Mountain.

On the 8th, I took both cars round the Mountain Circuit, the Magnette doing one minute four and two-fifths seconds, a lap speed of about 65 m.p.h., and the Bugatti a minute dead, with a note that the high wind made it almost impossible to stop for the hairpin at the fork so the wind was obviously blowing down from the home banking to the Vickers' sheds which meant that one would have been arriving there at, perhaps, 130 m.p.h.

All this activity was for the opening B.A.R.C. meeting on the 11th, which seems to have been earlier than usual that year. This time I had three races—one on each circuit, starting with the Magnette on the outer.

Reading back through these old log books—each car had its own—is, I find a bit disconcerting. I should like to think that weather conditions were responsible for the fact that the M.G. performed better in practice than it did in its initial races but I don't think that was true—I think I must have been 'foxing' a little, which wasn't a bad thing to do, if you wanted results, when driving a car you hadn't raced before.

I recall, earlier in this book, describing all the dreadful things that people did in order to win races, genuinely not recalling that I might have done almost the same myself but, on what I am seeing now, it does look very much as though I was just as bad as anyone else. Anyway, I'll set it down exactly as recorded and let the reader judge for himself. But it looks to me as though I did try hard to win a race with the Bugatti while 'marking time' with the Magnette.

The outer-circuit race on the Magnette received no mention in any of the press reports, which wasn't surprising. But the car's logbook says:

3-Lap Outer Circuit Handicap. Standing Start Lap. 84·27 m.p.h.

| | Flying | ,, | ,, | · 98·82 | ,, |
| | ,, | ,, | ,, | · 99·01 | ,, |

Race Constant. 5500.

| | Race Average. | 94·03 | ,, |
| | ,, Result. | Unplaced. |

And, in retrospect, I feel that it would be unlikely for the revs to have remained constant at 5500 unless by design. There just couldn't have been no wind at all that day.

And then this damning record goes on:

5-Lap Mountain Handicap. Standing Start Lap. 1 min. 13 secs

	Flying	,,	,,	· 1 min. 5·4 secs
	,,	,,	,,	· 1 min. 5·6 secs
	,,	,,	,,	· 1 min. 7 secs
	,,	,,	,,	· 1 min. 6 secs
	Race Average.	1 min. 7·4 secs
	Result. 4th.

There's nothing else particularly bad in the book but I don't see why the car should have gone slower in the race than it had in practice, four days earlier. *The Sporting Life* said:

'Fourteen turned out for the Second March Mountain Handicap. At the end of three laps, C. K. Mortimer (M.G.) led from J. L. Burton (Bugatti), Ian Connell (Darracq) and P. R. Monkhouse (M.G.). On the next lap Burton was in front of Connell and Mortimer, and on the final lap Reggie Parnell, making his first appearance since his suspension, and driving his newly acquired B.H.W., ran into third place by passing Mortimer.'

It rained although, by the time we were out again with the Bugatti, the rain had stopped, leaving the track damp and slippery at the hairpin turn at the fork. The *Autocar's* report said:

'A newcomer to car racing but well known to Brooklands folk as a racing motor-cyclist, C. K. Mortimer drove an M.G. well and stayed in the lead for the first three laps, eventually crossing the line in fourth place. In the final Mountain race Mortimer, now driving a 2·3 blown Bugatti started from the 17 s. mark, went like the proverbial bullet and not only got the lead but kept it to win the race by 6 s. from Parnell at 69·74 m.p.h. H. L. Brooke's Riley finished third. Stuart Wilton's M.G. went outside the barrels to avoid a collision, while Beadle with the Alta found the same trouble and continued on in the direction of Byfleet. Next lap Mortimer skidded and H. L. Brooke drove the Riley over the sandbank instead of round it.'

It really was very slippery at the fork hairpin that day, as everyone discovered. My 'moment' occurred on the last lap coming out into the finishing-straight. A bit too much power brought the tail of the old '2·3' right round so that one knew, at once, that to try correcting it would complete a hundred-and-eighty-degree-turn. There was always bags of room there so I just let the steering-wheel run light, momentarily, to let the old car go on, sideways, where it wanted to. The speed dropped and it gripped again and was away.

The standing lap this time was one minute six seconds and the best flying lap fifty-seven point eight seconds. I used to keep some sort of a financial record and, in the book, these notes read: 'Prize Money £25. Dunlop Bonus £5. Champion Plugs £1. Linton £25.'

Jack Linton was my bookmaker, a tremendous Brooklands character well known to all the drivers and patronised by them all. The other well known ones were Long Tom and George Cooper. Linton and Long Tom used to come down from town but George Cooper, a delightful rotund little man was, I believe, a local builder and contractor and a good bookmaker, too.

Once, on my way home after a successful meeting, I suddenly remembered that I had forgotten to collect my winnings from Linton. I didn't know him very well at that time and had the feeling that I might have had it for that meeting. Later I got to know him well and realised I needn't have worried. When I saw him at the next meeting I said, 'Jack, at the last meeting I had a few winning bets with you, and didn't get paid.'

'That's right, Guv'nor, and why was that? I'll tell you. You never asked me.'

'Can I collect now?'

'Of course. But you'll never get paid if you don't ask. Listen, Guv'nor, I'll tell you something. My old Dad used to say to me "Never pay until you're asked". He saved thousands of pounds that way and I have, too. When you gentlemen win these races, off you go to the bar after the last race and you often forget about it if you have enough champagne and caviar. That saves us money.'

He was quite right except that it was beer instead of champagne and caviar.

The day after that meeting I was talking to 'Mac' of Dunlops and he said, 'Charlie, I've got a couple of new tyres for the back of the Bugatti in the shed. I thought my money was down the drain on that last lap down at the fork. You nearly gave me heart failure.'

They weren't new tyres but they were Dunlop and they were better than those on the car and were free. The Dunlop Service at Brooklands was second to none. The company rightly had complete faith in 'Mac' and he ran it in his own way with two helpers, 'Fiddle' and 'the boy'. When 'Mac' retired, 'the boy' now became 'Reg' and another nameless youngster took his place, so it then became 'Fiddle', Reg and 'the boy'. It was clear and definite promotion for each of them. They worked in a well-equipped chalet-styled building with a little office at the back which dispensed hospitality all day in the form of tea and gossip. On non-race days, there was usually only one of the three of them working, usually 'the boy', while the other two acted as hosts to callers in the office but either 'Mac' or 'Fiddle' could do five times as much work as the boy if the necessity arose and there were occasions, in some of the long-distance races, when all three were working flat out, stripped to the waist, surrounded by mountains of tyres, when the necessity arose. If there was a World Land Speed Record attempt on by Cobb, Eyston or Campbell, 'Mac' would go with it to America and then there wasn't as much time for the hospitality.

Each day, they used to come down from the Dunlop Albany Street Depot in town, to Brooklands, always stopping at the 'Toby Jug' on the Kingston By-pass for early refreshment and the telephone number of the 'Toby Jug' was usually in the diary of most Brooklands riders. and drivers. But apart from their expertise in tyre-fitting, they were a superb public relations department and advertisement for their company and if super service was required, it was always to be had on the spot or, at worst, within range of the 'Toby Jug'.

And they really knew about tyres and wheels. I remember, once, seeing them fit a new set of tyres to the eight-litre Bentley-based Barnato Hassan, on the day before the 500-Mile race. 'Mac' had fitted the tyres and the boy was replacing the wheels on the car, banging up the rear hub caps with a copper hammer. Suddenly 'Mac' noticed him and ran out shouting 'No, no, no, lad'. Taking the hammer, he undid the rear hub caps and then turned them back gently, giving each cap one tap with the hammer, so lightly that it seemed they could almost be undone by hand. Then, turning to the boy with a grin he said 'Just that much, lad. No more. After two hundred and fifty miles those hubs'll be black hot. They'd never get the hub caps off, done up as tight as you'd got 'em.'

And they were so good to people like myself who were young and doing it on a shoestring. The top drivers like Earl Howe and Chris Staniland always started long races on new tyres so that 'Mac' had a good stock of tyres of most sizes that had been discarded although perfectly good for short races. If you were really 'skint' you received them, fitted, as a gift. If you'd just won a race, you gave the lads £1 apiece for them. If you'd been able to give them a 'tip off' about the race you aimed to win, the money was refused finally and definitely. There was a tremendous amount of barter in the paddock. A little favour was never, ever, forgotten—always repaid. Such a pity that life can't be like that and we have to be tied to the money ogre. But, for that sort of system to work, the people using it have to be fairly poor and have to be decent fellows as well. The 'Smart Alecs' wouldn't want it and it wouldn't work with them.

Early in April we took the Magnette out again, on the Mountain Circuit to see just what could be done. Before doing this, I phoned W. E. (Wilkie) Wilkinson of Bellevue Garages, from whom I had got the car because, when we had run it at the opening meeting, there had been a certain amount of unhappiness at the front end, particularly under braking from its maximum speed, down at the hairpin. There'd been some brake judder and, on the fast turn from the Finishing Straight, up under the Members' Bridge on to the home banking, there'd been some front wheel 'flap' which had slowed the car and made it a bit unstable. Putting the big wheels on the back and the small on the front had cured this but the gear ratio was then too high for the circuit and I felt that small wheels, front and back, would be a better set up and this was what I wanted to try. So 'Wilkie' kindly agreed to come down when we practised with the car, and was bringing another pair of small wheels with him.

We tried it, first, exactly as it had run in its last race and this produced a lap time of one minute four seconds accompanied by a lot of judder and flap. Then 'Wilkie', the expert, slacked off the front brakes and tightened the front axle cable tensioners bringing the lap speed down by a whole second although the wheel 'flap' continued and was, if anything, rather worse. Then we put his small wheels on the front of the car and went out again. This gave a lap time of one minute two point six seconds which, we felt, was probably good enough to win a race, provided no one else produced any horrid handicap surprises.

We had no great hopes for the Bugatti at the Easter Bank Holiday Meeting, in view of its win at the opening meeting and rang the changes by entering it for a race on the Campbell Circuit instead of the Mountain where it had scored its win. Our best previous lap had been two minutes point four seconds in 1938 and when we practised with it for Easter 1939, trying rather hard produced a best of one minute fifty-eight point four seconds which wasn't discouraging but not worth more than an 'each-way' bet. We had completed practising with both cars a week before the meeting which was good because it meant that we didn't have to give anything away regarding their potential in front of the fairly large crowd of spectators and other competitors present for the official practice periods. During this time, of course, we were able to sit in the stands and study form.

When practice ended, it looked as though the Magnette should be pretty well all right in its five-lap Mountain race but, on the Campbell Circuit, Percy Maclure stood out as an obvious winner and there was just nothing to be done except back him at the longest odds available which weren't likely to be great, since he'd practised in the official period which meant his form was known to all. But we did what we could by starting a rumour that we were quietly confident of beating 'Perc'. This gained ground like wildfire and brought the odds out no end, on the day so that, finally, we were able to get quite a lot of money on him at 'fours' while we also stood at 'fours' with every bookmaker present. 'Perc' was, of course, a super driver. His cars were always fast, he had works support and, this time, a very fast Riley indeed. In fact, it was virtually an E.R.A. for it had the original blown Riley engine on which the E.R.A. was based and it also enjoyed independent front suspension which most of the E.R.A.s hadn't. The five seconds per lap start which we were to receive from him wasn't nearly enough and we both knew it.

Despite the fact that my money was on 'Perc', I did drive the Bugatti as hard as I could in this race. He won by 5·6 seconds at 70·72 m.p.h. but several factors served to cloud the issue for us regarding the result. In the first place, there were a number of slower cars ahead for us both to get through. We were baulked badly, twice, the first occasion being by Tuson's little Fiat and the second by Stokes Roberts' Riley which, on turning off the Railway straight on to the Campbell Circuit, hit the bank and then spun right in front of the Bug on the second lap, bringing us right to a stop and causing our second lap time to be only three seconds faster than our standing lap time. On the other hand, 'Perc' must have been baulked too—it was an occupational hazard and in no way the fault of the 'baulkers'—just a matter of where you happened to come across the front markers. I first spotted 'Perc' in my mirror, on the second lap, as I came down the Railway straight and I thought then that the situation didn't look too hopeless. Immediately after that, the Stokes Roberts incident occurred and, on the following lap the blown Riley was a lot closer and came by on the lap after that, just after we had gone under the Members' Bridge. When he came by we were both flat out in top and there was a lot of difference in our top speeds, nothing in braking, but quite a bit in acceleration.

The Motor was very kind in its report of the race:

'The second similar race was really a battle between Mortimer (2·3 Bugatti) with 35 secs start and Percy Maclure (1500 Riley) with 10 secs start. Abecassis (1500 Alta) on Scratch, couldn't get into the picture. Maclure had the supercharged six cylinder engine taken out of Mrs Petre's old blue car and had put it into his own independently sprung frame. Mortimer drove remarkably well (Maclure always does) and, between them, they got to third and fourth positions in that order after three laps. On the fourth, Mortimer led the race but Maclure simply hooted past on the Railway Straight and won by 5·6 secs at 70·72 m.p.h.'

So, on that race, our bet won us more than our prize money—just four times as much, in fact, because the prize money for second place was £10.

The Mountain race on the Magnette turned out as we expected, thanks largely to 'Wilkie', now in the secret with us and, here, we got better odds so that the win put just over £100 in my pocket and something in 'Wilkie's', I hoped, and something, I knew, in Dunlop Mac's. The *Autocar* liked us too. Its reporter said:

'The second Road Handicap was won, as expected, by Percy Maclure. His chief rival was C. K. Mortimer who was as good on the 2·3 Bugatti as he is on a motor cycle but who was caught and passed on the last lap, while V. H. Tuson's Fiat, which had been travelling remarkably well, came home third. Again the scene shifted, this time to the Mountain Circuit where Mortimer won the first race in the single seater M.G. in most enterprising fashion, though Aldington with the white Frazer Nash B.M.W. as near as no matter caught him at the finish and Aitken did well with the E.R.A.'

Aldington was a surprise and quite a worry towards the end. He started seventeen seconds behind us and was in mirror sight for most of the way so that it really was necessary to 'steam on' and the Magnette's last lap was its best at one minute one second, or 69 m.p.h. The prize money was £25, Dunlop Bonus £5, Esso £5 for fuel and £3 for oil. Winning bets with every bookmaker on the site, including crafty old Jack Linton who would only give 'evens', added up to nearly £70 but, as I was known to most of them I had to get friends to put it on and, with so much interest, the odds kept dropping alarmingly because none of the Brooklands bookmakers ever liked taking much more than £10 stake money in the paddock.

Compared to today's astronomical figures these amounts seem laughable but, if one relates the income to the capital outlaid it's quite good because the two cars together had cost only £275, I had never been charged any storage rent for the Bugatti by Byfleet Motors who brought the car to Brooklands and looked after it for £2 per day, while the Magnette lived at the track in my shed, annual rental now £15, and this I maintained myself because it was not a simple car and I understood its six Amal carburettor set up.

My own dealings with the Brooklands bookies had by now reached such a science that I was approached by one of the less knowledgeable of them with a proposition that, rather than deal with him as a customer, I should settle for a lump sum paid on the morning of each

133

meeting in exchange for a list of anticipated winners, with a further sum to come at the end of the day if things worked out well. From a purely business point of view, this would have been more profitable and ideal, had it not been for the fact that, in doing it, I should have brought the odds down so disastrously that it would have made it not worthwhile for anyone, including my friends, to patronise the bookmakers at all. So, regretfully, and feeling immensely self-righteous, I turned the offer down but could never do any business with that particular firm again.

The Brooklands Automobile Racing Club ran an Aggregate Award system at all their meetings throughout the season, divided into two sections, races on the outer circuit and those run on the Campbell and Mountain circuits. Competitors scored three points for a win, two for second place and one point for a third in all short and long handicaps, the prizes being £25 for first place in each section and I found, now, that I was leading easily, the Aggregate for the two road circuits. I was quite keen to pull this off, not so much for the money involved as for the prestige value which would, I felt, help me in 1940. Had I known what was going to happen, I needn't have worried.

I knew, now, that I couldn't go much faster on the Bugatti on either of the road circuits and that there wasn't much point in running it on the outer. So the alternative was either to sell it and get something faster or to plug on and wait my turn to be favoured with a good enough handicap to win again. The latter didn't appeal at all and I began to think of a way round it. Was there a driver there who would fancy his chances on the outer circuit on the Bugatti, knowing its vices, and still be willing to drive it, in exchange for letting me use his outer-circuit car on the other courses?

In fact, there was one and it was, again, Charlie Brackenbury who found him. To drive a tricky car fast on the outer circuit, you had to have a certain 'hang on and hope' outlook which I had to some extent with bikes, but not with a car. Gerald Sumner felt he had it and was looking for a faster outer-circuit car than the 1100 cc. single-seater K.3 Magnette he'd been racing until then. I had no doubt that I should like his car better than he'd like mine but we met to try both. Very much to my surprise, it turned out the other way because Gerald took the Bug round faster than I had and didn't think it was bad at all. I didn't dislike the K.3—it was a very nice car indeed. But it wasn't much faster than my single-seater K.N. as I had expected and, while I felt that I could soon get the K.N. round the Mountain in a minute or under, I felt it would take me quite as long to do the same with the K.3. And on top of that, the K.N. was mine to break and I should have felt very bad if I damaged Gerald's.

I understood my six carburettor set up rather well. I knew quite a bit about Amals from the bike days and I had watched Dobbs at work on the six Amals fitted to his two-litre Riley single seater. I would have liked to study Fred Dixon's tuning of carburettors but the bonnets seldom came off either the two-litre or the one and a half Riley and if they were off and you went to have a look, Fred used to scowl frighteningly. The seating position of my Magnette was lower than Gerald's because while his seat was in the centre of the car and above the prop shaft, in true outer-circuit style, mine was offset to the right and sat down well between the propshaft and right-hand chassis member so that you really could whistle the old thing round right-hand corners like those on the Mountain.

With my M.G. the big snag was the gearbox. It was a manual box, which I preferred to a pre-selector, but the second- and third-gear ratios were too widely spaced which didn't matter once you got going but added up to poor standing-start laps. So this was the next thing to be dealt with, having decided to go on with the car.

In retrospect, all this careful thought and pre-planning seems rather comic. Everyone knew that war was coming but you couldn't just throw up your hands and wait, and planning ahead helped to put the thought of a war out of mind. And, all the time, of course, the German Auto Union and Mercedes Grand Prix teams were scooping the pool everywhere so that, when the crash did come, one knew how much of their pre-planning would be abortive.

I still hadn't driven the Magnette in a race on the Campbell Circuit so, at Whitsun, that was the choice. The Bug had scored on both so it didn't really matter. But I felt that, of the two circuits I stood a better chance of improving on the Mountain. This time, it was handicapped right out of the hunt. The lap time came down to fifty-six seconds and a fifth, just under 75 m.p.h.—the best the car had ever done, I was told—and for all that it only finished sixth. So I just had to find a buyer in order to get something faster which, while it might be just as stiffly handicapped, would be even more exciting to drive.

Again, the Magnette won. But, this time it was by courtesy of Reg Parnell who was carrying my money, so that my income amounted to prize money and bonuses only. I wasn't so pleased with Reg about this but, having backed me, there was nothing I could say that would upset him. This was the occasion when, having caught me up and actually come alongside to pass, he then 'lost' the big B.H.W. in a big way and took to the fields. Arthur Baron's 2·3 Bugatti was second and Beadle's two-litre blown Alta third.

Had I known it at the time, this was to be my last car race at my beloved Brooklands although there was still some fun to come on two wheels and three for I had been offered, by Francis Beart, rides in two races at the next motor-cycle meeting in July, on one of his 350 cc. Norton sidecar outfits, after which we were going for World Standing Start Mile and Kilometre Records with the same set up. Anything that Francis prepared and entered was always good and I was looking forward, no end, to getting back on a bike. By now, Francis himself held one of the most important and dangerous of all Brooklands' records. Difficult because you needed tremendous power allied to skill and dangerous because it was known that the record couldn't be broken without an accident.

Strange, you think? But true, because the record involved climbing the Test Hill faster than any before, which meant that, if you went up fast enough to break the record, the bike became airborne to the extent of six or more feet at the top, where the hill levelled out. The previous Test Hill Record Holder, R. Coes (Brough Superior) had found this out for himself and Francis, when he made his run, made all preparations for a 'heavy' landing, even to the extent of having the Brooklands ambulance in attendance at the top of the hill! Coes had made his run on June 9th 1925 and it was eleven years later, to the day, when Francis went for his record with a machine of just half the engine capacity, for his Grindlay Peerless was powered by one of the current speedway-type J.A.P. 500 cc. engines. The record stood at 7·3 seconds and, on his first run Francis eased slightly just before breasting the top of the hill so that the time was marginally slower. There was nothing for it—the power just had to be kept on regardless of the consequences if the record was to be taken. Down to the bottom again and, this time, a full-bore run all the way. The result was 6·99 seconds, the speed 34·35 m.p.h., no mean average for a standing start up a 1-in-4 gradient. The poor old rider did part company with his bicycle at the top but he wasn't hurt and it was worth it for the record was never broken and still stands today.

All this happened in 1936 and it was in 1939, July, when I had a go at some records on one of Francis' bikes. I was well into the car racing phase by that time but attended the bike meetings and the urge to have another ride was still there so I mentioned it to Francis and he offered me a ride on his lovely 350 cc. track-racing Norton and sidecar. Naturally, I jumped at it. Two races were planned, both short handicaps, at the July meeting and I tried the outfit for the first time on the day before the meeting. I never, for a moment, expected to find the slightest difficulty with it—but I was wrong—it seemed a very rough old lot from the point of view of controllability and I didn't like it. Francis was always frantically busy with customers' machinery on days prior to meetings and had no time to help me so all I could do was to keep trying different set-ups of tyre pressure and front fork adjustments, none of which seemed to improve it.

By mid-afternoon the three of us, Francis, the outfit and I had had enough of each other. I was sure I had slipped and become 'soft' and so had my entrant. I didn't think so much of his bikes but dared not say so and we were neither of us looking forward to the morrow. It seemed ridiculous, having had a lot of experience of riding fast and, sometimes, difficult bikes at speeds of over 110 m.p.h. on Brooklands to be unable, less than three years later, to control a 350 with sidecar set-up to lap at around 85 m.p.h. Towards the end of the day, Francis' business pressures eased and he came over to see me. We both stood looking at the outfit glumly. The body of the sidecar was a superbly streamlined shell with a tiny canvas tonneau cover over the top, where the passenger would have entered, if we had been carrying a passenger. We weren't carrying a passenger—we carried ballast in the form of a sackful of sand measured to the minimum weight, to the last ounce. After gazing at the set-up for several minutes Francis bent down and removed the tonneau. He peered thoughtfully into the depths of the sidecar.

'Charles, have you got a hammer, some nails and a bit of wood?'

I thought he'd gone mad but said, 'What size and shape d'you want the wood?'

He replied, 'That's important. I want to make a bulkhead to keep this ballast up in the nose of the body—its been slipping back and you've had no weight on the front wheel. That's all that's wrong.'

I believed him and, as usual, he was right. Which just goes to show that you think too much in terms of technicalities.

All the press were kind to us. *The Motor Cycle* said:

'After one lap, Leveson Gower led from the length of the Vickers Straight from C. K. Mortimer who it was good to see back again in the saddle of F. L. Beart's 348 cc. Norton and sidecar. Third place was held by R. J. A. Petty (246 New Imperial) with B. W. Smith (344 O. K. Supreme) fourth. With two laps covered, it was obvious that Leveson Gower was increasing his lead over Mortimer, while G. W. Field (498 Triumph) and L. A. Howe (497 Ariel) had separated from the pack and were coming up fast enough to battle for second place at the expense of Mortimer.

And this they did, so we were fourth, but the next race was better.

Again *The Motor Cycle*:

'For his audacity, Leveson Gower was rehandicapped in the second race, and, on the one minute six seconds mark was now giving twelve seconds to Mortimer and Petty and six seconds to N. Cox (249 Excelsior). Mortimer jumped away smartly at the start and held on to a good lead for two laps and for the greater part of the third lap. He looked like winning as he came off the Byfleet banking alone but, on the run up to the finishing line, V. N. Hood (499 Rudge) who had been eighth at the beginning of the lap, streaked past. About fifty yards behind Mortimer came R. Fazan (348 Velocette) followed by O. E. de Lissa (348 Norton) and J. M. Givons (348 Velocette).'

My very last race at Brooklands, had I known it, because war was to overtake it all within six weeks. I had had nearly ten wonderful years at Brooklands and, again, had I known it, my association with the place was to last throughout the war. I certainly hadn't set the place alight but had enjoyed success and, in odd ways, had made little bits of history. For one thing, there was the twelve-hour World Record run—that had been good. I had won Gold Stars for lapping at over 100 m.p.h. on both 500's and 1000's—and I had had the distinction of being the very last rider to conduct a belt-driven machine in a race at Brooklands.

And I had acquired some wonderful friends and met some unique people, seen some unbelievable things. I don't think, though, that there were many great riders competing at Brooklands, in my time, if, in fact, there were at any time. I think there are more today. It's difficult, I know, to draw comparisons because the problems of the rider are different in every period.

I never raced a machine having a sprung rear end but, since the war,

138

I have ridden two racing bikes, an A.J.S. 7R and Greeves Silverstone production racer at Silverstone on practice days and there's no comparison at all with the old rigid frames that we had. The problem is a different one altogether—in my day it was stamina, a question of how long you could put up with the pounding and still ride capably. With the sprung rear end, all that has passed and now it is a question of how far you can 'lean out of the window' without actually falling out and that, too, is tiring in a long race.

There were more potentially great riders in the era before mine, that is to say the mid-1920s. People like Denly, Lacey, Hicks, Staniland, Marchant, Le Vack and Horseman. I'll stick my neck out here and name those who I think could have made the grade in circuit racing today. What is needed? I think, mainly, superb judgement, grim determination, ruthlessness and an absolute refusal to 'take a back seat' to anyone, coupled with the ability to stay on board the machine and in control of it. So who can we rule out? Lacey for one because he had far too much respect for his machine. Machines have to be flogged to the absolute limit in today's short-circuit racing and Bill would have hated that for, above all, he was a superb engineer. Hicks the same, I would have thought and, possibly Le Vack because, today, you can't consider the bike. Eric would have fallen at this fence and so would Willy Worters. Les Archer would have had a go but I don't think he would have liked it and 'Pa' would have loathed it because he loved his bikes. I don't know about Bert Denly. I do believe that today's style of riding would have been within his capabilities but Bert has another drawback—he is a gentleman and you can't afford to be gentlemanly in racing today. Dougal Marchant and Chris Staniland would, I think, have made it. I'm far from meaning that they weren't gentlemen because they were. But Dougal was determined and I think to an extent that would have overshadowed his other characteristics and Chris enjoyed a beat up and had, too, possibly the most superb judgement of them all. On that basis Noel Pope ought to be included but, while he was a very very good rider indeed, Noel was at his best on big bikes at Brooklands and never shone dazzlingly in the Isle of Man.

Let me quote two specific things to illustrate the difference between racing then and now. I left the bike-racing scene in 1939 and never raced again on two wheels, returning as an owner/entrant in 1963. The rider I had then was a young man named Griff Jenkins and

Francis, who had never left the scene, prepared our bikes. Having just returned to the fold, I wanted to do as many races as possible including short circuits and the Isle of Man and the first shock I got was when Francis insisted that we had separate machines for the long and short races because, in his view, the short-circuit bikes received such a pasting that they just couldn't be brought to the standard of preparation he considered necessary for the T.T. So we had two sets of bikes, two 350's, two 500's, at between £500 and £800 each. Expensive when compared with the Manx Nortons we'd had new at around £100 but cheap today because they now cost up to £2,000 in a few cases!

Francis hated the short-circuit racing scene and, having done it, I now feel the same. Griff loved it, and said so and that was the start of slight friction between them. One of the things Francis used to complain to me about was the way Griff used the brakes because we had more than one instance of cracked front drums just from excessive heat. Griff cheerfully countered this by saying that if you didn't use the brakes late and hard, people who did went by you and, for a time, that was that. One day when we were racing at Mallory, Griff said to me, 'Where are you watching this race?' and I said I was going to be at the start. He said, 'To please me, will you watch somewhere else?' I didn't know what he meant but, then he explained, saying, 'Francis says I use the brakes too hard. I want you to go up to the hairpin, on the approach, about a hundred and fifty to two hundred yards from the apex. In that last race I followed —— for ten laps, as you saw. On every lap, at the approach to the hairpin, his back wheel came up nine inches off the ground a hundred and fifty yards before the hairpin and only touched the deck twice in that distance—that really is using the front brake!'

I went up and it was true. I told Francis and his comment was 'Disgusting!'

The other instance, illustrating improvement in machinery, and brakes in particular, happened in the 1963 Junior Manx Grand Prix, the first race after my return to the fold, involving a pit stop. Although I was the proud owner and had entered the bikes throughout the season it had never occurred to me that Griff would want me to do the pit, for I had no knowledge of my own bikes, mechanically. Francis couldn't do it for he had his own bike in that race so, in the end, I did. We never did rehearse the fill although I suggested it. Griff felt it wasn't necessary so there we were, all unrehearsed but lying sixth in the race when the time came to fill at half distance. I had always filled my own bikes in the Island when Jock Forbes had ridden for me in the thirties, of course, but now it was 1963 and as the bike became due I felt dreadful at the thought that I might let him down. Suddenly I saw him arriving and my immediate conviction was 'Holy Moses, he's overshot' because, all those years later, I instinctively recalled the exact approach speed at which a 350 arrived at its pit and could still stop there, forgetting that brakes improve in a span of thirty years. It brought me up to date with progress—and the fill was a good one.

But back now to 1939 and the Beart 350 sidecar on which we were scheduled to go for the World's 350 cc. Standing Mile and Kilometre. Although I was glad to be riding bikes again, I was more heavily involved with cars. We had had sufficient success with the Bugatti for it to be handicapped right out of the hunt, now, in every race in which we ran it. The Magnette was still a consistent notcher-up of wins and places, fun to drive but not exciting and I did badly want a much faster car. A buyer cropped up for the Bug and I took his money—all £125 of it and that, added to what I had in the bank, meant a price ceiling of £250. Even in 1939 £250 wouldn't buy an E.R.A. and I didn't want one anyway. What I would have liked would have been either an Alfa Romeo Monoposta or one of the big single-seater three-litre Maseratis that had been raced by Howe and Bira. I don't think either were for sale at that time and even if they had been, the prices would have been in the £500–£700 bracket.

Once again, Charlie Brack came up with the answer. 'The car you want is the big Sunbeam. John's car. That's for sale.' The Cobb twelve-cylinder Sunbeam. But even that was too much. He wanted £500 for it. Charles was adamant. 'Let me introduce you to him. He's a good chap. He'll take less for it.' So I did, although my limit was fixed.

It was a great piece of impertinence, really, to go and meet someone as eminent as John when one had only half the purchase price of the car that he was selling but I was twenty-six at the time and still possessed youth's optimism in matters of this sort and in some other matters as well. I hardly knew him and had only had odd cups of tea in his company when Charles had brought him up to the canteen, but the meeting was arranged by Charles, to take place at Thompson & Taylor's, at the track, where the car was kept. It was due to take place at eleven o'clock and this didn't leave much time because I was going to ride for Francis at twelve—we were having a go at the World's

Standing Mile and Kilometre records on the 350 Norton sidecar outfit, and all the track arrangements had been made and the timekeepers booked from that time.

Charles and John hadn't arrived when I got to T. & T.s but Ken Taylor knew about it and ushered me to the car which I duly tried for size. It was a great car—I had always liked it from the early days when Kaye Don had driven it and although it now looked very different after the modifications that Campbell had made, I thought that, if anything, its looks were improved. Ken told me all that he knew about its mechanical state and, as regards appearance, it looked almost exactly as it does today.

When they arrived, Charles opened the conversation by saying that it must be mutually understood that 'In the event of a deal ensuing, I shall require twenty-five per cent introductory commission' but John ignored this and said:

'Charles tells me you're interested in the Sunbeam. Would you like to try it.'

I put my cards on the table, saying that I certainly liked it but didn't feel I should suggest trying it although I had found that Ken Taylor had had instructions to the effect that I would be taking it out. The reason I felt that was that I hadn't got the sort of money he was asking for the car—although I thought it was perfectly fairly priced.

Instead of asking me what on earth I thought I was doing in being there at all, John said, 'What would you want to pay for it, then?' I felt an explanation was due, at this stage, and I gave it, finishing up by saying that, having sold the Bugatti and added a bit to it, I had just £250 in my pocket at that moment. That was all I had or was likely to have and that was what I could offer.

John's reply was, 'Well, if that's it and if you would enjoy driving it, why not have it?' Which put him very much on a pedestal as far as I was concerned. I then had a quick word with Taylor who agreed to continue looking after the Sunbeam for me, told him that I should like to run it at the August Bank Holiday meeting in one or possibly two short handicaps on the Mountain or Road circuits and then we went back to the paddock for a quick drink, after which I changed into leathers and reported to Francis who was waiting out in the lay-by on the Railway straight with the Norton outfit.

The idea of having a go at the standing mile and kilo had sprung from the fact that, in both races in which I had ridden the outfit, the standing laps had been rather good. This had caused us to get the F.I.C.M. Records Book out to see what the mile and kilo stood at. It was more the fact that we found that both records had been set up by Dougal Marchant in the 1920s, than the speed itself that made us decide to try to break them because it was logical to think that if those speeds could have been set up all those years ago on a machine having three speeds and hand gearchange, we must be able to dent them quite badly with more power, foot change and four speeds. It looked easy but it turned out to be surprisingly hard.

Marchant, who I had known quite well after he had finished with racing was a much more slightly built character than I but he must also have had more power than we realised and must have had everything dead right on the day he set up his records because we had to make four or five runs in each direction before we could break them by the clear 1 m.p.h. that was necessary, under the regulations. Riding wasn't really a factor because, unlike a 500 or a 1000, you couldn't bring the front wheel up so far that it would come right over and 'loop the loop' backwards—there wasn't that sort of power. And it was only necessary to point the machine slightly to the right, on the start-line, to allow for the 'crabbing' to the left that followed when the power went on—there was no question at all of the machine running round its sidecar anti-clockwise.

After two runs, with slight changes to gearing and carburation, we were only equalling the records, so a halt was called to consult. During the consultation which, till then had been rather barren, a quavering voice struck up from the back of the small knot of people who had turned out to watch. There were always people who liked to gather round when record attempts were in progress. There was nothing gratifying to see someone go out and break a record easily at the first attempt but it was fun to see others in trouble, having underestimated the task in hand and there was no doubt at all in the minds of those present—including ourselves—that this was exactly what we had done.

So having stifled the irritation at the sound of another voice, we listened, and it was a good job that we did, because the voice belonged to a very old gentleman who turned out to be a retired Brooklands' gatekeeper who was claiming that he had actually seen Marchant's attempt 'as close to him as I am to you now'.

Resisting the temptation to strangle him or, at least write him off

143

as an old fool, we did listen and this turned out to be the only wise thing we'd done that day. Marchant, said the oracle, had ridden 'a much lighter machine and had worn hardly any clothes'.

'Bloody old fool,' said Francis, 'hope you and I never get like that, Charles.' But we did continue to listen, partly because the old man had now got for himself the nucleus of an audience and partly because his reedy voice was so high pitched and penetrating that you couldn't do anything else.

The frame tubes of Marchant's machine, we learned, were 'half the thickness of ours, the front brake a quarter the size and he used a smaller engine, too. The rider was smaller, too—not a big chap like this gentleman.'

It began to dawn on us that the old boy was almost certainly right. The Chater Lea frame would certainly have been much more spindly and light than the Norton which was a lightened version of the very good but heavy Manx. Francis had always been cross at the idea of having to fit a front brake for the attempt. This was necessary under the regulations but, here again, Marchant would have had something the size of a sixpence when compared to ours. Although 'Gramps' was adrift regarding the engine, the Chater Lea engine was certainly much more lightly finned than our Norton and this would account for the 'smaller engine'.

By now Francis was thoughtfully removing surplus bits from the machine but there weren't very many and I was instructed to go back to the shed and change into something lighter. But what? I approached 'Gramps' who was now really in his stride—it was definitely his day.

'What did Mr Marchant wear?'

He looked at me blankly, through watery eyes. Someone said, 'He's deaf' so I bellowed:

'You said Mr Marchant wore hardly any clothes. D'you remember what clothes he did wear?'

He brightened at once. 'Oh yes, sir. He wore a crash-helmet—' long pause and for a moment we thought that that was going to be all, '—and combs.' There was a gust of laughter but someone said:

'I think he could be right. I did once hear that Marchant wore a skin-tight ballet dancer's costume for a short-distance record attempt.'

I wasn't going to try to copy Dougal's effort but I changed into the lightest pair of leather breeches I had, a thin roll-neck sweater, stockings and plimsolls instead of the usual fairly heavy riding-boots that

144

were the fashion at Brooklands and strapped myself up with the broadest body-belt I had. These belts were standard wear and I strapped this one up so tightly that I could hardly breathe.

When I got back I was met with an amazing sight. The supporters' club had increased and grandfather was now in top gear. The back wheel had been removed from the machine, there was no sign of Francis and four chaps were throwing buckets of water all over the start-line area. Gradually, I was put in the picture. Marchant, it appeared, had used a ribbed rear tyre instead of the block pattern we had and had had the start-area doused before his runs, with the object of getting maximum wheelspin for his comparatively low power-to-weight ratio outfit. If that worked for him it must work for us because, while we would have had a bit more power, our weight increase would have outweighed it.

The new rear wheel was fitted—one run as a test, one more and the record was ours—thanks to the good memory of our aged friend.

And thanks, too, to Francis who provided and prepared the outfit and who, like me, is today older and wiser and, also like me, readier and more able to see the humour of the situation in which we found ourselves that day. It didn't seem so funny at the time! We were always so broke, you see, in those days and the spectre of financial ruin stemming from an abortive record attempt wasn't funny then.

Had I known it, that was to be the very last time I was to ride a racing bike in any form of competition for, having ridden the outfit back to the Beart shed, I strolled round to my own, to change, and suddenly found that I didn't feel so good. I had a stomach ache which surpassed any I had ever previously encountered. It was worse when I took off my body support belt, better when I sat down and returned when I stood up again. In short, in breaking the records, I had given myself a hernia.

That was bad but what was worse was that both the doctor who I saw an hour later and the surgeon who visited me later in my nursing home in London said that I wouldn't be able to drive the Sunbeam at the August Bank Holiday meeting. The surgeon wasn't quite so positive. He said, 'You can if you want. But you won't want to.' And he was right.

I asked Charles if he would drive both cars for me, the Magnette as well. He couldn't drive the latter—he was already committed to another drive in the same race. And he refused to drive the Sunbeam, saying that if anything went wrong mechanically before I had had a chance to drive it, he'd feel unhappy. So the big car non-started and my old mate Jock West drove the M.G. and said he enjoyed it although, by then, its handicap was rather horrid and it wasn't placed.

By the time I emerged from the Duchess Nursing Home, in Beaumont Street, the War was upon us or it was, at least, within a very few days. I convalesced for a week or so, pretty depressed about everything, and then took a trip to the track. The War had made no impact on it at all by that time except that sheds were being turned out, cars and bikes were in process of coccooning for storage and a huge bonfire was raging on the waste ground between the paddock sheds and the River Wey. People were being optimistic and saying that the War would be over in a year, but no one said it with conviction and one knew very well that some would be seeing each other for the last time.

Strolling over to the bonfire I saw that the Club had had a turnout in the office for there were piles of blazing Membership Application Forms, Membership Rule Booklets and Lap Speed Booklets. Someone came along with some huge cardboard boxes and emptied the first into the flames where the contents fell with a jingling crash. It was the first of several boxes of brand new Members' Car Badges, unissued and, today, worth £50 a time. Even then, one felt that this couldn't be right and when someone else tried to rescue a few from the inferno, the chap who had brought them said 'Don't bother to fish them out. There are two more boxes here.' So everyone was alright for Members' —and Aero Club—Badges, it seemed.

I rescued one thing from that bonfire—a big bronze plaque that had been mounted on the outside wall of the Clubhouse for as long as I could remember. It read: 'On this Track, on the 15th of February. 1913, One Hundred Miles was first covered in One Hour by the Late Percy Lambert, Driving a Talbot car.' That was of special interest to me—I was born on February 15th 1913, in Byfleet, within a hundred yards of the Byfleet banking—so history was being made as I arrived and it wasn't surprising, I suppose, that I became involved later on.

I had the Percy Lambert plaque until the early 1960's when, in a moment of great enthusiasm I presented it to the Museum at Beaulieu. I've never seen it since then. I expect it will be in the archives and will, one day, be an exhibit. Maybe it is already.

Everyone knows what happened to dear old Brooklands. The 'shocking' story of how it was sold under the noses of those who loved it so much, and all that. It was sad but I never could see it as shocking. The trouble seemed to me to be the fact that Brooklands was very much taken for granted by those who used and loved it and the possibility that it might go, one day, just didn't occur—and I include myself in this.

In every sense of the word, it was a great place. I never thought it would go and was horrified when it did but, with hindsight, I never was a shareholder and I bet they had a lean time throughout all those great years. We used it, didn't appreciate what we had and we lost it. Serve us right. Maybe it could have been saved by public subscriptions but public subscriptions can be slow processes at the best of times and it wasn't the best of times, at all, when the moment of decision arose concerning Brooklands.

So it went, and I think it was sad that it went because, sentiment apart, I think it would have been valuable for a long time after the war ended and might even have a value now. It was bumpy and it was said to be out of date but so were the suspensions of the cars and bikes that used it. Even as it was, I would have thought that it would have been a good testing ground for suspension designs.

One door closes and another opens. It took time for doors to open after the end of the war but open they did and soon we had a new era of racing—and a good one. And, by courtesy of the British Aircraft Corporation, Brooklands can still be seen occasionally by Members of the Society—and that isn't taken for granted!

If one has to draw a moral from all this it must, I suppose, be to appreciate what you've got. We haven't got Brooklands but we have got other circuits, many of which we take largely for granted and any of which we could easily lose—if we cared to stop and think about it.

We probably won't but, if we did, we should howl just as dismally and probably be just as much to blame!

6

1939 to 1945

By the beginning of October 1939, motor racing seemed a million miles away. The Magnette had been towed away from Brooklands and stored at our family home at Dorking and then towed on again to Brighton when we sold our Dorking house in favour of a flat in Kemp Town. The Sunbeam was more of a problem and I had it transported to Capel and stored in the garage of my uncle's house there, visiting it from time to time, just to sit in it and dream of the time when one day I would be able to drive it, if we were both around at the end of it all.

Storing the M.G. was no problem. It was small and light and simple, but I soon began to worry about the 'Tiger' and made one more trip to Brooklands to seek out Ken Taylor. Everything had been carefully done, in storing it. The garage was heated but one could see that this might not always be so and when I asked Ken's advice it came at me like a bolt from the blue.

'Sell it! Why, Ken? It's a bloody good car.'

'Yes it is. But it won't be by the time this war's ended. Are you one of those people who think the war will be over in a year? I don't. I think it'll last five years, maybe more. That engine's got welded steel water jackets. They'll leak like a seive after two years, however well you store it. If you're wise, you sell it.'

I didn't take Ken's advice immediately although I accepted it gratefully, knowing it to be good. It was early in 1940 that I had a call from Robert Arbuthnot to say that he had a customer—a Mr James—who was interested in the car, and would I contemplate selling it. I did, and after the war I sought out Ken because when I next saw the car in action it was spewing water in all directions.

'What did I tell you? It was a great old car but it's had its day. No one will ever get it back now.' He was wrong there but there seemed

149

no reason to disagree with him then although I never did think that it was wrong to sell it. I just wouldn't have had the knowledge to do what had to be done, or even to delegate it to the right quarter, much less to finance it. Nor, I think, would I have had the enthusiasm, much as I loved the car.

I had one more good drive around Christmas time in 1940 for I heard of a K.3 Magnette for sale in London. This was one of the pointed-tail cars, never a famous one, but all the better for that because it had done very little running and was completely original.

Charles Brackenbury now had the garage outside Brooklands that Eric Fernihough had had until his death and Charles it was who came with me to London, equipped with trade plates to motor the K.3 down to Brighton. We shared the driving—it was very nostalgic but too short a trip altogether. And that really was the end for the time being.

It was time, now, to get down to the question of what I was to do. I had no feelings of gallantry but a strong desire to make a contribution to the war effort—but very little idea as to what I could best do. I saw a lot of both George Harvey Noble and Charlie Martin at this time. Both were Brighton residents and close friends but, of the three of us, only Charles really knew where he was going and that was into the Navy. Many of my friends were waiting and marking time in the Auxiliary services. Jock Forbes was in the Police Force in town and George Lane, a superb motoring artist, had joined the Fire Service.

Then Jock rang me and said that he was leaving the police and taking a temporary job at Cobham with the Admiralty and, if we could meet, there could be something for me. By the time we met, a week later, Jock was in his new job and we discussed it over lunch at the White Lion at Cobham.

The thing stemmed from the Railton Car Company which, itself, had followed on from the old Invicta Car Company, both of which had been presided over by Captain Noel Macklin, and both based at Cobham. On the outbreak of war, Noel Macklin had closed down production and made a prompt visit to the Admiralty to find out in what way his resources might be of use to them. Knowing him as I later came to know him, I have little doubt that had he been told 'nothing doing', Noel would have tried every other door of every Service Department until he got the answer he wanted. In fact, he got it clearly and at once. They wanted boats.

To be precise, they wanted a number of small boats to a standard design. Something around 110 feet long that could be easily adapted for different uses, such as air-sea rescue, harbour patrol or motor-gunboat and designed on a prefabricated basis for quickness of construction and repair.

This was right up Noel Macklin's street for although he had no facilities for boatbuilding, he had great powers of organisation coupled with an imaginative and active brain and, best of all, he was on his own in cutting through red tape and getting things done.

The Invicta and Railton cars had been produced in the small works at Cobham adjoining his private house on the Fairmile. There had been a tie-up, in the case of the Railton with Thompson and Taylor who were the Concessionaires and with Hudson Motors at Chiswick who supplied the engines.

His first action was to procure the services of Carol Holbeach who had been Sales Manager of T. & T.s and had been based at their depot in the paddock at Brooklands. Carol's job had come to an end with the outbreak of war and I knew him well for, in my 'dealer' capacity I had done odd transactions, mostly involving rather cheap and tatty cars that T. & T.s had had to take in part exchange when supplying new Railtons.

The first task that Noel Macklin gave Carol was to make a coastal motor-tour round England, Scotland and Wales and return with a list of small boatbuilders now out of work because of the War—'and please be back here with the list, within a week'.

On his return, which took a little more than a week, Carol, who had had no sleep at all and was looking forward to a day or two's relaxation, was met with, 'Now will you do the same thing again. Not boatbuilders this time. Small machine shops, even garages with machining capacity, who are in the same position, with no work on hand. Many thanks—see you in a week.' Somehow, poor old Carol managed this, too.

Noel was away when he returned, signing up the boatyards all round the coast, on Carol's list. He had negotiated arrangements with Hudson Motors and with T. & T.s so that they now had two vast stores, at Chiswick and in T. & T.'s new building at Brooklands into which the marine fittings of the boat could pour, direct from the garages and machine shops. And he had concluded a similar arrangement with a timber mill, Alfred Lockharts of Brentford, for facilities for making the prefabricated timber parts.

The next thing was transport and obviously the majority of the transport would have to be sub-contracted. This was where Jock Forbes came in, at Carol's suggestion—and this was where I nearly came in, but didn't. And how glad I was, later on.

The job that Carol offered me, through Jock, was in the department responsible for metering out the various parts for each boat to the boatyards. I was grateful to have been offered it but it was purely an office job and I just loathed the idea of an office. In vain, Jock cajoled me that it was a valuable contribution and a worthwhile thing to be doing. I knew he could be right just as well as I knew how much I'd hate it, so, sadly, I turned it down.

I thought that was the end of it but, three weeks later he rang me again. The thing was growing at a frightening rate under Macklin's pressure and Carol's drive. They now had 20 cars and 10 lorries of their own, a fleet of dispatch riders on motor-bikes and 200 lorries, from four contractors, ranging from 30 cwt to 15-tonners, on contract. Would I now join the organisation in the capacity of assistant transport manager? This would involve more work in the office at Cobham than outside, but there would be both.

This was on a Friday and I started with the company on the following Monday, touring round the whole organisation with Jock and meeting people to whom I should be speaking every day and all day, on the telephone. At first I spent more time at the various stores and yards than I did in the office but, almost immediately I could see that that was where I was needed and, once I could see that for myself, I didn't mind it.

The thing certainly was gathering momentum at a frightening rate and I had been there for little more than a week when both Jock and I were called to Macklin's office. We suspected the worst and it was the worst, but not in the way we had thought.

Noel looked grave, as he told us what was in his mind. One boat, the prototype, was completed and on builder's trials. The second contract was for ten—'B' Types—and although none of these were completed, they were desperately needed and it was his intention that they would be, at top speed. A third contract which would cover some hundreds, also 'B' Types, was on the way and on top of all that the Admiralty were concerned about invasion and how the Fairmile organisation would cope if that came.

If it did, building would have to continue but, even more important, there must be a constant flow of replacement parts to the naval bases on which the Fairmiles in commission were based. There was to be no mistake about this—a 24-hour service, nothing less. A plan must be drawn up immediately to ensure that, in the event of invasion, this happened. Stores must be dispersed, parts stored in smaller quantities anywhere they could be, even in fields if they were parts that wouldn't deteriorate in the open and it was our task to plan all this, in addition to our normal work, and to let him know as soon as we possibly could, exactly what plans had been made. How soon could this be done? Within a week? A week seemed to be about as long as he liked to wait for anything.

It was done in a week, if you could call it a week for, in terms of hours, it was really a fortnight. At the end of it, the plans were firm and either Jock or I were on call by phone day or night—a 24-hour service—for as long as the war, or we, lasted.

There was always a telephonist on the switchboard in the office and either Jock or I were around or one of us was on call at home. I had no house and it was obviously the wrong time to buy one for one never knew where one was going to be from day to day or what changes were in store so I moved into an hotel in Weybridge where I had a phone by my bedside although, to begin with, there were few night calls because so few boats were in service.

The great rush, at this stage, was to get materials and components to the builders on time—no matter what the cost. And it was the same when the first boats came into service. Sometimes the transport was shockingly wasteful and we pointed this out time and time again, always meeting with the same answer, 'Never mind—get it there'.

There was a ruling, for example, from the design department, that the prop shafts of the boat which were nearly twenty-five feet long, must be carried completely flat and supported along the whole of their length. When the early boats came into service, we sometimes got an urgent request for a single shaft, if one had been damaged in action and it frequently happened that the only available vehicle would be a 15-ton rigid 8-wheeler. Never mind—it had to be got there, so off would go the shaft, weighing 6 cwt on a vehicle capable of carrying another $14\frac{1}{2}$ tons, probably to Scotland at a cost, even then of between £50 and £60. We tried to justify our consciences by adding odd small items to the load, for delivery to builders in the area but the rush was always so great that even this was hardly worthwhile.

There were a number of well-known names within the organisation. Dennis May, the well-known motoring and motor-cycling journalist was in charge of the big store at Brooklands, 'Jumbo' Goddard whose lovely cars now grace the Vintage scene was an outside engineer and Granville Bradshaw of A.B.C. fame was also involved, to name but a few.

As time went on, speed of delivery began to be weighed, first against the use of petrol and diesel which was getting scarcer and, very much later, against cost, although this still seemed less important. And, of course, as the supply position improved, the bases were able to build up a nucleus of spares so that urgent calls should have become less frequent, but they weren't because more and more boats were coming into service.

Some of the loads themselves involved ingenious planning. The keel used to go out in a number of sections on one load, on big 15-ton rigid 8-wheelers, while the frames and bulkheads followed on another, a week or so later. Planking would continue and then would come the marine fittings. The funnel of the 'B' boats was a problem—it measured 12 feet by 6 feet by 4 feet and being light and bulky it didn't want to fit in any load although we tried many different permutations in an endeavour to economise as much as possible in the use of transport. Jock solved this one with the bright idea of wangling two funnels at a time into a 1,000-foot capacity furniture van and it was at this point that we met a wonderful friend.

Gurney Smeed was a gay and dashing member of a well-known family who had gone off on his way to acquire a small transport business. Living in the Southampton area, so Gurney told us, his business had sprung from the big air raids that smothered Southampton in the early part of the war and his first vehicle had been a Ford V-8 shooting-brake and the load—corpses of the previous night's raid from the scene of disaster to the mortuary. But the springs of the V-8 hadn't been up to the loads it was sometimes required to carry so he was compelled to invest in something altogether bigger.

I never saw another furniture van like his throughout the war. It was a rare make—a Reo Speed Wagon—and its cab was beautiful to behold with every possible modern convenience and a dashboard which glittered with dials and chrome. The seats were like a Rolls for comfort and, to drive, it was like a very high-quality car, with performance almost to match. The name of his business was S. Gwilt Ltd but Mr Gwilt had long since departed so Gurney was managing director of the company, driver and booking-clerk in the office. After working for us for a year, he told me one day, with delight, 'You know, Charles, you'll never catch me out with delivery complaints. You'll never find me, you see. There are three chaps in my business—Mr Gwilt, Mr Smeed in the office, and the driver. So if anything goes wrong, you can't win, can you?'

He did wonderful work for us. Runs to Scotland which used to take many drivers a week before we saw them again would take him three days, if the pressure was on. He became known to many of the crews of Fairmile boats at their Naval bases and, if he arrived late there was always something for him to eat and a bunk on board for the night. Like Jock and I, he remained with the organisation throughout.

The 'B' Type Fairmiles had two American Hall Scott twelve-cylinder petrol engines and these we carried crated. They were 9 feet long and nearly 5 feet wide in their crates and since our insurance limit was £20,000, we could carry four at a time on a 15-tonner at their value, apiece, of £5,000. Carried crosswise, they made an impressive load—one felt that one was getting value for money when four Hall Scotts left for Scotland!

When the contract came along for the 'D'-Type boats, the Hall Scotts were replaced by four Packards of identical value and almost the same size, per boat. It was just possible to cram five of these big engines on to a 15-tonner but we weren't allowed to do it because of the insurance ceiling.

I only once took a chance on this and spent three sleepless nights because of it. One of the Scottish yards, Silvers of Roseneath, were shouting for their four Packard engines to complete a boat. The engines were in short supply at that time but a batch had just arrived in the late afternoon and I was frantically searching for a suitable vehicle. Long after everyone had gone home from the office, I was still phoning round in search of a 'big 'un', still without success, when an incoming call arrived from Reg Parnell. Reg, in addition to being a pre-War Brooklands man, was also a haulier, in fact his business, Standard Transport of Derby, was one of the biggest and best.

'Charles, you'll have one of my chaps ringing you in an hour or so. Can you find him a load North in the morning?'

'What has he got, Reg?'

'Fifteen-ton rigid. Double drive. No sides.'

Just the thing.

'Can I get hold of him tonight?'

Reg whistled. 'Doubt it. I'll have a go though. He might be still offloading.'

Ten minutes later, he was back. 'Charles, he's on his way.'

Great. We were in business at last. A phone call to make sure that a loading gang and crane driver would be on hand and then the other phone rang. This time an urgent cry for one Packard and four tail-shafts, from a Naval base very close to Roseneath. It was too good to miss. The engines could be loaded crosswise, on timbers and the shafts slotted in beneath them.

I set off to Brooklands to see it done.

It was just beginning to snow when I left Cobham and by the time I got to Brooklands it was coming down fast—and laying. There was a wait of an hour and a half before the big Foden hove into sight through the gloom and it took about the same time to get the load on. Then I found that the driver didn't know the area at all and had no idea which way he had come to Weybridge and didn't know the route back to London either. At this stage the air-raid sirens started wailing and, partly out of sympathy for the unfortunate driver and partly because I had never before had a ride in the cab of a big diesel, I offered to go with him to town and aim him for the North Circular.

It was a memorable ride. The snow fell steadily and by the time we got to Sunbury, the bombs were falling too. The monster seemed incredibly slow but if you looked aft, out of the cab window, you could see why—the load really was vast. I left him at Chiswick, returning by underground and train—but it was three days before Reg's cheery voice rang to tell me that, despite being snowed up on Shap, he'd made it.

Another encounter with the drivers of the 'heavies' was stranger, almost macabre. My bedside phone rang loudly one mid-winter night. It was two o'clock and the night porter's booming voice informed me that there were 'four gentlemen' waiting in the hall to see me. On arrival I found four of our best drivers waiting for me with the weirdest of stories. Again, there was a big air-raid on London in progress but this time it was raining—teeming, in fact. The chaps told me that they had arrived at their yard, Cliffords of Brentford, after returning in convoy from the West Country, delivering Fairmile supplies. Instead of getting home to their warm beds, they had been met at the yard with top-priority instructions to proceed non-stop to Woolwich Arsenal where they were jointly loaded with nearly 75 tons of high explosive. They said it was chaos down there. There was a scare about the Arsenal being the number one target that night and, having got their loads on, they were given no papers or delivery instructions but told to get the hell out of it and go anywhere they liked—so, as they were under contract to the Fairmile company and had only been impressed for the one night, they thought they ought to come to me 'as you are on your own, Guv'nor, and we didn't want to knock up Mr & Mrs Forbes'.

I pictured, momentarily, the 'pop' there'd be if this lot went up and there seemed to be only one course of action. I got the car out, piloted the convoy down to Wisley Common, where we left it in charge of one man, and then I took the others back to their homes in Brentford and Isleworth before retiring sleepily to bed myself.

But if, at times, life was a bit intense, there were many lighter moments. There was a dance every Saturday night at the Oatlands Park Hotel, where I was resident, and this was always good. The 'pub' was unlicensed but permanent residents were herded into a small room called 'The Snake Pit' and did their drinking round a central table. The walls were lined with numbered lockers in which each resident kept his own bonded store and the official title of this haven was 'The Locker Room'. It really was a haven, for most of the residents were elderly and tended to be brittle and nearly all were terrified of air-raids, so The Snake Pit was the place to be at such times. Although its population was mainly young and middle-aged, there were some in the evening of life and all of these were welcome because they had humour and were, in the main, pretty steady drinkers.

I used to spend quite a bit of time chatting in The Snake Pit, mainly about motor racing, with Sir Thomas Bowen, whose brother, Sir John, had been killed when driving a Maserati at Donnington. Tommy had a number of girl-friends and so had I but I always rather coveted his number-one choice, Jean Summers, elder daughter of Captain 'Mutt' and Mrs Summers. 'Mutt' was a well-known Brooklands personality on the flying side because, for years, he had been chief test pilot for Vickers and, even then, had done more 'first flights' than any other living test pilot, including taking the first Spitfire off the ground on its maiden test flight.

Both Tommy Bowen and Jean were gay and great company although a bit scatty and unreliable, I thought, and when, one night, Tommy failed to turn up for their date in The Snake Pit, I whisked Jean off to dinner only moments after he was overdue. We had a good evening and agreed to do it again and, after doing it pretty regularly for a year or two, we married.

In fact, now I think about it, it was more than a year or two because this first meeting took place in 1940 and we finally tied the knot in October 1945. But Jean made a great difference to my life and so did I to hers. When we first met, she was sixteen and I was twenty-six but let me reassure the reader right away—this isn't going to be one of those 'lived happily ever after' things. Ours has been a tumultuous union, involving a family, a divorce, remarriage to each other and very nearly a second divorce, which actually started and was stayed half way through, I'm glad to say. We're still together today and it's becoming easier!

It wasn't at all a case of 'love at first sight'. We just enjoyed each other's company, and doing things together and, at that stage, seemed well adjusted although our temperaments were, and still are, very different. And we really have both got temperaments!

I was fascinated with the Summers family who were quite different to mine for ours was an orthodox family and they weren't. On one of my first visits for a meal at their house I expressed interest on hearing that they had horses. We were lunching at the time and before we finished that course, the best of the horses was brought in and led round the dining-table for my appraisal.

On arrival at the house on Christmas Day, for a pre-lunch drink, I was staggered and secretly appalled to see Jean's brother, Patrick, who was a very good shot and hadn't had a drink, shoot a hole in an apple, with an airgun. Not, in itself, so startling, had it not been for the fact that the apple was balanced on the head of Jack Firth, a friend of the family and a guest—and he'd had several!

So, later, when my dear mother-in-law to be, Dulce, won a pig by bowling for it at the local fête, I wasn't surprised when she refused to sell it to the local butcher although I did wonder if she was wise to keep it and lodge it with the dogs. She never seemed to doubt it but it did become a problem later for it became a habit to follow her wherever she went and grew to five times the size of their biggest dog before its departure became unavoidable.

My own family, of whom I was very fond, would never have got on with this and my father, who was also an extremely good shot, would, I know, never have visited the house again had he been present on the occasion of the apple-shooting episode.

Right from the start, I got on like a house on fire with Dulce who had, I think, a feeling that, being older, I was a good and restraining influence on Jean. In fact, we were good for each other, I slowing her down at times, while she speeded me up at others.

We didn't get on so well when drinking. We never have. It makes us cranky and cantankerous and brings out the worst in each of us and makes us see flaws in each other's characters which certainly weren't there the day before and somehow aren't there the day after. There had been some hard-drinking schools at Brooklands, when I was racing there and I had always been involved, even in the motor-cycle days. Never before a meeting but always afterwards—and a lot.

There was no less of this during the War years except that supplies were short and, if you were going to have a party, you had to delve into the local underworld to get supplies and, even then, the party had to be small. It never affected the work I was doing, though, for we restricted it to Saturdays but, on Saturdays, we certainly did hit it up sometimes.

Transport was no problem. It boiled down to a push-bike if the party was within a three-mile radius and a taxi if farther away. Jean's bike was a disgrace, red rust, no brakes, no lamps and almost un-roadworthy—the kind of machine which fathers, nowadays, impound if they find a younger member of the family riding it. Mine was the opposite, not new but glittering and a credit, I thought, to its owner.

She nearly got me into serious trouble, one night, with the bikes. We had met Jock and his wife, Vi, at Shepperton, had wined and dined well at one of the pubs in the square and then came the time to go home. The Forbes' were lording it in a taxi but we had biked there and when we were about to leave, it was dusk and I saw that, as usual, Jean had no lights. So, rather gallantly, I gave her my front light and we started back to Weybridge riding side by side so that my machine, on the outside, showed a red rear and hers a white front. We were chatting away merrily and as we reached the Ship at Halli-ford Bend, a policeman stepped out and hailed us to stop. I slowed instantly but with a shout of 'Ride on', Jean rode right round the man and disappeared ahead into the darkness. Feeling I couldn't stop after that, I did the same, whereupon the rosser jumped on his bike and gave chase. Jean had turned her front light off but my red rear was mounted low down where I couldn't reach it without stopping so I just pedalled for dear life. Across Walton Bridge and up Oatlands Avenue I could hear the policeman's laboured breathing getting closer and closer and felt what a fool I was to have got into such a situation. I thought of giving myself up but still kept on, turning off left into Oatlands Drive because there were some big houses there and I felt I might stand a chance by whisking up one of the drives. There was a car approaching in the other direction and he was obviously going to turn over to my side, into one of the drives. I could see he was waiting for me and, as he turned across behind me, I used him as cover and cornered into the drive of the next-door house as I'd never cornered before, crashing into the undergrowth, half falling off the bike and turning off the rear light as I fell.

The relief, as I heard the copper do the same, but into the drive whence the car had gone, was enormous. I listened to the conversation between him and the driver of the car. It continued and I realised he'd given up the chase for he knew the owner of the car and the owner of the car knew him. It must have been half an hour, at least, before I crawled dishevelled out of the shrubbery and pushed my bike, unlit, the rest of the way home. Jean was there, waiting for me—I could have killed her!

One of the best things about the Fairmile job was the encouragement and support we had from both Noel Macklin and Carol in cutting through red tape. There were far fewer people, then, than there are nowadays who revelled in saying 'no, it can't be done'. But there were some and when we came across them it was up to us to show that it could be and was done. A case in point cropped up in the latter part of the war when, late one afternoon, we had an urgent call for a set of propellor shafts from another Naval base in Scotland. Prop shafts were a transport headache throughout the whole period. They seemed to get damaged again and again when the boats were in action and we seemed never to be able to build up a big enough reserve stock at the bases. The rule about only carrying them flat on a vehicle with a platform length of never less than twenty feet made it harder because this usually meant a big diesel and fuel had become desperately short by that time. On this occasion we had no vehicle loading or about to load for Scotland and not enough other material to make up a load with

13. First post-war race: Maserati 4.C., Gransden
Lodge 50-Mile Race.

14. 1949. An 'eerie experience' with the Maserati
6.C., now owned and raced by Ray Fielding.

15. Brands Hatch, 1963—the Racing School. 'Fun, but no fortune.'

16. 1972: Robin Mortimer on a 350 cc. Ducati at Snetterton. 'But good sense prevailed.'

several drops. Jock and I talked it over and he jokingly suggested that the only way would be to load them in the corridor of the 'Night Scot' from Euston to Glasgow and let the Navy collect them there. The more we talked about it the less ridiculous it seemed so we rang up the Stationmaster at Euston who immediately said it couldn't be done. That was a spur, so we then rang the Admiralty Rail Transport Office and asked if this was right. We had a number of good friends there and, this time, we were lucky in getting hold of one who had helped us before. He was young, and disliked people who said things couldn't be done and particularly disliked 'high ups' who said it. He couldn't see any reason why it couldn't be done if the corridor of the leading coach was a straight one and not one of those cranked at the end of the coach to make room for the 'loo'. He felt we could only hope to get it in the leading coach because time was short and we couldn't hope to get the shafts to Euston before the train was backed down to the platform and this would mean that the rearmost vehicle would be against the buffers of the station. There would be at least twenty minutes elapsing between the train being backed into the station and the train locomotive being backed on to it so we stood a reasonable chance of getting the shafts aboard before the engine was coupled. His feeling was that we should somehow get the shafts to Euston and meet him there 'for a bloody good row with "L.M.S. Passenger"'.

It was agreed that I would go, too, and somehow get the shafts to the platform entrance gate where he would be waiting. We arrived at the gate barely fifteen minutes before the 'Night Scot' was due to depart with the shafts loaded on to three luggage trolleys connected in tandem, to find our 'R.T.O.' friend embroiled in a furious row with about half the station staff, including the Stationmaster who we identified by his bowler hat. Amid shouts of discouragement, we by-passed the row and proceeded, past a protesting ticket collector and down the platform to the head of the train. Once there, we found that the train engine had just backed on. Or rather, the engines had—the train was to be double-headed. So now the argument became more involved because two drivers and two firemen were in it as well. But oddly enough, they raised no objections at all to pulling forward to enable us to get down on to the track in order to 'thread' our awkward load into the leading corridor—it was the 'high ups' with their rule books who were kicking. In the end it was done, and thanks to our own staff and the engine crews, the 'Scot' left Euston not a minute late.

There were numerous adventures like this. Every one was a challenge and we were lucky in having friends in the right places.

The motor-cycle fleet that was used for communications between depots was a constant headache. The bikes, side-valve W.D. Nortons, were constantly in trouble but, in the end, we came to the conclusion that the real trouble lay, not in the bikes, but in their riders who were mostly school-leavers filling in time while awaiting their call-up. In the end we solved this one by contracting out the maintenance of the bikes to John Rowland who had a garage in Byfleet and, from then on, things were better.

7

By this time, the War was coming to an end and people were beginning to have thoughts about post-war motoring. I saw quite a lot of John and, when the War finally ended, we joined forces in buying and selling—pre-war cars, of course, because they were the only ones to be had.

But although they were the only ones, we concentrated on the best. Alfas, Bugatti, Bentley, Rolls, Mercedes and even racing cars such as E.R.A. and Alta. Prices had risen but they were still 'give away' compared with prices today.

I was keen to start racing again but there weren't any races. I had bought, from Robin Jackson, the 1½-litre supercharged Alta single seater that I had driven several times before the War and it was with this car that I first started competing in post-war events, mainly hill-climbs, because no circuits were yet open. The Alta was nearly an ideal car for this sort of thing, only bettered, I felt, by a good E.R.A. or hill-climb 'special'. But it was temperamental.

A trouble that mine had, and I noticed one or two other Altas suffered from, was a porous cylinder block. On its worst days, water would leak into the combustion chambers and the hotter the engine became, the worse the leak would be. It became quite a science to get the car warm enough to perform well without getting it warm enough to start a leak from the block. This didn't matter too much in hill-climbs unless one had to do two runs in quick succession. Little could be done about it at the time because spares were in short supply and there were no replacement blocks to be had. And, of course, there were still no races in which to run.

Geoffrey Taylor, the Alta designer, was always in attendance at these meetings, both in the capacity of a competitor and as a ministering angel to owners, like myself, and one item of equipment he always carried was a little round-headed peening hammer with which to slow down the leaks from the various Alta blocks. He was doing this, one day, at Prescott watched by an admiring audience, among whom was an elderly farm labourer who, having watched the operation, expressed the opinion that he knew a better way.

Geoffrey, who really was very good at this leak-stopping business, drew himself up to his full height. 'Really,' he said, 'and how would you do it?'

Scenting a challenge, the old man became secretive. 'I can stop that leak, Guv'nor, if you want me to.'

'Go ahead,' said Geoffrey.

The old chap strolled off across the paddock, returning a few minutes later with a large shovel full of cow dung.

'Open the radiator cap and start her up,' he said.

'You're not going to put that stuff in?'

'Not all of it. About a cupful. That'll do it.'

'Go on then.' And he did. And it cured the leak completely. From then on Geoffrey discarded his peening hammer and at future meetings spent the first half hour of practice looking for cows.

I found that five years away from racing hadn't made me any better at it. I was in the thirties by now and found that I had to work hard to put up times as good as the many young fellows, straight from the forces—names still unknown in motor racing. I never could get up Prescott quickly and never enjoyed competing there. The only thing I did enjoy was the delightful setting and the company of the nice people who ran the meetings—the Bugatti Owners' Club crowd.

The Alta had plenty of steam but the problem was getting it to the road for the car tended to be tail light. It hadn't got a Z.F. differential so the first thing I tried was elimination of the diff completely and the substitution of a solid rear axle but, while this always seemed to work well with the chain-drive Frazer Nash's, the old Alta tended to go straight on at corners however early you started to turn the wheel before a corner. In the end I invested in a pair of twin rear wheels and this did improve it.

By this time, Jean and I had tied the knot. She enjoyed the racing and had her first drive in the Alta at Shelsley, in teeming rain, putting up the fastest time of the day by a lady. I never should have let her do it— she became very keen and enthusiastic about it and rather too good at it so that my constant worry was that, one day, she might put up a better time than mine. I managed to stave this off by nagging her constantly about the awful things that could happen to racing engines if over revved, finally having to over rev the thing myself on most occasions in order not to be disgraced. In the end, the poor old Alta really did take a pasting for Jean's times became the same as mine and I knew that she couldn't be doing it on the revs I was suggesting. When it came, the explosion occurred while she was driving the car— in the Brighton Speed Trials. I would have liked to say 'I told you so' but hadn't the face.

The car had done us well although its history had been chequered and not particularly successful. The worst thing it ever did was to empty its sump all over the track at Donnington before the war, in a race in which all the big Mercedes and Auto Unions were competing so that more famous names glared at each other from ditches on both sides of the road than had ever been seen before in this country. That was during Robin's turn of ownership and, from memory, I think the driver on that occasion was Robin Hanson. We ourselves nearly lost it for good on one occasion. We used to tow it to immediate post-war events on a rigid self-steering bar behind a tender car. This time we had been running in speed trials at Hartlepool where the car had put up fastest time of day and when we were packing up to go home next morning, we thought we spotted a tiny hair crack at one end of the bar. We weren't sure about it and, as it was Sunday morning and no garages with welding equipment were open, we took a chance, backing the towbar with rope so that, if the bar were to break, there would be something to keep the racer with us, or so we hoped. A very stupid thing to do, really, even though it was early in the morning with very little traffic about in the immediate post-war period.

Needless to say, the bar did break—just as we were approaching Stockton on Tees. Fortunately, the rope did its job and the incident ended with minor damage only to both cars. It meant a long haul home on a rope and Jean had never before been towed. The rope was too light and broke five times, finally being so short that instead of appearing as one car towing another, the cortège gave the appearance of being one hybrid eight-wheeler. Rope was another thing unobtainable in those days, particularly on a Sunday!

We replaced the Alta with the nicest racing car I ever owned—the little 1½-litre single-seater supercharged Maserati that Teddy Rayson had raced so successfully at Brooklands before the War. The nicest thing about that car was that it didn't feel like a racing car at all. Most of the racing cars of its period, that I drove, felt like racing cars. By that I mean that they were sprung harshly, powered by units that always seemed to me fierce and harsh and felt as one imagined a racing car of the mid-1930s ought to feel—a rather savage old lot. The Maserati felt more like an extremely high-quality sports car. It was untiring and a thoroughly refined and pleasant car to drive and I loved it. Its only shortcoming was that it wasn't quite fast enough, being slightly slower than the E.R.A.s with which we competed most of the time. It gave me a super run in the first post-war race held in Britain after the War, a fifty-mile thing run by the Cambridge University Automobile Club at Gransden Lodge Aerodrome.

At that time we had a garage in Byfleet and besides buying and selling cars we undertook a certain amount of work for owners of sports and racing cars, among whom were a number of Cambridge undergraduates and it was from this source that we first heard that there was a possibility of a race being held for the first time. We were invited to go up to Gransden, meet Earl Howe, who was to inspect the circuit and take him round for a number of laps in a fast car but, at the time, we hadn't a fast enough car that had two seats. So I got on to George Abecassis whose personal fleet then included the 2-litre supercharged sports Alta that Cowell had raced pre-war. This car was fast. It was identical to the Alta we'd had except that it had a two-seater body and ran on petrol and not on dope and it was agreed that George and I would go up together and give the noble Earl his trip. In the event, we went up in convoy because I had to deliver a 'chain gang' Frazer Nash, on which we had worked, for one of the Cambridge people.

The Earl hadn't arrived when we got there so we did a few laps with the Alta and the circuit seemed good. He arrived in great form, George muttered to me, 'Now we'll frighten the old man, Charlie' and away they went, not for a couple of laps but for about a dozen. When they returned, the 'old man's' face was wreathed in smiles. 'Splendid, Abecassis, nice car. Nothing wrong with this place. Let's do it again as soon as possible.' A wonderful man who would always say 'yes' if it could possibly be done.

Unlike the Alta, on which we had had to work unceasingly at meetings, the Maserati was completely trouble free at Gransden. We got away to a good start, ahead of all the E.R.A.s and stayed in front of them to the end although, to be fair, it should be said that none of them were going as well as they do in Vintage events today. We were immediately swamped by Dennis Poore's big 3·8-litre Grand Prix Alfa, George's 3·3-litre Grand Prix Bugatti, Roy Salvadori's Alfa Monposta and Ken Hutchison's and Tony Rolt's similar cars, but these were all 3-litre cars or more with engines twice the size of ours. One found that, back on a circuit, one had regained lost form and it was Dennis Poore alone who began to disappear in the distance while the others were still in sight. Tony's Alfa went out quite quickly, Ken's wasn't as fast as the others and he and I began a rather nice little scrap with George and Roy disappearing gradually and Poore nowhere in sight. Coming up to half distance Ken's Monposta began to puff out smoke on the approach to the hairpin but, although it didn't seem to alter its speed, I still couldn't get by. The smoke got worse and I felt sure it would go with a bang before long, which it did, very noisily and expensively just after we had both been passed by Leslie Johnson in the big Darracq. So it was 'down one, up one' and we still lay fifth, the leading 1½-litre car in the race. We then fought it out with Leslie until the end and he got it. There was nothing in it between the top speeds of our cars, the Maserati was better under braking, the Darracq had a fraction more poke low down which helped out of the hairpin and I was surprised to find what a good driver Leslie was. Far better than I.

Although none of the E.R.A.s were in sight at the end, one had the feeling that it was only a matter of time before their owners got them going properly and it was at this stage that I made a mistake—I sold the Maserati and bought an E.R.A. This was the Technauto front-suspended car, originally owned by Embericos and subsequently raced at Brooklands and elsewhere by Pollack. It had now passed into George Abecassis' hands and it was from him that I bought it. George had done well with it, its record was quite good and I made the mistake of buying it without trying it beforehand. There was nothing wrong with it. In fact, I think it was probably the best of them all at that time —but, after the Maserati, I detested it. It was faster than the Maserati but, to me it felt a 'kit' car, harsh and with no feeling of quality. I practised a lot with it and, coming to the conclusion that I never would like it, I sold it to George Nixon, never having raced it.

I replaced the E.R.A. with another Maserati, this time a 6.C. independently front-sprung single seater which I bought from Charles Brackenbury, and liked it immediately although it was 'out of breath' when I acquired it and I wasn't able to try it. This particular example was one which had never raced previously in this country, having been brought in after the War. It was slightly different to the others in appearance, having a deeper radiator cowl which gave it more the appearance of the later 4.C.L. It is still being raced today, by Ray Fielding, still looks good, goes well and is better driven than when I had it. I get a fillip every time I see it race.

I had one eerie experience with it. We were running it in some speed trials at Stanmer Park at Brighton and I had practised with it and put it away to await my runs when I was approached by a man and a woman who asked if I would sell it. Instantly, the dealer image arose in me and, on being asked to name a price, I named one that would have suited me very well. To my surprise, two cheques were immediately written out, totalling the price I had named, one by the man, in the name of a firm of motor dealers whom I knew, the other by the lady in question. Then it appeared that they wished to drive the car in the event in which it was running that day and I refused to agree to this until I had cleared both cheques. The man was indignant and named several people present who, he said, would vouch for his integrity and after some discussion, it was agreed that I would talk to Roy Salvadori, one of those named.

Les Wilson, an ex-Thompson & Taylor man and a Maserati expert was looking after the car for me that day and, still feeling slightly doubtful about the thing, I told Les the form saying that, while I was talking to Roy, the purchasers could sit in the car if they wished, but not drive it. I journeyed up the paddock and found Roy who said that he would stand behind the dealer's cheque but not behind the lady's since he didn't know her and, in fact, had never before seen her. He knew the man and knew that he was a member of the staff of the firm whose cheque it was.

At this moment there was a burst of noise and the 6.C. appeared, being driven through the paddock at between 50 and 60 m.p.h. by the gentleman in question, disappearing out of the paddock trailing a string of marker ropes in its wake. Setting off in pursuit, I overtook Les and cursed him roundly as he breathlessly explained that, while he had turned his back for a moment, friends of the parties concerned had pulled the car out and started it. Meanwhile, it was nowhere in sight and I had a horrid feeling it might well be motoring round Brighton itself but, in the end, we did find it with the driver still *in situ*, stalled, among a vast bank of nettles. There were some harsh words and we loaded it into the van and went home.

Before we left, someone took a comic photograph of Les and myself discussing the episode and when I presented the cheques at the bank, next morning, both had been stopped. Then began a long series of acrimonious correspondence involving lawyers which went on for months, during which I had no racing car or enough money to buy one. In the end the deal wasn't completed and I was paid a sum of money mutually agreed by way of compensation, but the season had gone and it was an unhappy experience.

I still had the business at Byfleet and we were selling some lovely cars, all of the best possible types and quality so, for a time, racing receded into the background. At this point, I did a deal with Alastair Baring, also the owner of a 6.C., on an exchange of shares, he acquiring an interest in my car business and I an involvement in his business of home-grown timber.

We were quite busy and I was hardly missing racing but when, one day, Baring offered me a drive in his 2-litre H.W.M. I jumped at it. We had a lot on hand at the time and the car was entered for the Jersey International Road Race. If one of us had to be away for this, it was obviously better for it to be me. But there wasn't much time—the race was on Saturday and it was now Thursday and the car was already in Jersey with its mechanic, Buckle, so I dashed home, collected Jean who was good at lap scoring and we caught the night boat from Southampton. I won't dwell on that crossing but will just record that, on arrival at St Helier, we resolved never to travel on a boat again. We went straight to the garage and met Buckle whose first words were, 'I think you can say that we're over the trouble now.'

'What trouble, Maurie?'

'Oh, didn't you know? H.W.M.s have had an epidemic of losing wheels.'

I didn't know, but it did appear that mods had been made which would cure the bother.

The car was one of the earlier ones with a slightly wider body than the later cars, Alta powered, and pleasant to drive. It gave no trouble in practice and its times were respectable for what it was, an unblown, fairly heavy 2-litre. There was a strong entry for the race, Chiron, De Graffenried, Rolt, Parnell and Duncan Hamilton on Maseratis, Whitehead's Ferrari, Gerard, Shawe Taylor, Graham Whitehead, 'Cuth' Harrison and Joe Ashmore on E.R.A.s, Brooke's Special, Branca's Simca among them, while ours was the only H.W.M.

At the start, we were immediately behind Duncan's 6.C. and, at the fall of the flag, his rear wheels disappeared in a cloud of smoke and the car crabbed sideways, clobbering Merrick's Cooper with lumps of hub cap and rubber flying in all directions. The faster blown cars pulled away noticeably on the long run along the sea front but the H.W.M. brakes were super and we were among the pack again as we bunched for the hairpin turn-off to the right, back into the return run through the town itself. Duncan's driving was, I thought, lurid. The 6.C. wasn't fast and only had it over the H.W.M. out of the slower bends but its driver was giving it everything and one felt it couldn't go on for long. And it didn't. After about five laps of the nose-to-tail business, the Maserati spun a complete circle and for an awful moment I felt sure we were in it, too. But somehow we got through, by luck, and it was the last I saw of him.

From then on it was an unexciting but enjoyable race, enjoyable because the car was nice to drive and one got a good view of all that was going on, knowing that there was no chance of scoring and hoping that there would be a high retirement rate. Peter Whitehead's Ferrari won, followed home by Reg and De Graffenried in their 4.CLT Maseratis with Gerard's E.R.A. fourth, while we finished tenth behind Joe Ashmore's E.R.A. The principal entertainment came from De Graffenried whose car was throwing out oil so badly that, by half distance both it and its driver were black with the stuff. Even so, he went well, passing the H.W.M. at half distance and again, just before the end. The first time he came by, my goggles and the screen of the car became covered in oil from the Maser but, on the second occasion there was less so that one felt the sump must have emptied its contents by that stage. Saying his party piece at the prize-giving, with typical 'De Graf' humour, he quipped, 'I must congratulate my friend Peter Whitehead on his win. As for me—a leetle too much oil.'

My business associate, Baring, tended to change his cars rather frequently. The H.W.M. had replaced the ex-Rayson Maserati which I sold him and now, in turn, it was replaced by a Silverstone Healey, one of the original works cars that had been driven by Tony Rolt. Then he decided that the Frazer Nash was a better proposition so that, when the Healey became redundant, I bought it.

It gave us a super season of racing in sports car events, cheap, trouble free and fun to drive on the road. We got to know it well and were often able to give faster cars quite a run for their money. Up to the time of its first birthday, the Production Car Race at the Silverstone *Daily Express* Trophy Meeting in August 1950, no other Healey Silverstone had headed it in any race in which we'd run. This time, the works were running just one Healey, instead of the full team of three that they'd put out for the 1949 race so we did expect that it would be the fastest Silverstone we'd come up against, particularly as Duncan was going to drive it. At the end of the first day's practice, the X.K. 120 Jaguars of Tony Rolt and Peter Walker had put up fastest practice times at 81·24 m.p.h. while Duncan's and our own Healey tied for second fastest at 79·38 m.p.h. Reg was the fastest of the Aston Martins at 77 m.p.h. and Cuth Harrison did the same with the fastest of the big Allards. At the end of the second day, we had dropped to fifth fastest at 79·99 m.p.h. pipped by Duncan at just over 80 m.p.h.

Duncan won the class, for over 3-litre, at 79·22 m.p.h. followed by Raymond Somner, Reg and Eric Thompson, all on Aston Martin works cars with our privately owned car fifth. Then we went on to the Tourist Trophy in Northern Ireland.

Apart from routine service of the sort that any road car is entitled to, nothing was done to the car prior to the race apart from renewing the brake linings and, as things turned out, it would have been better if we hadn't done that, for the wrong lining was fitted and we had constant trouble throughout practice and in the race finally finished fourteenth overall and seventh in the class—the wettest and most miserable race we could recall.

It even began badly, when I was called to control during the first practice session and shown my medical form. It had been filled in by my doctor at home and in reply to the question 'Does the applicant suffer from giddiness or fits' he'd replied 'Yes'. So I was asked to undergo another medical then and there. This took place after I'd just come in from practice and the first thing I had to do was to stand with eyes closed, arms stretched out in front horizontally and one leg out in front. I was wearing plimsolls on soft grass, was a bit tired and swayed dangerously so was asked to do the thing that evening at the hospital in Belfast, where I made it without trouble.

We were sorry to see the old Healey go. It had done us well and Jean now held the Ladies' Lap Record at Goodwood with it at a speed slightly higher than I'd managed. We were now rather involved with a family and decided that the time for racing had passed. I wasn't enjoying the timber business and I got out of this and the garage at

171

Byfleet to go and help Robin Richards and an old school friend of mine, Dick Carr, in their car sales business in town. I'd first met Robin at the T.T. because Donald Healey had written to me saying that they wanted to field a works' team for the T.T. and would like me to be in it and Robin turned out to be one of my co-drivers. Jean's younger sister, Anne, had come with us for the trip. She wasn't too interested in the race but loved horses and we sold her the idea that Ireland was filled with horses. In fact, we didn't see many, but Anne and Robin got on well and subsequently married and still live nearby.

The early days at Richards & Carr were great fun. We were trading from a hole in the wall in Kinnerton Street and every deal was different and exciting but the bigger we got, the less variety there was and, by the time we expanded into fairly sumptuous showrooms in Sloane Street nearly all the fun had gone out of it and been replaced by worry.

We were, all three, diverse characters and although there wasn't friction, there wasn't always agreement or even harmony. The new car sales business was worrying at that time and this had a lot to do with it. I remember talking one day to Edward Mills of Knightsbridge Motors after seeing him and his partner, John Fuelling, stumping round Belgrave Square engaged in animated, even acrimonious conversation. I didn't stop—it seemed the wrong moment—but I mentioned it later. 'Yes', said Edward. 'That's right. We were having a bit of a barney. We always go out for a walk when that happens because when emotions arise you burn up your supply of adrenalin and that can only be replaced by exercise. Besides, it doesn't disturb the customers.' I told Dick and Robin about this—it seemed a good idea—but they preferred to thrash things out in the office and quite a lot of time was spent doing it.

But there were lighter moments. Dick was good company and Robin could be really amusing. One day, when Dick was out buying, I was in the showroom and Robin was at work in the office at the back. A customer came in, a man of around fifty or so, and seemed interested in what we had and I became hopeful of making a sale. Robin appeared and handed me a scrap of paper carefully folded.

'Sorry to disturb you, Charles. Could you just cast your eye over that?'

I opened it and on it was written, 'Elderly Nut Case. Has fits and calls in here when he feels one imminent. Waste of time. Get him out

172

if you can.' There was a postscript, 'Prelude to his particular variety of fit is rubbing his forehead. *Push* him out if you see this.'

Within two minutes the forehead-rubbing started, followed, immediately, by the fit. The man lay on the ground and Robin emerged from the office staring down at him unsympathetically. He turned to me, 'Pity I didn't notice him sooner.'

'What do we do now?'

'Don't know, really. On the other hand, perhaps I do.' He walked to the front of the showroom and out on to the pavement, stopping the first passer-by.

'Excuse me, sir. Have you seen a man having a fit?'

As well he might, the passer-by seemed astonished but admitted that he hadn't.

'Well do come in. We've got one here.'

Against his better judgement the chap came in and within minutes Robin had gathered up an admiring gallery of people who were seeing a man in a fit for the first time. Inevitably someone among them knew what to do but when the sufferer woke up he was confronted by a far bigger gallery of gapers than he'd ever had before and never again visited us for that purpose.

8

Trading became more difficult. Our best clients liked to buy and sell their cars on the way home from the office and this meant late evenings. Robin was good at this, but I wasn't, although I did it if it was essential. And to cap it all, I realised that something was wrong between Jean and I although I didn't know what it was and, somehow, couldn't find out because we seemed not to be able to communicate as we once had. It was now 1962, our older boy, Charles, was thirteen, Robin was ten and our daughter, Philippa, three. Had I known it, I was at the threshold of a very unhappy time.

There was someone else in Jean's life. Someone whom she wanted to marry but who was already married and, in any case, she still had feelings of affection, but not of love, for me and her feelings for the children were unchanged. My feelings for her were quite unchanged, even when I heard this. She told me who the other person was and I knew him and doubted whether they would be happy together. I confided in close friends and got conflicting advice, sincerely given, in every case. I just didn't know what course to take but I did know that I couldn't go on working in London for separation seemed inevitable and I wanted her to agree to let the children stay with me because I sincerely felt that that was where they should be.

There wasn't much acrimony except when we tried to solve the problem over drinks and we finally arrived at a sort of stop-gap formula. I would leave Richards & Carr, Jean would leave me. The children would stay with me and the door would always be open to her to visit or, as I hoped, to return one day. My dear mother-in-law, Dulce, somehow managed to steer a discreet middle course and came to live with me and help me until a nanny and some domestic help could be found. Having done this for us, Dulce moved back to her house, half a mile away and we saw each other on most days. She was absolutely wonderful and still is, thank God.

After a month or two completely apart, Jean began visiting home to see the children and I was happy to notice that she nearly always sought me out, too. Our meetings were sometimes difficult—she was torn between her lover and her children and we next agreed that, if they wanted to, the boys could visit her where she lived but that Pippa would still stay at home. At least we seemed able to agree about things like this.

I was, I suppose, stopped dead in my tracks by all this but, after a time I began to think about what I was going to do businesswise. Dulce suggested a holiday, saying she would stay at home in control for me and I opted for the Isle of Man in September, taking Charles with me to see the Manx Grand Prix. I'd always loved the Island when we competed there in the 1930s and although I realised I wouldn't know anyone competing, I would see places and, possibly some Manx people I hadn't seen for nearly twenty-five years.

It turned out to be a good choice for not only did I meet a lot of old friends, residents of the Island, I met one or two connected with the races against whom I'd raced in my day, among them Francis Beart whose bikes were being ridden by Norton star Joe Dunphy. For the first time in months I forgot the mess at home, decided to become somehow involved in motor-cycle racing again and began to feel better, particularly because, when I got back, Jean and I agreed that, if she would mark time for a year on the subject of remarriage, I would agree to divorce if she still wanted it. I hoped very much that by that time she might not feel the same.

I returned home feeling much better and within a week paid Francis a visit. We had a lot to talk about, not having seen each other for years and, on top of it all, Joe had ridden his Senior bike to victory in the Manx and, having seen it happen, I felt not completely out of touch.

I congratulated Francis on his Manx win and we mulled over the race together. Even before I left the Island to return home, I knew what I was going to do and had told him the rough outline which was that I wanted to get two good bikes, the best to be had, makes and capacities to be decided by him and both machines to be maintained by him. I aimed to sponsor a rider, recommended by him or selected by myself. His answer, in the Island, was that we could go into the questions of machinery when we got home but that quite a lot could be done about a rider while we were in the Island. He could make suggestions, but why didn't I get out on the circuit myself, during

17. 1968: Charles (Jnr). 5th Lightweight Manx Grand
Prix (Beart Aermacchi).

18. (*above*) 'Favourite of them all.' LMU 576, ex
'H.I.' 1947 Bentley H. J. Mulliner Lightweight.

19. 'Double Six' Daimler by Corsica. 'Something
of a setback.'

20. 1973: Back to Brooklands with the Society, forty years later. *Left to right:* H. Nash (New Imperial), Francis Beart, J. King (owner and restorer of the 498 cc. Bickell-J.A.P.) and the author.

practice, study form and try to make a selection myself? I didn't feel qualified to do this after so long a lapse but he pushed me into it, giving me a list of riders who were already sponsored which was a very short list, and left me a wide choice.

At first I just watched, feeling a bit confused and far from able, even, to remember any one rider on two consecutive laps. I wasn't helped by the fact that all this had to take place around six o'clock in the morning which is the time that Manx practice takes place. But soon I found I noticed the better chaps and started to make a 'short' list of possibles and by the end of the week I'd narrowed it down to one, a young man called Griff Jenkins who, it seemed to me, really could ride if he were better mounted.

I took all this paper work with me when I went to see Francis at his home. We discussed the machinery first and I asked whether I would be able to get 350 cc. and 500 cc. bikes identical to his and, if so, what would be the cost. I felt that the answer to this would be 'no', imagining that inside his engines there would be 'Beart specialities' that he wouldn't want to share.

'Same as mine. Umm, I don't see why not, Charles. No problem in setting up something identical to these. No guarantee, either, that it would go as well.'

'Why not?'

'Well you can't guarantee it. These two were always good even before I worked on them. You could buy the same. They might not go as well. They might go better. No two are the same however careful you are in setting them up or however much alike they look.'

'All right then, what would it cost?'

'About £500 for each bike; £500 spent on each. But I must tell you one thing. If you're going to do both short circuits, Brands Hatch, Silverstone, Mallory and road races like the T.T., the Manx and the Ulster, you must have two bikes for each class, one for short circuits and one for road-races. Many people do it with one but they seldom achieve much.'

'What makes?'

'Five hundred Norton, three-fifty A.J.S. The smaller Norton's a bit unpredictable.'

'Can we get them, spend £250 on each, test them and think again?'

'Yes. Quite a good way to do it. If we were lucky we might not have to spend much more.'

M 177

'Now, about the rider. What d'you know about him?' and I handed him my bit of paper.

'Oh yes. I know him. Friend of Joe's. Not bad at all. Nice chap to have around. One must consider that—you have to spend a lot of time with 'em.'

'Good, then we sign him, if he will.'

'No we don't. We find out what contracts he has with suppliers. They may not fit in. I'm with Shell and I hope you will be. If Jenkins is, too, then we can talk to him. But I'll have a word on the phone with Lew Ellis of Shell. He'll know.' And that was it.

I still couldn't see how all this could be applied businesswise although I wanted it to be in the end. In fact, that part followed logically. We tested the first machine in March 1963, or rather Joe did because he knew Francis' bikes and they wanted a direct comparison. The test was of the short-circuit A.J.S. and Joe felt that it was quite good but not as quick as Francis'. The following week we tried the road-racing 500 and Joe's reaction was that it was the quickest 500 Norton he'd ridden, faster, he thought, than the bike with which he'd won the Manx— but he didn't like the front brake which was standard Manx Norton.

'How much for a front brake like yours, Francis?'

'Three figures, I'm afraid.'

I asked Joe if he could live with the brake and he said he could but in such a way that one felt the ship was being spoiled for a 'happorth of tar' if you can call £100 that. So we had the brake and time and time again it saved our bacon—it was vital.

This 500 was a brand new bike which I bought from Harold Daniell—a standard Manx, worked on by Francis. We rehashed Griff's own 500 for the circuits and got another A.J.S. 7R. for the big races— a beautifully kept bike that had done only three races. It was indistinguishable from new in appearance but, despite Francis' hard work, it proved to be 'one of those'—it never had that final edge. One felt that it wouldn't have mattered if it hadn't looked so nice and sounded so good.

With four bikes to get right, we did an awful lot of testing in March and April 1963, most of it at Brands Hatch, and it was on one of these days that the next piece of the jigsaw fell into place. We were testing the short-circuit 500. It was a general practice day and all and sundry were out there and our bike was by far the fastest of anything running. Griff came in after a ten-lap session saying, 'Really, it's about time

178

someone showed those chaps how to do it. Why don't you start a racing school?' Till then one had thought only of allying the bike racing to sales but this idea was better. I spoke to Francis who agreed but felt we'd have to choose the bikes carefully. They ought to be two strokes because the boys would get the valves of a four-stroke tangled by over revving it, and they had to be light because they would be constantly 'dropped' and when a heavy bike prangs, it damages itself more than a light one. In the end the selection fell upon Greeves, the well-known makers of scrambles machinery, who had just announced a very ingenious little 250 cc. production racer which they called the 'Silverstone'. Francis knew them and was, in any case, going to run a Silverstone which Joe was to ride and, together we went down to Thundersley to put the plan before them.

I reckon the Greeves organisation must be pretty well unique. Bert Greeves was at one time an important cog in the Ford organisation at Dagenham. A relative of his, Derry Preston Cobb, had been an invalid from birth, consigned to a wheelchair which Bert thought ill designed so, off his own bat, he designed and made for Derry his conception of what an invalid chair should be. The result of this was that Bert's prototype literally brought Derry to life for it was well-powered and got him around as he'd never been around before. The design was clever. Derry never left the unpowered wheelchair which took him around indoors. The powered version stood outside in the drive, its tailboard down so that Derry could be pushed up into it, still in his unpowered plot, an aide would lift and secure the tailboard and from then on the intrepid pilot was in control even though the only mobile parts of Derry consist of his hands and fingers. Every control fell literally to hand and in his 'special' Derry began to take trips farther and farther afield, finally joining the Greeves organisation which had, by this time, secured Government contracts for similar vehicles for the disabled.

They both worked tirelessly, both have fantastic brains and enthusiasm and, since both thought on similar lines the manufacture of a sporting type of motor-cycle was the next thing to emerge from the fountain's head. Derry felt he could help in the testing of the engine so the one in his wheelchair was replaced by the prototype engine of the scrambles bike and this, of course, 'upped' the top speed by some 30 m.p.h. He is one of the most fearless men I've known and, of course, it was inevitable that some nasty 'prangs' would follow. Not always his fault, though. Not always the result of intrepid cornering under power. There was the nasty one on the Southend Bypass when the motor locked up between 60 and 70 m.p.h., hurling the 'tester' through a hawthorn hedge and on into a ploughed field where he remained, upside down until found some hours later by an astonished farm labourer. And there was the fire. On this occasion a fuel consumption test was being combined with a long hard test of the engine and Derry was sitting *in situ* at his local filling station as the tank was being refilled after the run. It must have been quite a run for, suddenly, the whole thing burst into flames. Not knowing how to extract the pilot, the forecourt attendant did the only thing possible—he emptied two gallons of foam extinguisher over the lot. Apart from being coated with virgin white from head to foot, the driver was unhurt and quite unperturbed, his only request being that a call should be put through to the works requesting a lorry being sent to get him back. The call caused a lot of anxiety among everyone at the works—Derry is very much loved and admired there—and his return was awaited anxiously by a large group of friends and employees.

As the lorry approached the works, the 'Tester' was seen to be waving cheerily from his high perch and a loud cheer went up accompanied by one employee's greeting, 'Crikey, the Fairy Snowman!' There have been many similar adventures and it's no wonder that he is so much held in esteem.

By the time we came on the scene, the racing engine had already done much road work in Derry's 'special', to which it gave a top speed of nearly 80 m.p.h. so that everyone was trying to snatch it back from him lest a worse disaster should befall. Both Bert and he liked the School idea and it was agreed we would start with four bikes, providing we could make the necessary arrangements for tracks and ensure that there would be a flow of customers. In the end, it was agreed that we would call the thing the 'Beart-Mortimer Training School' and that the bikes would be Francis' headache and the organisation mine.

I drafted a small advertisement and had it inserted in one of the motor-cycle papers under a box number. It read to the effect that the owner of a 250 cc. racing machine would be willing to hire it out for practice on circuits and would anyone interested please get in touch. Hundreds did, so we then knew the customers were there. Then I tackled the question of circuits.

The first two that we approached turned us down. They were nervous of the idea and so were we, slightly. It was Brands Hatch we particularly wanted and, with that in mind, we got the reaction of other circuit proprietors first. We didn't want to be turned down at Brands. We decided to think about this carefully before going further with circuits and switched to the question of insurance. This, too, was a headache, but not as bad and, fairly soon, we solved it. Then we made a stealthy approach to Brands, asking if there was a possibility of a day a week or even fortnightly when we could have the circuit to test out riders. The answer was a polite 'No' and they had good reasons—it was fully and solidly booked apart from maintenance days when it wasn't usable anyway. So we decided to be even stealthier and do it, uninvited, on their open practice days.

Francis and I had talked about the actual running of the thing. A charge of 10s (or 50p!) per lap was to be made, and we sat back complacently totting up the fortune we should make; 50p every time a machine passed us standing on the trackside! Ten laps—£5. Ten machines at the same time, £50. That was just one ten-lap session! We would be millionaires!

The snag to that turned out to be that in order to train one novice rider you need eyes in the back of your head, wits like a spiv, an ability such as few people possess to spot a disaster before it actually happens besides knowledge of motor-cycles and racing technique. We found that on a public day we needed one person per rider out on the circuit at any one time with an absolute minimum of three people at the trackside for four riders in action. You had to have, first, a lap scorer and timekeeper which was me. A mechanic to minister to the machinery. An instructing rider to lead them round, behind whom they had to stay and, if possible, a fourth man to give signals and messages to both the instructor and pupils via a blackboard.

For a time, I did combine all these functions, running the School single handed and twice weekly. It was slavery. We ran it at Brands on Wednesday and Saturday, so my week went something like this.

Monday: Clean all four bikes and repair ravages of previous Saturday.
Tuesday: Office day. Send out ahead notification to customers of when and at what track they would be having their next training session. Answer inquiries. Send out prospectus. Keep in touch with the Press. Make bookings for tracks ahead. Load machines and all gear for Wednesday session.

181

Wednesday: Leave home at 5 a.m. Brands 6.30 a.m. Unload bikes. Fill with fuel. Sign on customers. Get them kitted out (we hired them their gear, crash-hats, leathers, etc.). Brief them. Start all four bikes, etc., etc., etc.

Thursday: Clean bikes. Repair ravages.

Friday: Load up again. Visit to Francis at Guildford with badly damaged parts from previous week. Decide whether to repair or whether to re-order.

Saturday: As Wednesday.

By this time, nearly everyone liked us. They were good to us at Brands, we were steady revenue for them and, seeing this, the other circuits decided that they liked us, too, and invited us to come and 'let's have another talk'.

I was helped by Griff who did all the instructing in the early stages and by my older boy, Charles, during his holidays. It couldn't have been much fun for either of them but Griff was very good to do it and, even then, I think Charles really did enjoy it.

So, into this pattern, we had to fit our own racing. Griff, and his brother Alf, looked after the race bikes and very well they did it. Alf was extremely good at it and the bikes always looked good and went well. Griff rode exactly as I had always hoped he would and we began to win things almost every time we went out. We asked for and were given start-money at several tracks. It was great—but very hard work for us all.

We had set-backs. Griff's only fault, if you could call it a fault, was that he was far too anxious to please me and this became really frightening because the bikes were quick for their day and he began to ride them like a man possessed so that, while I felt sure a horrid accident was just round the corner, he couldn't see it—nothing was impossible, he felt. The crunch came at the first Brands Hatch International meeting in which we took part.

We had planned to run the A.J.S. and the Norton at the International Meeting at Brands on Whit Monday but, just before the entries went in, Griff phoned me to ask whether we could also get ready a 250 cc. Greeves—one of the training school bikes—for the small-bike race. This didn't seem a good idea—it was an international meeting and all the 'hard' characters were likely to be competing and the Greeves was nothing more than a production racer, not the sort of bike that would like the treatment it would have to have in order to remain even remotely in the picture. But he felt it would be a good advertisement for the School if our customers could see just what could be done with one of the bikes they actually rode themselves and, in the end, we entered it. But I felt sure it couldn't last the distance under the treatment it would get.

I got to Brands a bit late that morning for there was a big crowd and a mammoth traffic jam at the approaches. Practice had finished but I saw Griff and brother Alf and was told that the Greeves and the A.J.S. had put up fastest times in their classes at 1 minute 58·4 seconds and 1 minute 54·2 seconds respectively. The 500 had been a reluctant starter and had gone round in 1 minute 50·8 seconds so, since starting positions were based on practice times, we would be on the front row with the smaller two and in the second row with the 'big 'un' although they felt more confident of pulling this one off than either of the others.

Fifth at the end of the first lap, on the 350, he went up into second place at the end of lap two and led, third time round. The lead increased, from Peter Preston, and was 3 seconds at the end of the fifth, to nearly 15 seconds by the twelfth lap, at which point we slowed him, and we won our first 'International' by a comfortable five seconds.

I saw them both, in the paddock, after that race and, again, just before the 250 event. Griff was then in the starting-paddock, warming up the bike, and Alf said, 'He's got the idea, now, that he can win all three.'

'Has he, Alf. Well tell him "no". It's absurd. That isn't a winning bike and he can't win on it or even finish at anything like winning speed. To finish in the first eight would be fine or among the first six, even better. He'll hurt himself or break it if he tries anything else.'

'O.K. I'll tell him.'

'Yes, do. And make it strong.' He promised he would.

I was late in going up to the start and the race started just as I emerged from the tunnel from the paddock on to the infield. Griff was in the lead—by half a wheel—and I watched them round Paddock Bend. Seeing it, my feeling was 'That can't be done a second time'. I'd never seen anyone go round Paddock so nearly on the ragged edge. I stood for a minute, watching them disappear, the Greeves still leading and, instead of going to the pits, began strolling down the hill to the bottom of Paddock because I felt sure that that was where it would end and I would then be on hand to pick up the pieces. Then I thought, 'If he's like it round here, he's like it everywhere else. This accident can happen anywhere on the circuit', and I stopped, wondering whether he would be still in it second time round. Yes, and still by half a wheel.

I watched it again, marvelling that it could be done, even twice, wondering how many times he could get away with it. Lap three provided the quick answer and I was running down the hill even before they'd started rounding the bend. Griff didn't depart from the bike at the bottom of Paddock—he was already leaving it at the entrance. Half way round, the bike was on the floor and bits of it were flying in all directions. It all ended in a cloud of dust, on the opposite side of the track to where I stood. I saw that there were willing hands, Alf among them, saw Griff lifted over the railings to Alf, which he wouldn't have been if he'd been badly hurt, and made my way back to the paddock. There, I purposely kept out of the picture—it seemed to be the best thing.

Presently, Alf sought me out. 'I don't know what you'll think. He still wants to ride the five hundred.' I didn't know what I thought, either, but one had to admire him.

'D'you think he wants to, Alf, or feels that he ought to?'

'No. He really does want to, he feels he can do justice to it.'

'Well, if he feels that, he'd better. But forget "doing justice to it". Just have a nice steady ride and get back into the groove a bit.'

That 'nice steady ride' was the most ragged that Griff ever rode for me but it was also the gamest. He must have felt like doing anything except race a motor-bike. Fourth at the end of the first lap, third on the fifth, second and on Peter Preston's tail at the end of the sixth. Then a moment, when he got on the grass at Bottom Hill Bend, dropping him to sixth again. But he fought back and, in the end, finished fourth. He was a very game chap.

From then on, we had a lot of fun and it was intriguing to see how the scene had altered from that of the 1930s. Everything had changed— circuits, machines, personalities, procedure—literally everything.

If one had to name one thing that had changed less than another, one would have said the trade 'barons', and then, I think, the machines themselves. The trade reps were like their pre-war counterparts, always enthusiastic and helpful, and still had the same problem of keeping their riders happy on tight budgets. To me, Lew Ellis of Shell was very much like Reg Tanner whose Esso fuel I had used at Brook-lands in the 1930s. There was always the same amicable pantomime at the start of each season when, not even having talked to any other fuel company, one inferred to Lew that stupendous rival offers had come one's way and that, if one was going to stay with Shell, things would have to be very different from now on. It was never true and Lew knew it, knowing also exactly what his rivals were offering, who they wanted, and how they would ensure getting them. But, to his credit, Lew played it along, pretending to be very impressed with it all and, finally increasing the finance minimally, which was all that you hoped for. Perhaps you did hope for more, but you knew you wouldn't get it—there were too many good bikes and riders around.

Lew was very good to us and as generous as he could afford to be both with the racing itself and in the support given to the racing school, by Shell. He was always friendly, hard when he had to be but always helpful. And so were all the trade people with whom we were in league, notably Avon and Ferodo.

One saw little of this in the attitude of some of the race organisers. Perhaps nothing is to be gained by going farther down this road. Every meeting was oversubscribed, from the entry point of view and the organisers were in a strong position. But one sometimes wondered why one bothered to bring several thousand pounds worth of highly tuned machinery in return for peanuts, when it was tacitly inferred that one was fortunate to be allowed to do so and even more favoured in being allowed to stand at the trackside in half a gale and pouring rain before going home to pay the bills. Two exceptions still stand out. We always got a nice reception from Bob Havers at Snetterton and from Charles Wilkinson at Cadwell. In the years that followed, I never failed to leave Cadwell without thinking what nice people ran it and we enjoyed racing and running the Racing School there in a way that we never enjoyed elsewhere. There is no doubt at all, in my own mind, that private ownership has something to do with it.

The machinery had altered less in character than it had in appearance. From time to time, when Griff had done his stuff, I used to climb aboard the A.J.S. or the bigger Norton and enjoy a short canter on one of the runways and, apart from the obvious improvement in brakes and suspension both felt very little different to the bikes we had raced in the mid-1930s. They were a lot faster but didn't feel it partly, I think, because they were rather more flexible but also, when I was aboard, because they were carrying more weight! There was still the nice slogging old single-cylinder engine and still the pleasing change of exhaust note on the over-run. No, they didn't seem to have changed much in those conditions but the change would quickly be seen when they were being motored 'in anger'.

The riders were different. As a group, they were younger than the chaps one had raced against at Brooklands where I, myself, had been one of the youngest. And they were a different generation, of course. At first I didn't feel completely at home with them. They were always friendly and helpful but I had been a bit of a recluse for some time and it took me a little time to get used to the jargon. If you had ridden well, you were 'chuffed' and if not, you were 'choked'. If, in my day, the machine had performed well, we would have said that it was 'cracking'. Now it was said to be 'flying', which was more descriptive, really. A dangerous rider at Brooklands was described as a 'Menace'. At Brands Hatch, he would be a 'nutter'. But I soon got with it and, today, having had two boys of my own through the same age bracket, I would be with it at once. I liked the definition once given to me by a rider of mine, concerning another rider who was generally agreed to be really dangerous. 'He's an accident looking for a place to happen.'

The two most changed things were the race procedure and the circuits themselves. At Brooklands, for instance, the Scrutineers visited the competitor in his paddock bay, and provided one was *in situ* by ten o'clock no other action was needed. Thirty years interim had changed all this and it was a bit of a shock to find that not only had one to be at the circuit by eight o'clock on the morning of race day, but that the competitor had to go to Mahomet. Not only that, but he had to queue to do so, often waiting for half an hour or more in pouring rain or shrieking wind.

I didn't think much of this arrangement but accepted it as gracefully as I could, partly because everyone else did, never having known any other way of doing it. And, anyway, one realised that, to some extent, it was necessary because of the enormous entries.

I found that, at every circuit, the Scrutineers were good chaps and much more in the Brooklands tradition than anyone else. The vast entry lists presented them with appalling problems and one couldn't fail to be impressed with their skill and patience.

But the same thing didn't apply to some of the minor officials. Sporting an 'Entrant's' Pass at one of our first Brands Hatch meetings I was stopped abruptly by an exceedingly large gentleman who told me that my pass didn't permit me to go through the tunnel and down to the start of a race in which we were running. Shoals of others wearing the same pass were streaming through the tunnel and, presumably, were known to him but, when I pointed out that besides being an entrant, I was also a sponsor, I got the reply, 'Oh, that's nothing, we've got plenty of sponsors.' It was the first of a number of things that made me wish I hadn't bothered and one of a number that finally decided me to pack it in.

I think, really, that this was one of the principal differences between racing at Brooklands in the 1930s and racing on the short circuits, particularly in the South, in the 1960s. Nobody was rude at Brooklands but quite a few people were at Brands and one soon learned to cultivate a rude veneer in order to get what one wanted and where one wanted to go. It was difficult, at first, but became easier when one discovered that, with a few officials the ruder one was, the more one got what one wanted. In the end, when they discovered that one could be rude, there was no more bother.

Lest it be thought that I am denigrating the short circuits in the South, I must say that I very much doubt whether the track proprietors themselves were ever aware of this and in any case, it wasn't a problem sufficiently big to bring to their notice, being easily dealt with in the manner described. All the permanent staff at every circuit leant over backwards to be helpful on race days and even more so when we were running the School. They became great friends without whose help life would, at times, have been difficult.

The 1963 season was good and enjoyable for our equipe on the short circuits and we notched up successes almost everywhere we went, up and down the country. I wouldn't suggest that we always won or even that we were always in the first three but we did have wins and plenty of places and we were always there or thereabouts. The bikes were good, Griff rode them better and better as the season wore on and our organisation was all right as well.

We looked forward to returning to the Island, for the Manx Grand Prix, in September. Since it was the 500 that Griff really enjoyed riding, Francis felt that it would be a good idea to run the bike in one race prior to the Manx in case, being a brand new bike, it decided to play any tricks. The obvious race was the Ulster, a very tough nut, in which all the big boys would be running and, in the end, it was decided that Joe Dunphy would ride it, instead of Francis' own bike for, besides being a first-class runner, Joe was skilled in diagnosis and the setting-up of a bike. We did this and he finished eighth in the 500 cc. class—a good result in extremely tough company.

The Isle of Man, that September, was a busy place for Francis and his right-hand-man, Phil Kettle, for in addition to looking after our Junior and Senior bikes, Francis had four entries of his own, Peter Darvill and Jimmy Guthrie, son of the famous Jimmy Guthrie, in both races. But although a lot of hard work went on during the week of practice preceding the race, troubles were few, because the machinery had been so well put together beforehand.

The Junior race was a good start to the week, Peter winning at a record average of 92·48 m.p.h. Griff was sixth on my 7R at 89·78 m.p.h. and Jimmy had been well placed until brake trouble dropped him down to finish twentieth. But good as it was, the race wasn't a patch on the Senior.

All three runners had gone well in practice and when the day came we did feel that our chances of good placing were promising. The Island, of course, is not the place for a massed start. Competitors start in pairs at ten-second intervals and when the starting-positions were out we found that Peter and Griff had been allocated consecutive numbers, 58 and 59, while Jimmy was a later starter—number 98.

But although these two had consecutive numbers, they weren't paired, Peter being due to leave the line ten seconds before us. It did mean, though, that we had adjoining pits and this was great for me because, after nearly thirty years' absence, my pit lore was rusty by modern standards and I could draw confidence from being able to talk with Francis who was doing Peter's pit.

No book is more boring than the one which continually chronicles race result after race result and up to now, I've avoided it. But this race was so good and so close that I think the full story should be told.

Like any good race, the result was open till the very last minute and, in this case, even beyond it. The first drama occurred right at the start, when instead of starting instantly in the manner of all Beart-tuned bikes, Peter's engine coughed and spluttered twice as he pushed off. The effect of this was that five or six seconds of his lead on the road, over Griff, was lost, since our Beart-prepared bike fairly leapt off the line in the approved manner.

One knew that if, at the end of the first lap, they came through side by side, Griff would be leading Peter on race time by ten seconds and that if he was ten seconds behind Peter, they would be dead-heating. As their scoreboard clocks moved, you could see that there was very little in it. Griff was a few seconds astern at Ballacraine, seemed closer at Kirkmichael and closer still at Ramsey. In fact, when they came through at the end of that first lap, they weren't side by side, quite, although very nearly.

We waited for the official results at the end of lap one. When they were posted on the scoreboard they read:

1st	David Williams	Norton	23 mins 23·0 secs	96·81 m.p.h.
2nd	R. Hunter	Matchless	23 mins 26·4 secs	96·58 m.p.h.
3rd	G. Jenkins	Norton	23 mins 49·2 secs	95·45 m.p.h.
4th	S. Griffiths	Matchless	23 mins 49·2 secs	95·04 m.p.h.
5th	P. Darvill	Norton	23 mins 53·2 secs	94·78 m.p.h.
6th	M. Kelly	Norton	24 mins 08·2 secs	93·79 m.p.h.

Very interesting. The boys were going well but so were a lot of others. At the end of the second lap, the order was the same. Williams had pushed his race average up to 97·34 m.p.h., well above record speed for the Manx, an amateur race officially. Griff was now marginally ahead of Peter on the road and led him on race time by eleven seconds and Griffiths had dropped back a bit.

One could see that refuelling, at the end of lap three, was going to be not only exciting but would probably have a bearing on the race result. This applied not only to Williams and Hunter who were pulling away from us, albeit slowly, but also to Griff and Peter—and how I wished that someone other than myself could be in command of the pit. The Manx pits are small and I remember discussing with Francis the problems of keeping our respective runners disentangled when they made their stops for it was now obvious that both would be in together —and within a second or so of each other.

Even now, ten years later, the memory of that fill is vivid for me. Both chaps appeared, our bike leading Francis' by a wheel and then they were with us. In the Junior race, Griff hadn't managed to get the filler-cap open when we filled but it was open on the Senior bike although all that you could see was a mass of fuel vapour as you peered down into the huge tank. I remember the smell of the bike and the awful discovery that, having had to come round us to get to his pit, Peter's rear wheel was overlapping our front and blocking our exit. Yelling at Griff to pull the bike back, we completed the fill and both left as they had arrived—virtually together. It was the most exciting pit moment I ever had in racing—but it would have been worse if we had realised that we were, in fact, refuelling the winner of the race and the runner-up.

Coupled with all this, Mike Kelly, the popular Manx rider, whose pit was next door, had been keeping company with our two on the road and he, too, was in at the same time. There could hardly have been a second's difference between any of the three stops—they all left as they had arrived. Although he was laying farther back in race order, Mike was desperately trying to stay with our chaps and this had paid dividends for, at the end of the third lap, he came up to fifth place behind Peter. But Williams and Hunter still kept pulling away slowly.

The order changed a lot at the end of the fourth. Hunter now led Williams, we were still third, Peter fourth, Ron Chandler fifth and Denis Crane, another Manxman, sixth. Poor Mike had tried too hard on the climb up the Mountain from Ramsey, had overdone it and was en route for Ramsey hospital with a broken arm.

By the end of the fourth lap, Williams had gone. The commentators had assumed that the change of race order between him and Hunter had been due to refuelling but crafty old Francis knew he was slowing and told me long before the scoreboard showed it. We were now second to Hunter and Peter third, eleven seconds astern. But Hunter led us by more than a minute after 185 miles of racing.

Throughout the season I had never put out a 'faster' signal to Griff and this obviously wasn't the moment to do it. There was no sign that Hunter was slowing and it was inconceivable that we could make up a minute on him on that last lap. But I was certain that he was really on the ragged edge and knew that, like ourselves, he had signalling stations all round the Island. I felt that, if we could close the gap even a little at a stage of the race when he wouldn't expect it, it might produce some dramatic effect although I knew it might boomerang on us.

I didn't ask Griff to go faster. Instead, I gave him the only untruthful pit signal I ever gave anyone. I could only do it once—it was the last lap—and I told him he was second, which was true, and that he was very close indeed to Hunter, which wasn't. Hunter then went out and we won, at a record average for the race of 96·10 m.p.h.

That Peter was second was good but what followed was better and I never saw anything like it in racing before or since. There was some delay in deciding who was third while the timekeepers waited for any

190

likely third placemen to finish. Then it was announced that the third placeman was Denis Crane and he it was who joined the others in the winner's enclosure. Photographs were taken of all three and then there was a stir. Something had happened to change the results—and it involved poor Denis. Jimmy Guthrie on Francis' second-string bike, never at any time on the leader board throughout the race, had put in a phenomenal last lap and had pulled it off. Three Beart-prepared bikes entered. First, Second and Third in addition to winning the Junior. One couldn't recall anything like it.

This posed quite a problem. All three engines had to be stripped so as to be measured. Jimmy had had a friend looking after his pit which had meant that Francis' right-hand-man, Phil Kettle, had been given the day off, since he wasn't required in a pit. And Phil, having understandably had enough of racing motor-cycles for a bit, had gone as far away from it all as he could, and was way up somewhere on the Mountain.

Somehow it was done, Francis stripping Peter's engine, and handing tools to Jimmy and myself, together with instructions and encouragement. Mercifully, in the middle of it all, the Norton factory fitters arrived, out of interest to see how the motors looked when stripped, to find that they had inherited more work.

The official results for the six-lap race, thirty-seven miles round each time, were:

1st	G. Jenkins	Norton	2 hrs 21 mins 21·2 secs	96·10 m.p.h.
2nd	P. Darvill	Norton	2 hrs 21 mins 47·2 secs	95·81 m.p.h.
3rd	J. Guthrie	Norton	2 hrs 27 mins 35·2 secs	92·04 m.p.h.

Many times, subsequently, people have said to me, 'Lord, how you must have enjoyed that race.' But I don't think it works that way. I would have enjoyed it more while it was happening had I been an uninvolved spectator. It was enjoyable afterwards, but not at the time because it was far too worrying.

Although I enjoyed the races in which I rode myself, I never regarded even the successful ones as exciting because I think one was always too busy and involved to be excited. Nor, in this later period of sponsorship did I enjoy the most successful of our races at the time— I just found it increasingly worrying as we met with more success. But one enjoyed the success when the worry of attaining it had receded.

By far the most exciting races I've seen have been those in which I had no active interest and no involvement. Under those conditions you really can enjoy it, I think.

If one feels like this, one ought to seek the reason to continue doing it. I did this, never really getting to the bottom of it. I would have missed it if I hadn't gone on. I am sure it becomes a way of life.

It may seem strange to say this but the races I actually enjoyed were not the big and important ones where we had success but the earlier ones on the way up. I got a tremendous kick, in the early days with Griff, watching him ride bikes that were better than any he'd had until then and enjoying comparatively small successes that were surprises to us as we climbed our way up the ladder together. Once we were there, the worries overshadowed the enjoyment.

Later on, when my own boy, Charles, started racing, I had it all over again, selecting the machinery with him, watching its preparation in the capable hands of Francis and others nearly as skilled and getting a tremendous kick when he won or scored a couple of seconds at a club meeting. But, even in the case of Charles, the enjoyment faded and the worry began to creep in when we had reached a stage at which we were disappointed if he didn't win. Since then, he has become British 125 cc. Champion, has won two T.T. races in the Isle of Man, the Senior Spanish Grand Prix in 1972 and narrowly missed the 125 cc. World Championship. I am very proud of him and of his achievements but I've never seen him do any of these things although I sometimes think it's time I did. He himself, is much better suited to it than I ever was, and can accept reverses and disappointments in a way that I never could.

A race which—absurdly—I enjoyed more than most in 1964 was the Lightweight 250 cc. Manx Grand Prix. Griff and I had continued our partnership on the short circuits that year and he had ridden my 500 into a rousing fifth place in the Senior T.T. in the Island in June, finishing astern of Mike Hailwood who had won on a Norton at an average of 100·95 m.p.h., the first time a single had ever averaged over 100 m.p.h. By now, Griff was getting offers of rides from many directions and since I no longer felt keen about short-circuit racing, we called it a day at this stage.

I wanted to do the Manx again but, having won it in 1963, he wasn't eligible to compete in it any more, so I had to look around for a replacement, finally choosing Mike Kelly who had gone so well the previous year, partly because his 1963 ride had impressed me and partly because I always did like the Island and liked the idea of having a Manxman ride for me. Francis was the middle man in this arrangement. When I signed with Mike, I'd never met him and didn't even know what he looked like. All I knew was the flying figure I'd seen in the 1963 Senior Manx. And everyone told me what a nice chap he was.

Mike rode the same two bikes Griff had ridden for me in 1963, finishing fourth in the Junior and 3rd in the Senior so, with Griff's good ride in June, it was in some ways a better year than the previous. But it was the Lightweight Manx I really enjoyed, despite the fact that the very best we hoped for was a finisher's award.

One of our pupils in the Racing School was Ron Eldridge. We got to know Ron well during the time he rode with the School and, subsequently, he came along from time to time, helping us run the thing, particularly with the machinery, with which he was good. Later still he came on the permanent staff and worked with Charles who, at that time, had no mechanical knowledge, despite the fact that, even at that stage, he was fast becoming proficient as a rider. Ron, too, was a good and neat rider and, for fun, we decided to take one of the School Greeves production racers over to the Manx and run it, ridden by Ron, in the Lightweight race. All the School bikes were a sorry sight at this late stage in the season. All had been pranged, repaired, and pranged again and the thought of running any of them in a long race was rather ridiculous, but Ron selected one, took it home and stripped it. When I next saw it, it just wasn't recognisable and I felt, at once, how awful it was that he should have put in so much work on the poor old thing with so little chance of even finishing.

I became interested and it really mattered to me, very much, that Ron should have as good a run as possible for his money after all the hard work he'd put in. He asked me to run his pit and I was delighted to do it and, in the end, he somehow nursed the poor old relic through the Lightweight race and got his coveted finisher's award. I never thought he would and, towards the end I was sure he hadn't, for his last lap was slower by far than the first three. But when I asked him why, he replied, 'Well, you see, having got that far, I just dared not push it too hard up the Mountain from Ramsey. So I just let it go at its own pace to make sure of getting home.'

To me that was an enjoyable and rewarding race not, perhaps, as exciting as the big events but free of the tensions. It marked the end of the 1964 season and, at the time, I had few thoughts of continuing sponsoring and thought only of running the Racing School and widening its scope. But, as the winter wore on, I began to feel that, if I didn't keep on racing, interest in the School might flag, so even though I had sold both the A.J.S.s and the big Norton, I ordered a new 350 cc. Aermacchi and entered into a contract with Paul Smart to ride it, partly because Paul had been one of our School members, partly because he was obviously, even then, going to be good, but also because he, Ron and Charles got on well together and I knew they'd enjoy it and, perhaps, notch up some results.

At this time, my domestic life was even more rugged and chaotic than at any time previously. Jean and I had had a divorce, had stayed that way for a year and then, neither of us having remarried, we got spliced again. We found we had done the right thing but at the wrong time. In other words, we had done it too soon. Had we waited longer, there would have been a better chance of it working. But we didn't and, although it worked better, it was still far from right. This was my fault because I never wanted the divorce and was much surer that there was nothing fundamentally wrong with the marriage than was my poor old mate. She took off for the second time and we very nearly untied the knot once more but finally decided against it. That was seven years ago and when we got together again for the third time, we decided to try a change from living together under one big roof, and try the effect of living close to each other under two small ones. A strange solution to the problem, it must be admitted but, for both of us, it has its advantages and one day, who knows, we may end up sharing the same fireside.

But, in 1965, I really had no idea where I was going domestically and this was certainly one reason why I continued to be involved in racing. And, although he was only sixteen, it was in this year that Charles started racing, while working full time with me in the running of the School.

Looking back, 1965 was an enjoyable year. The School did well, I enjoyed managing Paul with the Aermacchi despite the fact that he was still in the 'hairy' stage and gave me numerous frights. And I thoroughly enjoyed Charles' early efforts at the Club Meetings, at first with the School Greeves that Ron had ridden in the Manx and later with one of the five-speeders. Paul rode the Greeves R.D.S. five-speeder for me also and he and Charles were competing against each other a lot of the time on these bikes.

You really needed eyes in the back of your head to manage these two together. No greater couple of menaces ever rode under the same banner together and what one didn't think up, the other did. A case in point was a race in which they both rode Greeves for me at Snetterton. Both had gone well in practice and, in the race, Paul led from the start with Charles well placed but laying back a bit. At this stage of his career, Paul was parting company with his race bikes regularly and frequently while I was trying to din in to him the importance of staying in the saddle in order to win races. Sometimes, the two of them would go off together to a meeting. One would part company with the bike and, on their return, the other would cover up when reporting to me so that, whatever happened, I wouldn't know about it.

The race at Snetterton was a ten-lap thing and when about three had been run, another rider came up to talk to me as I watched it. Suddenly, as we chatted, it looked to me as though Paul was missing but, two laps later I saw he was back in the lead. I wasn't really concentrating on the race and, the lap after that, he again appeared to be missing. But, finally he won it and Charles was second. I drifted over to the bar and they joined me there but when I told them I had found the race pattern hard to follow, they expressed surprise. It wasn't until a year later that, convulsed with laughter, they picked the right moment to tell me that, in that race alone, Paul had fallen off three times!

Although, even then, one knew that, one day, both would be really good riders I never thought I would see them rated sixth and seventh best riders in the world. But in this week's Motor Cycle News I see that this is the rating given them by racing expert John Brown, so I was obviously very fortunate to have them both riding for me at the same time although it didn't always seem so when it was happening.

Ron, who looked after the Aermacchi, used to cover up for them both if things went wrong. If I hadn't gone to a meeting I could always tell whether things had gone well or not so well. If the day had been good, I would get a call from Ron on Monday morning. If I didn't get the call I would phone him and if he had 'just slipped out to get some cigarettes' I knew that someone had fallen off!

On one of these occasions, the first I knew of the 'accident' was when I opened Motor Cycle News, four days after the meeting. There it was—a photograph of Paul lying in the middle of the track alongside Tom

Kirby's rider, Pat Mahoney, while both machines lay tangled together in the ditch. I rang Ron who had gone out for cigarettes, so I left a message to say that, if he didn't ring me back in ten minutes, I was coming over to Tonbridge as there were some questions I had to ask. He rang back three minutes later to assure me that, although he hadn't seen the prang, he understood that the fault had been Pat's since it was he who had fallen and brought Paul down.

I thought that Tom would probably ring me to express apologies since this was usually done in such cases. I thought no more about it till I saw Tom at the next meeting, only to find that he had expected me to ring him as it was Paul who had brought Pat down!

At this time, Paul, being slightly older and more experienced than Charles, was definitely the better of the two and, when they were both riding for me, he had the better bike whenever one was felt to be better. Everyone in the equipe was happy about this, including Charles, who always gave his number one good backing and, one day, I discovered how it worked for them mutually. I won't name the circuit but it was one that had a long straight not very accessible to spectators and, in this particular race they were lying first and second and Charles, whose bike was not a lot less good than Paul's, that day, was being hard pressed by another rider. They finished in first and second places but, later in the day, an elderly spectator asked me, in a rather shocked manner, whether I approved of their riding tactics.

According to him, he had made his way across country to the remote straight where, he said, he had seen Paul 'towing' Charles during the race in question. And when he said 'towing' he didn't mean slip-streaming for what had happened was that Paul had literally towed Charles along the back straight, riding alongside him at over 120 m.p.h., pulling him along by holding on to the rear of the seat of Charles' bike with his left hand. At first I could hardly believe it. I felt that, if it had happened, the rider who had been pressing Charles must have protested for no one would have had a better view of it than he. So, instead of talking to Paul and Charles I spoke to him, only to find that it was true. Why hadn't he put in a protest? He laughed and said that they were a couple of characters, both good friends of his and he had had as good a laugh about it as they had. He was a very nice chap.

Both 1965 and 1966 were seasons of the sort that I liked best, working with young riders who were unspoiled and were starting to climb the ladder and having a lot of minor successes on the way. There were times when they nearly drove me to drink and I must have appeared just as irksome to them. But I had tremendous regard for them and for what they were trying to do and they knew that and knew, too, that having raced myself, I appreciated their problems.

The laughs that we had far exceeded the times that weren't so good. The 'petrol' joke was one of them. At that time Shell had a gimmick advertisement running—'Super Shell with I.C.A.' 'I.C.A.' stood for Internal Combustion Additive and one saw posters emblazoning every Shell filling station in the country that proclaimed 'Super Shell with I.C.A.'. The boys would select some remote little filling station on the way to a meeting or a Training School session, pull in and ask for a fill-up. Often, the attendant was a very old man and, just as the refill was about to start, the driver would say, 'Without I.C.A. please.' The effect was always the same. After asking for the request to be repeated, the attendant would say that he couldn't serve it without I.C.A.

'Why not?'

'Well, you can't. It's mixed in. Why don't you want it, anyway?'

'The engine seems better without it. We had some without I.C.A. at the last filling station we stopped at.'

By now the poor old chap was scratching his head. 'How did they get it out?'

'I didn't see. Filtered it I suppose. Hey, Paul, how did they take out the I.C.A. at that place we stopped at on the way up?'

'Filtered it. Through oiled silk.'

'Blimey. I didn't know you could. We've never had anyone ask for it without I.C.A. And, anyway, we haven't got any oiled silk. It must be a slow business. How long did it take?'

'Oh, I don't know. About half an hour.'

'No, it was longer than that, Charles. We had a meal while they were doing it, remember? Nearer an hour.'

At this, the poor chap would almost explode. 'An hour? Well, what's going to happen to my other customers if people start expecting me to start messing around filtering a few gallons with oiled silk. I don't reckon they did it. I reckon they took you for a ride.' And so it went on. You wouldn't believe that anyone would fall for it, but a great many did.

The café joke was another. They would go into a café and look at the fare for a few minutes. Paul would say:

'Cup of tea, please. You having tea or coffee, Chas?'

197

'I don't want a drink. I'll have a packet of crisps and a rock cake. And a ham roll.'

'Right, then. I'll have a cheese sandwich, a packet of biscuits and a bun.'

'Oh biscuits, I didn't know they'd got them. I'll have some.'

'Tell you what. You have mine . . . I'll have crisps.'

'On second thoughts I don't think I want crisps. You can have mine.'

By this time there would be a little pile of oddments on the counter, in front of each. Nothing had been moved during the agreed swapping and each would be told how much he owed. Then the charge would be queried.

'But I'm not having crisps. He's having mine.'

'But they are on your plate—in front of you.'

'But I'm not going to eat them. I'm only taking them over to the table for him.' Fortunately, they never did it unless the place was empty and, again, it was so ridiculous that you wouldn't have thought anyone could be confused by it. They were though, quite often.

Despite all this, their racing was taken seriously. Charles had graduated from the old R.A.S.-type four-speed Greeves, via the 1965 and 1966 five-speed R.D.S. and, in the middle of 1966 we became more enthusiastic and fielded two watercooled Bultacos, a 125 cc. and a 250 cc., both new bikes. A wrong thing to do, really, and I should have known better. You should never change mounts in mid-season if it can be avoided, and this could have been. For some reason, the watercooled 250 was constantly prone to engine seizure and it wasn't the only one of its type to suffer from it that year. But the 125 cc. was a superb little bike and was a big step up the ladder. But as it wasn't any good for the Lightweight Manx, we took two R.D.S. Greeves, one for each runner and a third as a spare. Charles had had one previous ride in the Manx and had gained a finisher's award thanks to valuable help and advice from experts like Joe Dunphy and Griff. But Paul had never been there and this was a bit worrying because, although they were such good mates, one felt that Paul would want to be at least as quick as Charles, right from the start.

Looking back, it isn't surprising, really, that both have got to the top for both had that essential thing, dedication, which seems essential to success in any sport. Paul went over to the Island that year utterly determined to learn everything he possibly could about that tortuous thirty-seven-mile circuit. Like every one of us who become involved in racing, climbing up the ladder had left him 'skint' but when I met him in Douglas there, outside his digs, stood the most disreputable scooter imaginable and it was on this that he firmly intended to circle the T.T. course all day and every day while the roads were open. To me, the scooter was a very impressive demonstration of real enthusiasm although I'm sure it never seemed that way to him. In fact, he didn't need to use it much for, again, we were able to get much help and good advice from top riders who were in the Island either to ride or to spectate. I rather doubt if anyone ever had more concentrated T.T.-course cramming poured in to him than Paul did in that fortnight. Everyone was on his side and he listened to advice from mentors ranging from Austin Munks, all the way down the line to Charles with his one year's experience of the Island.

He astonished everyone with his fast practice times and delighted and amazed us by lying second in the Lightweight race at the end of the first lap. Unfortunately, the bike let him down. But Paul had arrived, with no doubt at all.

At that stage, there was a great deal more difference between the two boys than there is now. Both were dedicated but Charles' approach was more calculated and he was prepared to take time to learn. Paul never was. Today was the day and it all had to be absorbed instantly before passing on to the next lesson.

All the time I tried, constantly, to check both of them from making more and more changes of machine. I was happy to be allied to the Greeves equipe. Their bikes were ideal for the School and it was obviously right for me to enter Greeves in races. Unfortunately both Charles and Paul now knew enough to realise that, while this might suit me, the Greeves had been designed as a production racer to sell at a competitive price which meant that it was by no means the best in its class if price were disregarded. That was a battle I fought and lost. They were grateful for what the Greeves had done for them but they meant to move on to something better.

The watercooled Bultaco was the next step but that soon went, in favour of a 125 cc. Honda. This was Charles' own property and really was a super little bike.

It was always a mystery to me how he managed to acquire this little bike. Although I had been able to help him in providing race machinery the bikes had always been my property and the only money that

Charles had accrued had come from his earnings at work in the Racing School. The School was by this time flourishing. We were running it all the year round at Brands Hatch on Wednesdays and throughout the summer we paid monthly visits to Oulton Park, Cadwell and Mallory Park. The bulk of the office work I did myself while Charles and Ron dealt with the machinery and as a rule, when we were going up north, we would take three vans with a big trailer attached to mine. In this way we could carry four bikes in each van and five in the trailer.

On our 'away trips' we would usually have a big school, sometimes amounting to thirty members, and this took a lot of getting through if it was to be done in the day. We would load up on the Thursday, travel northwards on Friday, stop the night in a pub near the circuit and be at the circuit by six o'clock on Saturday morning. While Ron, Charles and Paul unloaded the machinery and dealt with things like fuel, oil and tyre pressures I would set up the office in one of the Club buildings, talking to each member individually and then having a final briefing with them altogether.

The next operation was to show them the track to describe the technique of each bend telling them where to brake and make gear changes, and this we did by taking them round in the vans, sometimes stopping at each corner to underline important points. Then the first batch of six or eight would go out for a twenty-lap session with instructions to sit behind the Instructor for the first ten laps, after which they could continue circulating on their own. The problem was always the same. It was to ensure that at the end of the day the lads felt that they had had value for their money, and yet at the same time make sure that we had not ended the day with too much damaged machinery. The way we tried to achieve this was by letting the Instructor set out with him riding, as a rule, behind the class instead of in front. Occasionally we would have dramatic moments, and one of these occurred on a visit to Oulton Park. This time we were using the short circuit and half way through the morning Charles told me that a rider, not a member of the School, had arrived in the belief that there was an open practice day at the circuit. He had come a long way and was asking whether he could use the track at the same time as we were using it. He knew the chap and knew that he was a proficient rider and it was agreed that he would go out at the same time as the next class. What we did not realise was that he was under the impression that we were using the long circuit and it was several laps before we discovered that we were meeting him at the intersection.

Having taken over 1,000 members through the School in the years that we ran it we were lucky never to have had a fatal accident. Maybe it was luck, although we did take a lot of trouble to avoid anything of this nature. We did have two bad accidents; one at Oulton Park which left a member in hospital for many months and the other at Brands Hatch. The Brands Hatch Trackside Authorities could not have been more helpful to us and I had an arrangement with the ambulance people that if at any time one of our members appeared seriously hurt the driver would flash his lights to me from the point on the track at which he picked the boy up. We had so many minor prangs that one had almost come to the point where one thought that this would never happen but it did and we called the whole class in to await the return of the ambulance. When it arrived back at the start one knew it was serious because the driver did not even stop to tell us the form. In fact, the victim was sitting up and taking nourishment the morning after the accident with no broken bones and no serious injuries but we were told by the ambulance crew that on picking him up from the track they found that his heart had stopped and although they were able to get him going again it stopped twice more on the way to the hospital.

With the big numbers we used to take on our visits up north a tremendous amount of work was involved, partly in keeping an eye on the boys, but mainly in keeping enough machines operational throughout the day. We often had to cannibalise machines and although we kept a log of each bike we frequently came home with one machine less than the number with which we had set out; its component parts having been used to keep the rest going.

We also came back on these occasions with a stack of money but so much of it was used in replacing damaged machinery that the net result was nothing like as good.

We had many amusing incidents, of course. Sometimes during the winter Brands Hatch sessions we would arrive to find the track iced-up and to pass the time we used to walk round the circuit with the school members describing to them the technique of each corner. On one occasion, when Rex Butcher was the Instructor, we were doing this and as we approached the paddock I said to Rex:

'What speed do you reckon you could do round the paddock on your 500?'

He replied, 'When I'm in the groove, I suppose eighty to eighty-five.'

On this occasion one of the members was a huge chap and as he approached Paddock Bend on his first lap it was obvious he was never going to make it. The accident that followed was one of the most spectacular I ever saw; the machine ending up at the bottom of the hill, its throttle jammed flat out, still in third gear, and lying in about three inches of mud and water, although the rider was obviously unhurt. Talking to the chap afterwards, I said:

'What made you think you could get round Paddock at that speed?'

He replied, 'I just thought that if Rex could manage it at eighty to eighty-five I ought to be able to manage it ten miles an hour slower— I now know that I was wrong.'

We became expert in spotting the chaps likely to do themselves a mischief. You could nearly always spot them on their first lap without an Instructor, and the problem then was to get them in before the prang happened and one had to be very quick about this because it usually happened pretty quickly. One could often spot them during the briefing and, immediately after the briefing and before letting them out on the circuit, Charles, Ron and I used to get together to see if we agreed on who the 'nutters' might be. Having spotted them, we would mark their sheets with a red cross which indicated 'special observation' and it was surprising how many prangs this saved, for we were often right at this early stage in the proceedings. The most obvious sign was over confidence, not to be confused with forced jocularity, which usually indicated nervousness, but another type we came to look for was the quiet, moody character, who was often transformed into a wild man once aboard the machine and free from the clutches of his Instructor.

We always rather dreaded lap eleven of each session, the one on which the Instructor, having led the class for the first ten laps, signalled them to go on ahead on their own. Very close liaison between Instructor and those of us in the pits was called for and this we certainly had. In fact, we had an agreed code of signals from pit to Instructor and vice versa that was so good that we almost held long conversations throughout each session. Charles was absolutely magnificent in this way. The class would perhaps be circulating on the first of their unchaperoned laps when Ron would sing out to me 'Nutter on number nine' and, at the same moment we would see Charles shoot forward from his post at the rear of the procession, for all the world like a mobile 'cop', pinpointing bike number nine and slowing its intrepid conductor down with hand signals. Although we had very few training sessions free of prangs, we must have saved hundreds and hundreds of shunts that way.

Most members had their second training session about a month after the first and this, too, was one to watch for, although we knew a bit about each by now, they would be going out on their own from the start, this time, and had already gained quite a bit more confidence than they had knowledge, during their previous ride. So, when we briefed them this time, we used to emphasise the importance of staying on board the bike, adding, 'If you've set your heart on falling off, do it on lap one, because we don't refund any money or allow any additional laps to 'droppers' so we shall then have been paid for nineteen laps which you won't get'—and this had the effect of slowing them more than anything else we could possibly have said!

By the third time they came to us, we knew them well. Almost to a man, they turned out to be good chaps and many became firm friends. We had always agreed that if we came across a chap temperamentally unsuited to racing, we would tell him but, in fact, out of a thousand boys, we only had two. Both were nice young fellows and both told us they felt they weren't cut out for it before we had to tell them. We had a lot of slow riders who knew they would never be good but enjoyed their rides. They weren't, as a rule, slow enough to be in the way of the faster chaps and some of them were our best customers because they didn't assassinate the machinery as did some of the others. When we could, we tried to devise special classes for riders whose lap times were in the same bracket.

We always gave members strict instructions about what revs they could use. Most were very good about this but we had a few habitual 'over-revvers' and, for a time, this was rather a headache because, for all their denials, we knew the bikes so well that we always knew when one was being over-revved. In the end, the solution proved to be to send them out on machines with rev counters reading 1,000 revs high and this cured it. They could see 7,000 on the clock—we could hear 6,000, and everyone was happy.

We encouraged dads and mums to come and watch, and why not? After all, they had payed our fees in nine cases out of ten. And wonderful friends many of them turned out to be, some, like Mr Aucott and

Mr Notley becoming temporarily part of the organisation, when we were hard pressed.

Many of the big names gave us help, among them Griff Jenkins, Joe Dunphy, Rex Butcher and Bill Ivy. Charles, of course, although up and coming at that time and invaluable as an Instructor, occasionally found that he was coping with a member who was as good a rider and might be better for all we knew. We always had the spectre hanging over us of finding that the pupil was better than the master and would have hung our heads in shame if it had ever been made clear for all to see. Once or twice we suspected it and, on those occasions we would shout for the help of 'special instruction' at the hands of Griff, Joe, Rex or Bill—and we were never refused. This was a great draw, of course, for the members liked meeting their idols and liked, even better, being taught by them. We reimbursed the idols, however unwilling they were to accept their dues, and it cost the member concerned no extra.

Speaking generally, the School members could be slotted into three categories, the first being the chap who was thinking about taking up racing but wanted to try it before laying out capital. Most, in this section did take it up, some so quickly that we only saw them ride in the School once. Others stayed with us, usually owing to problems in building up capital. Next came the chaps who just weren't sure whether they'd enjoy it or not. About half of them did, and continued to be good clients. But it was the third lot who formed the basis of the membership. These were chaps who had no intention of racing at all. Mainly, ardent and knowledgeable spectators of the sport, they just wanted to see what it was like to be the other side of the fence and, having sampled it, they then knew how good their idols were, thereby becoming among the most appreciative spectators of motor-cycle racing. Usually, boys in this category rode with the outfit when it was run on their home track but a few journeyed all round the country with us, sampling every track in turn.

We also became pretty crafty at squeezing the last drop out of the orange, as regards the machinery, once we had found that the engine life of the Greeves Silverstone was in the region of 1,000 miles between overhauls. A new or rebuilt engine needed a 100 miles at reduced revs before it could safely be handed to a member with virtually no risk of it seizing so, for the first 100 miles it stayed in the hands of the Instructor who ran it in as he rode with his class. For the next 800 miles it would be in the hands of members and—assuming it lasted that long—it would then go back to the Instructor's pool for another hundred miles or more for, although it was worn out from a racing point of view, it was quite adequate for this use.

At its peak the School had fifteen machines operational, components for another five and several additional spare engines. Sheer necessity made us become expert at trackside rebuilds and replacements and, in the end, we could change an engine in twenty minutes. After one particularly exasperating day, Bob Mills of the Greeves company once removed an engine from its machine in four minutes flat. No one ever improved on that and, on that occasion, Bob had had enough of it and wanted to get home! We never, at any time, refused to buy a privately owned Greeves Silverstone, should one be offered to us, no matter what its condition. The company was more than good to us in the supply of spares, and with technical help, but secondhand usable spares were invaluable for the mileage we were covering annually was astronomical.

A log book was kept for every machine in which every lap was entered, every change of setting, every replacement and every mishap recorded. This was essential and took a lot of time, being one of poor old Charles' many chores. He, more than any of us, dreaded the arrival of certain members whose riding habits loaded him with numerous extra entries to make in the machine logs.

From all this, over a period of six years, there emerged a number of good riders, some very good, a few excellent but only two, Paul and Charles himself, better than that. We used to discuss this sometimes, feeling that there had been one or two who, had it not been for problems of family or finance, might also have come to the top. And there were others who might have done if they had had this thing called dedication. But lack of dedication isn't, necessarily, bad and may even be a good thing if, for instance, a lad decides that to be dedicated to motor-cycle racing doesn't add up to good sense.

I was never dedicated, but never reached the heights. Our younger boy, Robin, was, at one stage, dead keen to become a top-notcher on two wheels but, after several quite successful seasons, good sense prevailed in his case. He packed it in, finding that there were other things in life, as enjoyable and a bit less demanding and time consuming. So I don't think that anyone who went through our training school and didn't keep on with it through lack of dedication, need have worried.

Somewhere around 'half time', when the Beart-Mortimer Training School had been running for nearly three years, Francis told me that he felt he would like to give up his interest in it and, although I was sorry, I realised that his own business interests kept him sufficiently busy. Charles was well in the picture by this time, so we re-formed the thing and re-named it the Charles Mortimer Racing School. By the time we reached the five-year mark, I felt as Francis had, for the thing had grown constantly and, even with the hard work that Charles and Ron put in, running it was tiring and a strain. And there was another thing. When Charles had been on the way up, on the racing side, he was riding, mostly, machines that were mine and his racing didn't conflict with the running of the School. He was still not at the top but had reached a stage when he was riding a variety of machinery for a number of different sponsors and it was clear that, sooner or later, either the School or his racing must take precedence. It seemed clear that it would be his own racing which would mean that one day I would find myself back on square one, running the School as a one-man band or with new people to help me. I had enjoyed the past five years more than I had realised and the thought of running it without Chas wasn't worth considering. So I told him that I proposed to pull out and to make the whole thing over to him, lock, stock and barrel for he had worked really hard at it and was just as much responsible for its success as I. And I made it clear that I didn't expect him to go on running it. He could dispose of it either as a going concern or let it freewheel to a finish and then dispose of the assets.

He did continue to run it for quite a time. But it became clearer, every day, that he had to turn one way or the other and there was never any doubt in either of our minds as to which way that would be.

Our last year of being associated together in racing was an Aermacchi year. I had always liked the Aermacchi since Paul had ridden my 350 and, in 1968, Chas and I plumped for the 250. We could have done worse, but we certainly could have done better. It was a nice, reliable little bike but not fast enough. But one good thing did come out of it, for Francis was impressed with Chas' riding and, having a similar machine himself, spoke to me about the possibility of Chas riding his bike in the Lightweight Manx Grand Prix in September. This was a great thing for Chas and for me. For him it meant recognition of the fact that, as a rider, he had come a long way. For me it was a splendid ending to our association in racing that he should be riding for Francis, my oldest friend. And it meant that Francis would become the only one in the business to have had a father and a son ride for him.

I did wonder, before we went to the Island, whether their two personalities would clash. They did, a little, but only a little. Not enough to prevent it being a worthwhile trip for they finished fifth in the race, easily the best placing Chas had had in the Island so far.

So now I was out of it. I would have expected, really, to be sadder than I was. In fact I felt relief at having off-loaded the burden of the racing school which I had enjoyed no end when I was doing it. But I had had enough of standing on windy tracksides and enough of long hauls up and down the country.

But, better than that, I felt that with luck and God's guidance, Charles could well make the goal for which he'd worked so hard. The year had given him his first win at a National Meeting, riding Frank Sheene's 125 cc. Bultaco and one felt sure it wouldn't be his last.

He hadn't won a Manx Grand Prix but he had won the British Clubman's Championship with the Greeves and later, the British National 125 cc. Championship. His aims now, he told me, were first a win in the T.T. and then to win a World Championship. The sights seemed high but not impossible.

9

All this involvement in racing added up to a big annual mileage on open roads which, over the span of forty years, must have been substantial. One sometimes wishes one had kept more records of cars and the distances covered in each.

To me, the road motoring has been only slightly less enjoyable than the racing. I can't understand the chap who says that all the pleasure has gone out of motoring and sometimes wonder whether he says it just to underline the fact that he has been motoring for a long time.

Like everyone else in my age bracket I have been extremely lucky to have owned, in the 1930s, many cars that are now held to have been great creations, so it may, perhaps, be amusing to take a look back at particular examples one owned throughout the period—the 1930s to the 1970s. I've tried to list them alphabetically, including only those that were mine in the sense that they were not cars bought with a view to re-selling, but bought, owned and used, most of them for many months and others for years. The size of the list is a bit of a surprise to me but forty years is a long time, so perhaps it may be forgiven.

My very first car was new, and a present from my mother, shortly after my father's death in 1932. It was a 1933 Austin Ten saloon, registered JJ 3211, and it was an absolutely first-class car in every way when one takes into account the year in which it was made and the selling price. It took me everywhere, never failed to start, never once broke down on the road and is something that I should quite like to own again. I'm quite lucky here for, even at today's absurd prices, I could afford a 1933 Austin Ten!

I can only recall one temporary stop on the road with JJ 3211, in 1935 or 1936. It happened in Belgium when I was trailing my Norton 500 down to Dinant to compete in the Grand Prix des Sambre et Meuse. Noel Christmas was with me and his 350 Velocette was keeping my old Norton company on the trailer. The Austin had never sampled Belgian pave before and, to register this, it broke two 'U' bolts holding the front springs. It was a trip that went wrong all the time although we had planned it carefully, selecting the race at a time we knew the Norton team, Woods, Guthrie and Hunt, etc., would be engaged elsewhere. Our two bikes were among the best of the privateers and we felt optimistic when we set out.

The Velocette engine, in every way the equal of the Norton when it came to reliability, blew itself to smithereens in the final practice session, the start of the trouble being the collapse of the piston crown, and this meant that poor old Noel didn't get a ride at all.

The engine of the Norton developed an intermittent misfire at peak revs and nothing we could do would correct it, not even changes of magneto and the entire fuel system including the carburettor. And, on top of that, two works F.N.s turned up for the race on race day itself, to be ridden by Milhoux and Charlier. Wonderful looking bikes, really fast and quite a worry to the works' Nortons, they were the kiss of death to us. For the riders, it was one of their home circuits and they made the first few laps their practice period before proceeding to make mincemeat of everyone.

What other 'A's? Only Alfa Romeo. I had a 2·3-litre blown straight-eight in the immediate post-war period. A nice car with a pretty two-seater body by Zagato, and we ran it in the very first post-war motoring event held in this country, not a speed event but something which became very much like it. The thing happened at Cockfosters and I think Rivers Fletcher was the brain behind it. It was just what everyone wanted at the time. Under the same banner, I later had a Guilietta Sprint Veloce Coupé and, later, a similar Guilia 1600 cc. But none of these leave lasting or deep impressions.

Alta. Only one and it has been covered already. Although I don't remember the new price of the 1½-litre blown Alta single seater, I suppose it must have come under the heading of 'the poor man's E.R.A.' In certain circumstances and over a short distance it could give the E.R.A. a run for its money but if it wasn't a lot cheaper than the E.R.A. one wonders why people bought them. Particularly people like Johnny Wakefield, who had an E.R.A. as well. But it was good that there were buyers for the Alta and made the pre-war race scene more interesting.

I had a lot of Bentleys over the years and it was when driving through Hammersmith Broadway, in 1934, that I spotted the first of the marque that I was to own. Parked outside a pub was a really pretty Speed Six,

Freestone and Webb foursome coupé. I was slightly less 'skint' than usual at the time and, although the owner of the Speed Six was merely slaking his thirst, I somehow had a feeling that the car might be bought —I didn't know why.

There was only one customer in the bar—it was around mid-morning—and he turned out to be the owner. Mr Edgar was a local builder and he was also a very good businessman when it came to selling cars. When I had admired his Bentley, he had countered with words 'D'you want to buy it?', and when I said I would buy it if the price was right, he obviously decided that here was a raving lunatic or some sort of juvenile crank with more money than sense, because, in 1934, people just didn't walk into pubs and say, 'I should like to buy your Speed Six Bentley.'

Sensing that he had put himself on to weak ground, Mr Edgar then went into reverse, deciding that this was the best car he had ever had and that he didn't want to sell it. He didn't want to although he should, really, because it was a bigger car than he needed for his work. I had quite a background of dealing, by this time, and felt well able to cope so, for the next ten minutes, we dropped the subject of the Bentley and went on to discuss sport. Suddenly, he drained his glass and said:

'If you really do want to buy that car, I'll sell it to you.'

'How much d'you want for it?'

'Well, it's two-hundred-and-fifty-pounds-worth of motor car.'

That seemed a strange way of putting it and, in any case, was just five times the amount I hoped to pay.

'It may be. But not to me, I'm afraid.'

'What's your idea?'

'Fifty.'

He raised his eyes to Heaven.

'Where can you buy a car like that for fifty pounds? Go on, now, tell me.'

'You can, you know.'

'Not like this one. There's nothing to be done to that car. Not a spanner to be laid on it. It's taxed for nine months. The tyres are nearly new. But I must get back to work. Tell you what. Give me a hundred and you can drive it away.'

'Sixty, then.'

'A hundred. Not a penny less. Come on. I'll take you for a run.'

We went out on to the Kingston Bypass and back and I worked on him all the way. It was a good Speed Six and we both knew it so that, in the end, I paid him £90 for PG 6345—by far the highest price I'd ever given for a used car. I never regretted it. It was a very good Bentley. It just didn't notice the trailer, loaded with bikes, but it was thirsty.

Its end came suddenly. We had a successful day's racing at the track and then went up to town to celebrate. Noel Pope led the procession as far as Esher but, once on the bypass, the Speed Six took over and was still there when we ran down to the traffic lights at the bottom of Roehampton Lane. The lights began to change at that awful moment of no return, and I decided to be good and to obey. It was a wrong decision. With a deafening crash, Noel's 3-litre charged into the back of the Speed Six and, a moment later, he was standing at the side of my door—holding out his hand.

'Money,' he said.

'What d'you mean, money? You rammed me.'

'Yes. Now I want payment. I've done you a good turn. In one simple operation I've given you the quickest conversion a Speed Six ever had —from a long chassis to a short. Much more valuable.'

It was true, too, the chassis really had taken it. The 3-litre had come off much better, but I still didn't like them—I much preferred the Six.

Temporary repairs were effected to PG 6345 and it continued to be used. But, not long after this, I went to the Used Car Show which, at that time, was held annually at Islington and there I came across GJ 3811, a sister car, but fitted with a rather exotic three-seater coupé body by Gurney Nutting. This car had originally belonged to Barnato and subsequently to one of the Dunfee brothers. It was a striking-looking car and all sorts of legends surrounded it. I owned it over a longer period than any other pre-war Bentley and covered a big mileage in it. The only fault that I can recall, during my period of ownership, was a rather bad engine vibration period that crept in at peak revs and this, I was told, was due to a fault in the crankshaft vibration damper if, in fact, there is such a component in a Speed Six. Whether there was, or not, I never knew. It sounded expensive and wasn't something that I contemplated tackling.

GJ 3811 wasn't a good tender car where bike racing was concerned. The boot held virtually nothing and there was very little room inside the body. But it became a great favourite and I enjoyed every mile I did with it. We had a regular weekend routine whereby I would go up to town, from Dorking, late on Saturday night, collect my girl friend from her late show at the London Casino and drive down to her parents' place at North Bersted where we would stay the weekend, returning in time for the first show on Monday evening. And in between shows, we had a good holiday in the Isle of Man with the car although loading it on to the deck of the *King Orry* proved a bigger headache than either we or the Isle of Man Steam Packet Company anticipated. I was glad to see that the car is illustrated on page 54 of Johnnie Green's *Fifty Years of the Marque*, as it should be, its present owner, Hugh Harben, having done a wonderful restoration from the decaying wreck that it became during the war years. It was a good car when I bought it and rather better when I sold it to J. S. (Willy) Worters, ex-World Record Holder on motorcycles and, later, tuner of Chris Staniland's famous Multi Union. I saw it again, last year, at Silverstone, and the sight of it did me good.

Two other Speed Sixes followed GJ 3811. The first was UW 4989, a Le Mans Replica four seater that I bought from Ken Waller, the Brooklands test pilot. Nicer than GJ 3811 only in that the steering was lighter, my period of ownership was shorter because I never was a diehard of the type that enjoys open motoring all the time.

The last of the four was a Barker-bodied, two-seater, boat-tailed, drophead coupé. A nice car that was said to have been the actual Show model of its year. But it hadn't the steam of the others which may have been due to the weight of the body.

I liked all these four cars at the time although I wouldn't hanker after one today for road conditions were ideal for them in the 1930s with fewer clottish drivers and no morons to remove mascots and radiator caps.

Sandwiched between these four Speed Sixes and the outbreak of World War Two were two 8-litre Bentleys, the first of which was a four-seater drophead coupé bodied by Gurney Nutting. It wasn't a car that I meant to keep—I bought it purely for resale, imagining the 8-litre to be in all respects a scaled-up version of the Speed Six. But the short run I did with it, collecting it from the vendor, surprised me and it seemed in many respects a much nicer car with a chassis that seemed to me to possess more rigidity. Unfortunately, one of my customers felt the same way and my ownership of it was short. But I did then look around for another and found a short-chassis sports saloon which I had for nearly a year and liked the best of them all.

A number of 3- and 4½-litres came and went through the business but the charms of the pre-war four-cylinder Bentleys have always escaped me and still do, with the exception of the Dorothy Paget blown cars, all of which seemed to me to have the same aura of glamour as did the Sixes—rather more so, in fact, in their way.

My last ownership of this era of Bentley was another 8-litre, this time a long-chassis H. J. Mulliner sports saloon, in 1962, and this car gave me quite a lot of enjoyable motoring, even though the roads were now becoming so crowded. James Tilling and I made up a party to support the Veteran run, John Bolster particularly, but by the time we reached Brighton I had had enough of 8-litres. James drove home and a very spirited run home it turned out to be, especially the final *piece de resistance* round Berkeley Square!

Pre-war Rolls Bentleys? Only one. A 1939 4¼, Freestone & Webb razor-edge saloon. A really lovely car in its day and, even now, I would think, a car that would be a pleasure to own and drive. This became mine immediately after the war and was one that, at the time, I felt would stay with me to the end of its days. The reason it didn't was that, while owning it, I saw, for the first time 'HI'.

'HI' was a 1947 Mark 6. In its way, nothing to get very excited about if it hadn't been for its body which was an ultra lightweight 'one off' by H. J. Mulliner to the special order of its original owner, a Mr McLeod. I never, at any time, met Mr McLeod but his conception of a lightweight body on a Bentley chassis was my ideal. He had dreamed up a similar style, again by H. J. Mulliner, on a 1939 4¼ and I had seen this car many times over the years and often yearned to own it. In many ways I liked it even better than the Mark 6 version but 'HI' 1939 never came my way, much to my sorrow.

The registration plate 'HI' was *in situ* on the Mark 6 when I first saw the car in the mid-1950s but although the car was for sale, its owner was retaining his exclusive number. Not that this mattered very much to me at the time because the price of the car was many thousands more pounds than I had to spend, anyway. I was delighted to come across it, though, for it was the first I knew of a similar body to the pre-war version, being fitted to a Mark 6. Maybe I would never own it but at least I would try to keep in touch with it in the hope that, one day, it might come down to my price bracket.

And, of course, it did and, to my surprise and joy, reasonably soon. This time it was being offered for sale by Knightsbridge Motors, a delightfully personal little firm run by John Fuelling and Edward Mills, both friends of mine who dealt in the type of car that I liked. They knew my feelings about the car and I always believed they must have bought it with me in mind as the 'victim' although they both denied this strongly. Be that as it may we did the deal and for a long time I was again feeling that I now owned the car that would take me to the end of my days even though it was no longer 'HI' but now LMU 576.

Of all the cars I have been lucky enough to own for use on the road, this one stands out as my number one choice. It wasn't outstandingly fast although its performance far surpassed the standard version but it was the way it did what it did that remains so vividly in one's memory. I really did intend keeping it for good but, one day, one of my customers saw it and went mad about it, making me ever-increasing offers for it until the profit motive reared its ugly head so high that it went— and I regretted it once I'd done it. I bought it back again a year later and sold it once more for the same reason and this time it seemed to have gone for good. At this stage of its life it was becoming a little bit 'off'. Not mechanically, although the brakes could have been better, but bodily. The two big doors were beginning to rattle slightly and, in heavy rain, water would creep in through the edges of the perspex roof panel.

When I next saw it, this time in the 1960s or late 1950s, money had been spent on it so that it had regained its former glory and even had some additional glamour in the shape of the later-type wheel trims. It was for sale again—at a higher price than I had ever obtained for it but, once more, I jumped in. By now I had the feeling that I could keep on doing this with LMU 576, owning and using it and then taking profits on it at will. I did feel that, this time, my ownership would be long, in view of what I'd paid for the car but when an attractive offer came along I opted out again, in the sure knowledge that, when the car came home to roost again, I would be waiting. Sadly, it never did and, now, I very much doubt whether it will. It was a super car, really great, and I hope it has found a good home— it certainly deserved one!

I replaced LMU 576 with a 1953 'R'-type, Standard Steel, manual, a very nice car on which I covered quite a big mileage. The Standard Steel 'R'-type still seems to me to be under-priced, even in today's absurdly inflated market. Good examples are hard to find and the rust bug is ever present but I liked mine and looked after it and it served me well.

All my Bentleys gave me good motoring and none of them provided any serious headaches. The only quaint thing I can recall in connection with the make occurred with an 8-litre that I bought, jointly, with Edward Mills and John Fuelling, as a car for stock and resale. We had to collect it from Pangbourne and Edward and I went down together in LMU 576, coming back to town in convoy with Edward driving the bigger car. We had tried it before buying it and it seemed to have no vices. But on the way home, we got in rather heavy traffic in Reading and this became worse as we neared the city centre, finally becoming a solid block. It was a warm afternoon and we were stationary, side by side, in the block and Edward was telling me what a nice car it was when suddenly, there was an explosion via the radiator cap, which was a plain cap with a hole drilled in the centre to take the mascot had there been one. Without warning, there was a noise rather like a rocket and a jet of boiling water shot up through the hole rising ten or twelve feet or more, not momentarily, but in a continuous boiling stream which sent pedestrians scattering and cascaded down over both cars. I was appalled by the performance but Edward, always unruffled, wound up the windows of the 8-litre and sat watching calmly with a half smile. When the phenomenon had abated, he wound down the driver's side window, leant across to me and said, 'Now I think that's rather nice, Charles, don't you? We'll keep that, I think.'

I always enjoyed deals with Edward, who was a super salesman of the most sophisticated and intelligent kind. We both liked the same sort of cars but he was far more skilled and professional than I, often knowing, when he bought a car, exactly to whom he was going to sell it and taking endless pains to make sure that he did sell it to the particular customer he had in mind. The cars we both liked were the 'white elephant' type, mainly big Bentleys, Rolls or Mercedes, the sort of car that terrified the average trader but which would show really handsome profits, provided you took care in buying them and provided you had nerves of steel when it came to resale—because if things didn't go as planned, you could find yourself the owner of such a car for a very long time.

I much preferred buying the cars to selling them. Edward was good at both but was, I thought, right out on his own when it came to selling. Sometimes I would find a car, try to buy it and arrive at a stage where I just wasn't sure whether it would be safe to buy at the final price at which it was offered. On such occasions I would ask for twenty-four hours to think about it and would drift round to see Edward. I always knew, as I was describing it to him, whether we were going to buy it or not. If the answer was 'yes' he would say, thoughtfully, 'Well now, Charles, I think I know a man who would like that car.' And we would buy it and, invariably, the man did like it.

On the rare occasions when he didn't, we were stuck with it for a time—but only for a time because, before long someone would go along who Edward would decide was the man for the car even though the man himself might not be aware of it. All he had to do was to express admiration for the car on seeing it and not everyone who expressed admiration for it was deemed by Edward as the man for that car. But once he was convinced that the man fitted the car and vice versa, he would go to work to cement the deal, no matter how long it took—and he was patient. I found it absorbing to see him do it. He would find out where the man did his drinking and would drink there, find out his interests and become interested in them himself, all the time with the one object in view and, in the end, the deal would be done. But the strangest thing about it was that, not only was the man delighted with the car he had bought, Edward really did become interested in the interests of his customer whether it be vintage motoring, yachting, tennis or anything else.

He had a fantastic ability to assess a customer and to know how to handle him. Once, we were sitting and talking in the little office in Knightsbridge Mews that overlooked the 'showroom'. A prospective customer strolled in and stopped to look at one car—a 540K. Mercedes. He looked a most unlikely client for such a car, ungroomed, untidy, almost rough. Edward didn't get up immediately but went on talking, watching him. Then he said:

'Mr Right, I think, Charles.'

'D'you really. I wouldn't have thought so.'

'I think so. But it wouldn't do to try and sell it to him. Anyway, we'll see.'

He strolled out into the showroom. 'Morning, sir, can I help you?'

'I was looking at your Mercedes.'

'Beautiful car, sir. But I wonder if it's the car for you.'

'How d'you mean?'

'Well, it's a lovely car. But it's a connoisseur's car. I would have thought possibly a car like this (a 1939 4¼ Bentley) would have been more your sort of car.'

I would never have dared to try that line. But Edward was right. That one remark decided the man—if he was going to buy a car at all, that day, it would be a 540K., and Knightsbridge Motors were, at the time, the only people in London who had one. He bought it, kept it and sold it back to them years later. That's salesmanship.

I enjoyed his dry sense of humour. Once, I found a Phantom III Rolls, not a very pretty car but one which had been stored and was in lovely condition. I wasn't sure about it and called Edward in and it was agreed that he would make a separate approach to the vendor, go down and see the car and try it. And buy it if necessary. That night I rang him.

'Did you try that P.3, Edward?'

'Yes, dear boy. I bought it for us. But it gave me a fright.'

'Really. How come?'

'Well, Charles, dear boy. That P.3 is the only car I've ever driven that suffered shattering wheel wobble standing still. It's a lovely car but I took it out and did a run of about ten miles with it. It didn't boil as they sometimes do if they've been stored for a long time. But coming over Sunningdale level crossing it went into the worst attack of wheel wobble I've ever had with a car. So bad that I had to stop just over the crossing. But by that time, such a mass of metal and rubber was wobbling that, even when stopped, the wobble continued. it was quite an experience, dear boy. But it's ours and we'll make sure it doesn't do it again.'

I enjoyed the deals that I did with Edward and John more, almost, than any others. We would go in 'fifty-fifty' on buying these huge 'white elephants', sharing the profit evenly and, although I was buying the same type of car myself and reselling them on my own, I tended to worry if one hung around too long. They never worried or, at least, appeared not to. In fact, at times, it hardly seemed important that the cars should be sold, and there was certainly no apparent hurry. Even when the customer hove into sight and it was agreed that he was 'Mr Right' there was still no hurry. The whole thing was done in the most pleasant and unhurried way. Quite a lot of socialising accompanied every deal including visits to some lovely homes, often with the car,

218

so that the customer's wife could see and appraise it. Wives can be a bit of a trial on such occasions but not, I found, when one was dealing in this type of car or in this price bracket. Usually the wife's attitude was that it seemed a vast, even rather useless, car but, if it was what the 'Guv'nor' wanted, it was all right as far as she was concerned. The reason for this was, clearly, that even if he did buy it, they could afford it and she could still have the new carpet for the hall.

It was trading in the grand manner, elegant, sophisticated, civilised and very much like the pre-war stuff. And they were all nice people with great interests like yachting, fishing and horses, who really did like these fine old cars and knew how to use them and look after them. So different from the dealing that one sometimes had to do in the purchase and sale of the bread and butter stuff where nothing except the part-exchange price for the 'trade-in' counted. Rather snobbish, all this, but that's how it was.

Alphabetically, the next car on my own list was the Invicta, discounting Citroen of which I had many in the course of business, ranging from the Light Fifteen to the I.D.19. All were good and I did a fair mileage in them, particularly the I.D.19 which was the firm's demonstrator.

But I really loved the low-chassis 4½-litre Invicta and had a number of them both before and after the War, all open two/four-seaters and all of them good. If, like myself, one doesn't worship at the shrine of the early Bentleys, it is hard to justify enthusing over the Invicta but, to me, it really did have something and I enjoyed every mile I did in each one of them. A strange old car but one I would still like to own.

Lagonda. I had a 1938 twelve-cylinder short-chassis saloon which I bought immediately after the War when its mileage was nominal. I had never, till then, been able to think of W. O. Bentley as a great designer but this was, to me, a really great car. Its thirst for fuel was a headache in the immediate post-war period but, when Jean and I got married, it was our honeymoon car and a very comfortable and luxurious one, too. Repairs could be expensive. We had few troubles with ours but a friend of mine bought one, egged on by both of us, and within a month was cursing us over the phone because he alleged he'd had to outlay nearly a hundred pounds in having a new exhaust system supplied and fitted. If true, that was expensive around 1946–7.

Mercedes have totalled four. One 36/220 open four-seater and a

38/250 Corsica-bodied foursome coupé before the War. Both very husky and exciting cars and very thrilling to own. But, at the time, I could only just afford to own and run them and a major repair would have been a disaster because, while there were many Bentley Speed Sixes in the breakers' yards and a copious supply of used spares, there weren't so many Mercs being broken and, on this count alone, one used the blower sparingly. There have been two post-war examples, a 1966 200 which did a big mileage and gave us our first trip to Scotland, and a 1967 250SE. I loved this car but can't progress sufficiently to prefer automatic to manual boxes. Even so, the marque Mercedes is one of my two great favourites and if I had to limit myself solely to one make, I could rub along easily with a stable of Mercs!

But Rolls Royce were always number one favourite from the moment I first owned one. This was a beautifully maintained 20/25 h.p. H. J. Mulliner sports saloon. Such a slow old car by today's standards but so comfortable and enjoyable to drive no matter how long the journey. We did an enormous mileage in AYR 199 which included our first post-war Continental holiday to see the Swiss Grand Prix at Berne. Travel allowances were minimal at that time and tyres were a worry as new ones weren't to be had. But we had five new remoulds saved up which can't have been best quality for, by the time we arrived home, the rear ones were bald and we'd had two punctures on the return trip. Tyres were a real problem in the immediate post-war period. On our return trip, we came across George Abecassis, also involved in tyre troubles with his Light Fifteen Citroen. His problems were worse than ours for he'd run out of tubes! I was a bit concerned about George and rang him, a couple of days after our return, to make sure he'd made it. His tyre story was great. 'Yes, Charlie, we did make it, but by the skin of our teeth. We really were down to rock bottom with every tube a mass of patches and one literally in half. We couldn't get one anywhere but in the end we found a garagiste in Amiens who said he'd lend us one. The fee was astronomical and a condition was that he accompanied us to Boulogne to make sure that we didn't take his tube back to England. We agreed to all this but nearly fell through the floor when we saw the ruddy tube. Honestly, Charlie, it wasn't a tube. It was just one mass of patches held together by what had once been a tube. It did get us to Boulogne, though, but no sooner was the car on the boat than the chap was at work removing it to take back to Amiens. We had to leave the car on the quay at Dover when we got back.'

Businesswise, many Rolls came and went during the 1950s and 1960s. I liked them all and it really was hard to part with some of them; 20/25's, 25/30's, Wraiths, Phantoms 2 and 3, all great cars. Two emerged as great favourites, AYR 199 and GW 1151.

The latter became absolute favourite. A Phantom 2 Continental, it had originally been owned by Kaye Don. Both he and its subsequent owners must have looked after it because, when it came my way, it was way ahead of others of its type I'd had previously. We fell for it, hardly having to spend a penny on it during a long period of ownership. A lovely car. Something I should still like to own. Good fun as they were, I never could see how the big six-cylinder Bentleys of that period could be thought of as in the same class.

During the time I was dealing in them, I sold a number of these cars to owners in the States. Not everyone thought highly of this but it didn't seem wrong to me for the new American owners really did spend money on them, bringing them back to the superb products they had once been. One couldn't help noticing that some, in this country, who criticised, were the very people who, while owning the cars here, had let them run down until, in some cases, they were nearly driven into the ground. I couldn't understand their philosophy. They professed their love for the cars and would often boast of owning four or five different types. But when one saw them, there wasn't a well-maintained one among them and it would have been far better to have sold four from a collection and have spent real money in bringing back the fifth to its former glory.

Gradually, the supply of big Rolls in marketable condition began to dry up and one had to look around for other white elephants of interest and it was in doing this that I really did burn my fingers badly with one. Although one seldom came across one, I had always remembered and admired the big 'Double Six' Daimlers, a few of which had been modified and lowered by Thompson & Taylors when they were new. A great modification, which made them look rather like an outsize low-chassis '$4\frac{1}{2}$' Invicta. I read, one day, that Bill Boddy had discovered one of these in a derelict state, lying in a breaker's yard at Tring, so to Tring I went hotfoot. The car was there all right and, although it certainly was derelict, it was still a magnificent-looking thing, tremendously long and low, and fitted with an extremely elegant four-seater drophead body by Corsica. I decided to have a go at it, bought it for £50 and sent transport to bring it back to T. & T.s after having had a word on the subject with Ken Taylor.

Ken was rather lukewarm about this before seeing the car and more so when it arrived but, having started the project, I overruled him—which turned out to be unfortunate, for me! I'd established, before parting with my £50, that the engine was solid and hoped that this might be nothing more than the rust of years. It wasn't! Others, before me, had tried to turn the engine and, in doing so, had wrecked its sleeve valves so that, at this point, we couldn't even depart from square one! Ken said, 'That's it. Cut your losses. You'll never find another of these engines.' And what good advice it was. But I couldn't, or wouldn't accept it. It seemed such a shame that such a magnificent-looking car should go under for good and I asked him to store the car for me for a month or two while I thought about it. I didn't just think about it. I scoured the country for an engine, never believing I'd find one. But I did. A good engine, in a near derelict limousine of gigantic proportions and not far from home, either. This horrified him more than anything but I persisted and, in the end, the engine was removed from the limousine and fitted into the coupé and finally ran. For all this I got a very large bill which wasn't, really, surprising.

Then the bodywork had to be done. Another big bill and I sat back to assess the situation. It was a unique and wonderful-looking car but, compared to a Rolls or a Bentley, no great shakes once on the road. But I still felt sure it would sell and sell well.

It was something of a setback, therefore, to find that, while everyone rhapsodised about its magnificent lines and giant proportions, no one felt like parting with cash. At first, I mentioned it around then advertised it and finally tried hard to sell it any way I could. No takers! Literally none! I stored it, pretending to forget about it, hoping that somebody else wouldn't and would come along with cash in hand—but no one did.

At that time, Vintage car auctions were just getting under way and I put the car into one of these, at Beaulieu. It wouldn't be wrong to recall the price it made—it was sold under the hammer at Beaulieu for £500. I don't think, though, that my professional pride will let me reveal, in print, the net loss on the Daimler. Suffice it to say that it wasn't a two- or a three-figure loss!

In their class, no cars I ever owned approached the Rolls or the one

Bentley LMU 576. But there was one other marque that had a special appeal for me and this was the Roesch-designed Talbot and especially the works' car that had been raced by Fox and Nicholl with such outstanding success in the early 1930s.

With Anthony Blight's great book, *Georges Roesch and The Invincible Talbot* in print, it would be absurd to enlarge on these cars but I had seen a lot of the works' cars at Brooklands during their heyday and had later owned one of the team 90's. It had always seemed an anachronism to me that so much fanfare and ballyhoo should be lavished on so many mediocre Bentleys while the much more successful and efficient Talbot team cars had sunk into oblivion and I decided to plan a search to see if any of them still existed.

I remembered their distinctive registration numbers, GO 51, 52, 53 and 54, and recalled that there had also been the successful single-seater track car so much loved by Arthur Fox that, when its racing days were over, he replaced its body with a saloon, using it on the road as a car for business, registered as APF 999. I never really thought I would find any of these great old cars but, one by one, they came up, APF 999 among them.

I became deeply involved in the racing Talbots, even to the extent of starting to write about them. In doing so, I met Anthony and realised, at once, that it was he and not I who should be writing. Throughout my era of motoring I've known many great cars and owners but I don't know anyone who has remained so unswervingly faithful to one make as he has to his Talbots. At the time we met, I had just made contact with Roesch and it gave me enormous pleasure to sit he and Anthony down at the same lunch table. And even more so when I discovered that, after the first five minutes, they were so much in harmony that they had almost forgotten my presence. I shall always remember that lunch. Roesch was a brilliant and unusual man. But he required careful handling and understanding. I could never have done it in the way that Anthony did.

It was logical, then, that the two Fox and Nicholl Talbots I had, together with the basis of the Pass and Joyce car, BGH 23, should join his other team cars and this they did, not all at once but from time to time over a period. His reforming and rebuilding of the complete team and unravelling the cars' histories has been a masterpiece of dedication, determination and patience. And how interesting and revealing it has been, now that the cars are back in competition again, to see history repeat itself all over again. A great fillip for the Vintage scene today.

Many good post-war cars, mostly owned from new, came and went in the 1950s and 1960s. Citroen Light Fifteen, six-cylinder and I.D.19; Jaguar XK.120 and 150, Marks 7, 8 and 9; 3·4- and 3·8-litre Rolls Silver Dawn, and others. All good cars in their way, a few already becoming classics.

Looking back on it all, if I now had the opportunity to gather a stable from the cars I've been fortunate enough to own, it wouldn't be big. It would consist of the McCleod Mark 6 H. J. Mulliner Lightweight Bentley LMU 576 for daily use, the Rolls Phantom 2 Continental GW 1151 for high days and holidays, the best of the low-chassis 4½-litre Invictas which was, I think, KXD 142, for days when the sun shone, and my first car, the little 1934 Austin Ten, JJ 3211, for sentiment.

The fact that I shall never again own any of them causes me no headaches. I was lucky to own them when I did. I enjoyed them all but it is the road and the motoring which is, to me, nearly as enjoyable as the cars themselves. My present stable is modest, a 1970 Cortina 1600E and a Fiat 850 Coupé of the same year. Not even up to date, but I get pleasure from a long run and an early start in either. And new and better cars come along every year.

10

Now, it is 1973 and a lot of water has flowed under the bridge. But the story doesn't seem to have ended. I'm no longer a dealer in cars but will still buy one to sell again if I like it and feel that I can sell it well. I am out of the racing scene in the sense that I don't take any active part. But even here both Jean and I are more than a little involved in Charles' racing, whether we like it or not, and most of the time we do.

He is successful and good at it and since during the racing season he is never in one country for more than ten days or so, we are his base into which messages pour from race organisers, manufacturers and accessory people, all of which we pass to him while receiving from him messages that he wants passed on.

He has achieved the first of his aims, in winning two Isle of Man T.T.s, in 1971 and 1972. Both were a great thrill to us and particularly the first because, after all our personal upheavals, we sat alone together, listening to the BBC report of the race. We did for the second one as well and that was good—but the first somehow stands out.

He missed his aim of a World Championship in 1972 after leading on points nearly the whole way through the season so that the last round, at Barcelona, became the decider. At that meeting, the Spanish Grand Prix, the disappointment of not becoming 125 cc. World Champion was quickly offset by his winning the 500 cc. Grand Prix in the absence of Agostini who didn't attend, having already amassed enough points to have clinched the 500 cc. Championship.

We are lucky in seeing him reasonably frequently for, when he races in England or the Isle of Man, we have the joy of his two-year-old daughter's company—and she really is a joy. And when the season ends, he takes up residence in Amsterdam, near the Yamaha head-quarters, so that inter-family visits become easy.

It is tempting to write more of Charles and his racing but I don't think it would be right to do it even if only because the day will come when he may decide to do it himself. Naturally we are pleased and proud of what he is doing but, obviously, we see the risks and worry when the racing season is on. One can do nothing about this so we do what we can to help.

It has been great for me to have been given the opportunity to look back and write about all these things and I have been more than fortunate to have been able to enjoy so many fine machines and experiences. Right up to this very moment, life has been good, both to Jean and to me for although both boys have grown up and now have their own lives and homes, we still have our fourteen-year-old daughter, Philippa, living at home.

'Pip' is a valuable liaison between home and the race scene for she is a dedicated aunt to our grand-daughter, Tanya, and very much on a beam with Charles' lovely Finnish wife Marianne so that, during her summer holidays, she gladly accepts their invitation to journey round Europe with them for a month, during which time she sees countries she would never otherwise see and 'gets with' the race scene in a way that isn't possible unless one lives with it. She has helped me a lot with this manuscript when it has come to details of people and places.

But it is Jean who is really Charles' 'Secretary' and she who deals with his mail and problems during the season. And, sometimes, there are knotty ones to unravel. The worst, this season, cropped up in a telephone call from him two days before a big Italian race at Pesaro. He had lost his competition licence and, without it, wouldn't be allowed to start in the race. This one involved a frantic dash, by Jean, to the head-quarters of the Auto Cycle Union in London, where a duplicate was issued, followed by the boarding of an Italian-bound plane by 'Pip' at London Airport—and the day was saved!

Robin, too, is a valued member of the 'equipe', spending part of his holidays travelling with the 'circus' as it wends its way from country to country.

All this goes on round me as I pursue my daily task of a dealer and purveyor of motoring books and miscellanea. Even when I had the cars themselves, I always enjoyed reading about them. I had quite a good motoring library before I was twenty and, over the years it grew to almost unmanageable proportions before I realised that quantity must give way to quality. I pruned it, bought the motoring libraries of friends whose interest had waned and, in selling off the 'unwanteds', soon found that I had the nucleus of a business.

When my own involvement in racing came to an end I had more time to give to books and I pushed this along a bit so that, now, it is well on the way to becoming a retirement interest. It always seemed to me that, if one wanted to buy something, it was better to go out and find it than to wait at home for it to be brought to you, so I spread the word around that, if anyone had motoring books or miscellanea to sell, they needn't bring them to me—I would come to them.

In this way I've been lucky in unearthing some interesting relics of the past and luckier in meeting many extremely interesting and nice people. Yes, and in meeting old friends with whom I'd lost touch over the years and, in a few cases, sons of old friends. Many of them with famous names like Rex Hays, Alan Hess, Michael May and Terry Barnes, son of the late Donald Barnes of Austin racing fame.

A great life for someone like me for I like the things I deal in, enjoy meeting the people with whom I deal and enjoy the travelling involved and the country through which it takes me. If there is a snag to it, it is that books are made from paper, and paper in large quantities is heavy. Apart from being a valuable piece of property, a comprehensive motoring library is heavy and the movement of it does involve physical exercise—but, perhaps this may not be entirely bad!

Sandwiched between my family and my customers I get many opportunities of comparing the old and the new—the racing scenes of yesterday and today. It's wrong, of course, to live in the past but I'm glad to find I'm not alone in having not the slightest interest in the modern Grand Prix racing scene. To me, the cars, while undeniably efficient, lack individuality and glamour, as do their drivers who, sometimes, appear to be a rather spoiled and pampered lot. There seem to be no Nuvolaris or Fangios among them and the whole scene appears to me commercial and colourless.

And sadly lacking in quality. This, I think, is largely the crux of it for it is quality and craftsmanship that has gone by the board in favour of cheapness. Rather sad, it seems to me, but one has to hand it to the designers and manufacturers for their ingenuity in dishing out the appearance of quality without it being the real thing. The thing they deliver is efficient, of course, but to relics like me, who have known quality, it's no substitute.

So there it is. Nearly forty years spent in dreaming, planning and taking part in motor racing on two, three and four wheels. In terms of enjoyment, a great life, and how fortunate I've been to live it. So much excitement and variety, so many colourful personalities, so much worry and some heartache. A full life.

Regrets? Very few. There were times when one may have spent a bit too freely although, at the time, it didn't seem so and many wonderful memories and the fact that, as a family, we're not on the bread line, must mean something. Some of my contemporaries are now in comfortable retirement and I can't afford to be but, on the other hand, others who can afford to be are still working as hard as I am and they seem to thrive on it, as I do.

I rather wish that there were more car race meetings to watch, of the sort that ex-racers, like myself, can enjoy. The only ones, now, are those of the Vintage Sports Car Club, at Silverstone, Oulton and elsewhere. At their meetings you can see good racing, good driving and, although they may be inefficient by today's standards, cars which are interesting and look different from each other. And the car-parks, filled with great old cars are, to people like me, almost as absorbing as the racing itself. When attending one of these meetings one feels a sense of gratitude to people like Tim Carson and others like him who have worked so hard to make the Club the success it is and to members like Neil Corner, Anthony Blight and others whose burning enthusiasm contributes so much to the racing scene. It's good, too, to see so many young and knowledgeable Vintagents both among the competitors and in the public enclosures.

Time and again, one sees flashes of what I can only term the Brooklands approach at V.S.C.C. meetings and a case in point was one of their Oulton Park meetings which I attended a year or two ago. On this occasion, James Tilling had rung me a week or so before the great day to say that, at this particular meeting, there was to be a parade of historic racing cars. John Bolster had been invited to attend with 'Bloody Mary' and was anxious to have one or two helpers around who understood 'Bloody' and remembered her whims so could we go up to Oulton together and help. It was agreed that we would do this and, in discussing the arrangements, I suggested a certain pub in the area at which we might stay.

'Lord, no,' said James, 'we can't stay there. John's banned from that one.'

'Is he, James? Why?'

'Well, you know. Rather silly, really. It's one of those big places with night porters and all that jazz. John arrived late and there was no one behind the reception desk. He waited and rang and still no one appeared. Then, an elderly couple arrived and, mistaking him for the manager, asked him if they could have a nice double room for the night. You know John. That was enough. He looked at the book, signed them in, pulled a key off the rack and sent them up in the lift with their luggage. It would have been all right if he and they hadn't happened to be leaving the pub at exactly the same time next morning. They met at the reception desk and the fat was in the fire.'

So we stayed somewhere else. John was in great form but, after a longish sojourn at Beaulieu, 'Bloody' wasn't, the main bother being that her ancient rubber petrol lines were perished so that, after making a meteoric start and leading first time round, she then didn't appear again. James and I were at the start and, presently, Tim Carson arrived, in his 30/98 Vauxhall. We explained that John was missing and Tim agreed to take us on an exploratory lap, during which we found 'Bloody' with J.B. working furiously to clear the blocked fuel lines. By now, the 'parade' had reached the proportions of a fairly hotly contested race and, as we arrived on the scene, we saw that 'Bloody's' designer/driver had turned her round and was about to restart by running her downhill the reverse way of the track. Tim, with a lot of responsibility on his hands, said, 'He can't be serious.' But he was, of course and, just as the field hove into sight, 'Bloody' fired on all four and restarted lustily. Seeing the approaching horde of Alfas, Bugs and E.R.A.s, John gave her full power and, spinning her in her own length on the road, disappeared back up the hill, still in the lead. Tim was cross and you couldn't blame him!

So, carwise, it must now be the Vintage scene for me because things like this don't happen in Grand Prix and Formula racing and it wouldn't be right if they did, of course. Even to start 'Bloody' was an experience, John lecturing us all, beforehand, 'Don't forget. What ever you do, you mustn't stop pushing when she fires. Keep on till you can't keep up with her. If you're doing it properly, you should be laying flat on your face on the tarmac when she goes. If your nose is bleeding, it means you haven't lost your touch.' Nothing like that, I think, in modern racing!

Another thing, of course, is that one quickly gets out of touch.

One may meet old friends at the British Grand Prix but, no one, probably, at other meetings. But there are always kindred spirits at the Vintage 'do's' and this is a lot of the fun.

On the bike side, I am luckier, having been involved in it more recently and still having an indirect connection. If Charles is taking part, one is 'in' from the start, meeting all the big names as well as the ones who have shot up the ladder recently and who, until now, have only been names to read about.

This is great and it's surprising to see how much has altered in such a short period of time. Good, too, to hear the latest happenings in the domestic lives of the people one knew and to see the changes in the machinery.

While I've enjoyed it all no end, I must confess, now, that if I have a leaning at all, it must be slightly towards the two wheelers and the people who ride them. I still love every aspect of motor-cycle racing from those great days organised by the Vintage Motor Cycle Club to a modern National or International race, whether or not I have an indirect interest.

I do think that, despite its obvious hazards, motor-cycling in most of its forms is a splendid interest for a young man, and, particularly, road racing. It's very hard but the chaps who come to the top are splendid fellows and if they can do it and still remain unspoiled, they are the cream. Most of those who do, manage to remain the same sort of chaps they were when they started and they're the ones I enjoy listening to.

And, by the time you reach the ripe old age of sixty, you should have been listening for some time. As Francis said to me not long ago, 'I had a visit from Chas the other day. It seemed only yesterday that we used to cuff him over the head and tell him to listen to his olders and betters. Now one has to keep quiet and listen to what he has to say.'

One realises, when one thinks about it, how lucky one has been to have enjoyed all these things when one was younger, and to still be made welcome by the next generation when their turn has come. Yes, I really shall have to see some good bike races as well as the 'Vintage' things this year!

Epilogue

The year 1973 began as well as 1972 had ended. The Christmas had been the best we could recall for a long time and we had all the family with us.

During the holiday, Charles said, 'I shall be racing on my birthday this year, Dad. At Mettet, so why don't you come along?'

I said, 'I raced at Mettet in the 1930s. I took a five hundred but it gave trouble and, in any case, two of the works' F.N.s turned up and they were faster than we were, so it wouldn't have made any difference, anyway. I can't remember one of the riders, but the other was Tacheny.'

'Tacheny? The circuit is named after him now. Circuit Jules Tacheny. And he's the big chief there. He's got a motor business there and lives in Mettet.' This was a coincidence and, as we continued talking, we found that it was the same circuit and that, therefore, it must be the only one on which Charles and I had raced. So I really felt I must go down and watch. I had never met Jules Tacheny and, since the F.N.s had been last-minute entries, I had only seen him on the line, in his war-paint, the lower half of his face covered with a mask. But he was famous and had held numerous long-distance records riding F.N.s at Montlhéry with Milhoux and Charlier in the 1930s. Apart from wanting to see Charles' efforts, I felt I really would like to meet him. So when Jean and Philippa were keen to go, we decided to do it.

We caught an early boat from Dover on April 13th (a Friday!) and motored from Calais to Ostend and down the motorway to Brussels, arriving at Mettet in the afternoon. Marianne and our grand-daughter, Tanya, were in the paddock waiting for us, but Charles was on his way back from Amsterdam where he had been collecting a race bike from the Yamaha headquarters there. We all dined in their caravan and it was a super evening.

We decided to leave them to it for practice on the Saturday and motored down to explore parts of Luxembourg, where we lunched well before returning to the circuit in the evening. We attended a party for the riders in the restaurant under the grandstand and this was great, for they laid on a super 'do' and had somehow discovered that it was Chas' birthday and produced an exotic cake with twenty-four lighted candles. After that, we were taken into the inner sanctum where M. Tacheny and his committee were enjoying their own party. At this stage my French isn't good, but they had even laid on an interpreter, a dear Belgian girl who spoke perfect English and taught it in their School. We were entertained again and had so much to talk about, finally leaving around midnight, armed with V.I.P. passes for the morrow. They were very very good to us.

It was the usual race weather on Sunday, steady rain, which became heavier as we arrived at the circuit around eight o'clock. But it didn't deter us and, of course, it was a godsend to have the family caravan.

First came the 125 cc. race and, from the 'Mortimer' point of view, this was a bit of a flop for the bike was obviously off-song; although it led for the first lap, it quickly faded and retired on lap three. The races were run in two heats, all the competitors going into each heat and the result being decided on a combination of points and aggregate heat times. From now on, the racing was really good and very close indeed in the 250 cc.

Initially, Chas led the first 250 cc. heat by a whisker, but was passed by Borje Janson, similarly mounted, and they ran away from the rest of the race so that the result was:

Borje Janson	Sweden	Yamaha	19 m. 40·6 s.	106·725 m.p.h.
Chas Mortimer	England	Yamaha	19 m. 40·7 s.	106·715 m.p.h.
Dieter Braun	Germany	Yamaha	20 m. 35·2 s.	

The rain was now heavier than ever, making riding conditions really bad, so that the runners were half frozen even after a comparatively short ride and Janson and Chas departed for the warm showers which formed part of the super facilities for the riders beneath the grandstand. Dieter Braun decided against this since the second heat was due to follow shortly, and many would have agreed with him, for a warming and comfort-making process doesn't always keep a rider right up to the mark. Griff Jenkins, when riding for me, would seldom even allow himself the comfort of a cup of coffee, alleging that he preferred to brave the elements between heats so that he could stay 'mean and nasty' for the next wet one!

But it didn't work out that way on this occasion. This time, Chas got a super start and, inch by inch, increased his lead so that, in the end, the second heat result was:

Chas Mortimer	England	Yamaha	19 m. 09·2 s.	109·640 m.p.h.
Borje Janson	Sweden	Yamaha	19 m. 11·3 s.	
Dieter Braun	Germany	Yamaha	19 m. 29·6 s.	

Chas' aggregate time for the two heats gave him a clear win at an average of over 108 m.p.h. It was enlightening, to me, to see 250s *averaging* speeds in these conditions, higher than the *maximum* speed of the 500 that I had run at Mettet—and that had been a good bike in its day!

After a mini jolly-up in the caravan, Chas was summoned to the rostrum to collect his laurel wreath and, to my surprise, the summons included me, so that I was rather proud to be photographed with him alongside M. Tacheny. It was a nice thought and very kind.

As I had now painlessly entered the start area, I thought I would remain there for the start of the first 500 cc. heat and I watched the line-up with interest. Agostini, who hadn't yet ridden, apart from practice on the previous day, asked Chas what the conditions were like. Chas proceeded to demoralise him, fairly skilfully I thought, emphasising how bad things were and that he should avoid the white lines which were the worst parts of all. As this was virtually impossible at racing speeds, it was probably the right line to take, although Giacomo was clearly not fooled by it.

But he did start cautiously. He could afford to, because the M.V. was probably ten clear miles an hour faster than the big Yamaha, which is virtually a bored-out 350 and not a full 500, like the M.V. 'three' cylinder. Agostini won that heat, averaging 112·7 m.p.h., with Chas second, just under four seconds behind him at 112·1 m.p.h. But Chas really had to work for this one as the third man, Dieter Braun, was just one-hundredth of a second behind him. Back in the caravan to dry out again, I said, 'I really don't see what you can tell him after that, Chas. He knows the form now. Your headache seems to be to hold off the rest of the field,' although the fourth man, Kim Newcombe, had been thirty-six seconds behind Braun.

'No, Dieter's the real headache. But I think I'll work on Ago a bit, if I can. I've got some Italian lira. They were a bit lower yesterday than they have been. Maybe I'll cheer him up by telling him the lira has crashed. He's got rather more of them than I have.'

Agostini won the second heat but had to go a little bit faster to do it, averaging 114·17 m.p.h. This time Chas was slightly closer to him —the gap was 3·2 seconds. And, once again, the determined Dieter Braun was third and, again, one-hundredth of a second astern of Chas. So this, of course, was the final result of the 500 race.

After the race we dined *en famille* at our pub, the Hotel de la Citadelle in Dinant and, early next morning, set off for home. It was a very happy and enjoyable little trip and seems a fitting epilogue to this story. Really, if it hadn't been for the fact that writing this book revived so many memories, I might never have recalled the race I had had at Mettet, and that would have been my loss.

No book relating to Brooklands would be complete without reference to the Brooklands Society, formed in 1967 by a small group of enthusiasts headed by Bill Boddy. The Society has gone from strength to strength and now includes in its membership of 550, the names of almost every living Brooklands driver, besides many others who were devotees.

Its functions include regular meetings throughout the summer, at which many of the old track cars and motor-cycles can be seen in action, occasional reunions at Brooklands itself, social get-togethers and film shows, and a superb dinner during the winter. Dudley Gahagan's hard work has been well rewarded and is reflected in the healthy state of the Society, which has no less a celebrity than T. A. S. O. Mathieson as its President.

For those interested in Brooklands, the Society is a 'must'. Details can be obtained from the Society's hard-working Secretary, J. H. Dunn, 'Summerlea', Pinewood Avenue, New Haw, Weybridge. Telephone Byfleet 46199.

Index